THE TRANSPORT DEBATE

Jon Shaw and Iain Docherty

First published in Great Britain in 2014 by

Policy Press
University of Bristol
1-9 Old Park Hill
Bristol
BS2 8BB
UK
t: +44 (0)117 954 5940
pp-info@bristol.ac.uk
www.policypress.co.uk

North America office:
Policy Press
c/o The University of Chicago Press
1427 East 60th Street
Chicago, IL 60637, USA
t: +1 773 702 7700
f: +1 773-702-9756
sales@press.uchicago.edu
www.press.uchicago.edu

British Library Cataloguing in Publication Data
A catalogue record for this book is available from the British Library

Library of Congress Cataloging-in-Publication Data
A catalog record for this book has been requested

ISBN 978 1 84742 856 1 paperback

Cover design by Policy Press
Front cover: image kindly supplied by www.alamy.com

To Phil Goodwin, whose encouragement reaches well beyond the back row of the lecture theatre

Contents

List of tables and figures

Tables

Figures

List of abbreviations

ABP	Associated British Ports
BA	British Airways
BBC	British Broadcasting Corporation
BCR	benefit:cost ratio
BR	British Rail
CAA	Civil Aviation Authority
CBA	cost-benefit analysis
CBI	Confederation of British Industry
CfIT	Commission for Integrated Transport
CO_2	carbon dioxide
CO_2e	carbon dioxide equivalent
CR	Chiltern Railways
DETR	Department of the Environment, Transport and the Regions
DfES	Department for Education and Skills
DfT	Department for Transport
DLR	Docklands Light Railway
DRT	Demand Responsive Transport
EGIP	Edinburgh–Glasgow Improvement Programme
EU	European Union
GDP	gross domestic product
GHG	greenhouse gas
HM	Her Majesty's
HQ	headquarters
HS1	High Speed 1: the UK's first high speed railway line, from St Pancras to the Channel Tunnel
HS2	High Speed 2: the planned second high speed line, from Euston to Birmingham, Manchester and Leeds
HSR	high speed rail
ICE	Inter City Express services run by Deutsche Bahn
ICT	information and communications technology
IEP	Inter-city Express Programme

LED	light emitting diode
NAEI	National Atmospheric Emissions Inventory
NATA	New Approach to Appraisal
NFC	National Freight Consortium
NHS	National Health Service
NIMBY	Not In My Back Yard
OECD	Organisation for Economic Cooperation and Development
OEF	Oxford Economic Forecasting
Ofsted	Office for Standards in Education, Children's Services and Skills
ONS	Office of National Statistics
PDU	Plan de Déplacements Urbains
PPP	Public Private Partnership
PTP	Personalised Travel Planning
RAC	Royal Automobile Club
RDF	Route Development Fund
SACTRA	Standing Advisory Committee on Trunk Road Assessment
S-Bahn	Urban rail services operated by Deutsche Bahn in Germany
TfL	Transport for London
TGV	Train à Grande Vitesse
tkms	freight tonne kilometres
TOC	train operating company
TRACY	Transport Needs in an Ageing Society
UK	United Kingdom
US	United States
VAT	Value Added Tax
VED	Vehicle Excise Duty
WCML	West Coast Main Line

About the authors

Jon Shaw and Iain Docherty have published four books together on various aspects of transport geography and policy. Most recently, they edited *Traffic jam: Ten years of 'sustainable' transport in the UK* (Policy Press, 2008), a comprehensive critical review of British transport policy. In addition to *A new deal for transport? The UK's struggle with the sustainable transport agenda* (Blackwell, 2003), they wrote (with Danny Mackinnon) *Diverging mobilities? Devolution, transport and policy innovation* (Elsevier, 2008) and edited (with Richard Knowles) *Transport geographies: Mobilities, flows and spaces* (Blackwell, 2008).

Jon is Professor and Head of Geography at Plymouth University. He has been Associate Editor of the *Journal of Transport Geography* and a Specialist Adviser to the Transport Committee of the House of Commons. He researches issues associated with mobility, transport policy and governance and he is widely published in the academic and policy literatures. His current research activity includes a large European Union-funded project on the mobility needs of older people. He is the author of *Competition, regulation and the privatisation of British Rail* (Ashgate, 2000) and co-edited *The Sage handbook of transport studies* (Sage, 2013) and *All change: British Railway privatisation* (McGraw-Hill, 2000).

Iain is Head of Management and Professor of Public Policy and Governance at the University of Glasgow Adam Smith Business School. His current transport-related research focuses on the delivery of low carbon transitions. Iain has advised a range of private sector, governmental and other organisations in the UK, US, Canada and Sweden. He served as Non-Executive Director of Transport Scotland, the national transport agency for Scotland, from 2006 to 2010, and in 2011 was appointed as one of the inaugural members of the Royal Society of Edinburgh's Young Academy of Scotland. He is the author of *Making Tracks: The Politics of Local Rail Transport* (Ashgate, 1999).

Both prefer to go to work on foot or by public transport, and they also own cars (German and French respectively) and travel a lot by train. Jon's bike is stashed in his mate Andy's garage and Iain never learned to ride one. The carbon intensity of their work schedules means that both are Silver members of the British Airways Executive Club.

Foreword

Christian Wolmar

We all want things to get better. Or at least to live in the hope that they might get better. But what does that mean in terms of transport? In the past, this has tended to mean more transport. And more specifically it has tended to mean more and better facilities for cars. It is barely a century since the car first started to impose itself as the dominant form of transport and yet it seems like the whole world has been changed to accommodate this most significant of inventions (although my view is that the railways were more significant but that is for another debate).

In the UK we have been particularly accommodating or even subservient. As the authors show, in Europe not only have governments routinely invested more – much more – in transport infrastructure over the past 40 years, but they have done so in a much more balanced way – balanced that is between the various means of transport. The book demonstrates the sharp contrast between the decision in France to invest quite determinedly in tram systems in towns of even quite modest size as part of a national long-term policy, while the vague plans for 25 tram schemes across Britain promised by John Prescott in his 2000 White Paper materialised into, euh, just one! Nothing could be more telling about the difference in approach between ourselves and our Continental neighbours.

Those of us who have been writing about transport for a long time, whether like me as a journalist or like the authors as academics, know most of the answers (although we may differ on the details, as the authors are a tad more enamoured of the idea of building more roads than I am). But finding new ways of outlining the problems and setting out a series of solutions is no easy task. So I hope readers of this book will enjoy as much as I did the clever use of a fictional family to breathe life into an old story in a way that shows how and why people make specific transport choices. This device enables the authors to raise all the relevant issues in a novel form.

Despite our occasional differences, the principle basis for all solutions – whose impact incidentally goes far beyond transport policy to encompass health, obesity, the environment and our very way of life – is to reduce car use and the impact of the car. No sensible transport planner could do anything else but start from that point, if only to save the planet and the world's resources for their grandchildren. It is the little matter of winning over the public and indeed many politicians to that point of view which is the difficult task.

In their research for this book, incidentally, the authors have dug up the most startling transport statistic that I have seen in a long time. In 1934 there were more than 7,300 deaths on Britain's roads and if today there were the same ratio of deaths per million cars, there would be more than 822,000 fatalities annually. Now if that were the case, one suspects our love affair with the car would be, quite literally, fatally tarnished.

That raises a rather more serious point. The crazy Mr Toads of the thirties have been reined in by a series of legal and, indeed, social changes. We have to some extent accepted the need to fetter the car. Yet somehow we have got stuck in a sterile debate about whether further impositions, notably road tolling and congestion charging but also measures such as universal 20 mph zones in towns and cities, are 'anti-car'. Such things have always been posed by the motoring lobby as restricting choice. But here the authors demonstrate so well that there is an Achilles heel in that argument. The reality is quite the opposite. Encouraging car use actually limits choice in numerous ways, from leading to reduced bus services to making it harder for cyclists to use the roads safely.

Therefore the message for policy makers and politicians is be brave. The car is already being tamed but it is still like a newly caged tiger, snarling and restless. We need to tame it far more, turn it into a purring pussycat meeting our needs rather than its own insatiable appetite for more resources. Enjoy the adventures and travels of Paul and Susan and their family.

30 August 2013
(on a plane between Seoul and London)

Series editor's foreword

Michael Hill

As someone who has no expertise in this area of policy but who, in common with many others, has a variety of prejudices or at best ill-informed opinions about transport policy, I am delighted to welcome the addition of this book to the Policy and Politics in the Twenty-first Century series. I enjoyed reading it, welcoming its lively style and its exploration of the issues about the transport system in terms of the issues likely to be encountered by a middle-class family of the kind that politicians listen to. Jon Shaw and Iain Docherty's original 'journeys' approach is used brilliantly to contrast this perspective with those of others, and to bring to light the complexity of the transport system and of the options for improving it.

Drawing on the work of Jillian Anable, Jon and Iain identify three main opinion categories – 'car complacents', 'malcontent motorists' and 'aspiring environmentalists'. Seeing myself as someone who would like to think he belongs to that last category Jon and Iain's lively analysis helps me to see the many inconsistencies, indeed even perhaps hypocrisies, in my point of view. Living near Gatwick I am fervently opposed to the building of a second runway. But I relish the access it gives me to cheap national and European air travel and often travel there by taxi through a village with narrow streets, spoilt by the building of a nearby motorway access point. I use a free bus pass but turn to the car whenever I am in a hurry. Moreover I am troubled to observe that local buses run half empty largely for the benefit of pensioners, when perhaps, as Jon and Iain point out, a subsidy providing a low flat fare for all would be both more efficient in taking cars off the road and offer a better deal for low-income people below pension age. I could go on about the many expedients that govern my own selective use of the transport systems on offer. The point that this book brings out so well is the complexity of the issues and the many difficult trade-offs that affect the politics of transport.

But that is not to say that Jon and Iain argue that it is all too difficult. Their book is full of suggestions, across the board, of ways in which all aspects of the transport system might be improved and better integrated. They surprise the reader with ideas they commend but with caveats, for example making a case for tolls and road pricing but only if road improvements are first carried out. They indicate ways in which transport policy innovation needs to be linked in with other policy developments, in relation to health and education for example. They praise developments in London, and suggest things that might be learnt by other areas, and they look outside the UK to France and Germany at useful developments from which we might learn.

This is book tackles a complex cluster of policy issues in a lucid and sometimes even entertaining way. It is to be hoped that it will secure a wide readership.

Preface and acknowledgements

We were asked to write this book not long after the publication of *Traffic jam*, our previous volume with Policy Press. Given that works in the field of transport policy and travel behaviour are numerous, we did not immediately see the need to write something else about the topic from a UK perspective. But as we learned more about the Policy and Politics in the Twenty-first Century series, it seemed there might be an opportunity to provide a different kind of introduction to key transport issues for anyone interested in how and why we travel in the ways that we do. Broadly speaking, recent transport policy offerings say that modern transport, especially the plane and the car, has brought great benefits because it enables us to get between more places, more quickly and with less hassle than ever before. Then, in almost indecent haste, they caution that the disadvantages of modern travel systems are such that there is an 'urgent need' – that most wonderfully earnest and often disingenuous of academic phrases – to spend a far greater number of words investigating the downsides of modern transport than the upsides. Especially in 'traditional' transport studies books, the layout of the argument also tends to be a bit predictable, with the contents usually categorised by mode (the tactic we largely adopted in *Traffic jam*) or theme or policy concern (economic development, pollution, social exclusion, gender and so on).

Our approach in what follows differs in two main ways. For a start, we actively embrace the virtues of a modern transport system. We want to acknowledge and indeed to celebrate that modern transport brings huge advantages. This is not to deny that there are resilient problems with pollution, congestion, social exclusion and the like. But it is more than perfectly fine that mechanised transport is, and by any grounded imagination will remain, central to who we are and what we do. Certainly we need to promote more inclusive and more sustainable transport, but doing this is not just about serving minority interests or responding to negative externalities. Quite to the contrary, it is about making things (even) better for all of us who use the system as a means of going about our daily lives – rich and poor, able bodied and mobility impaired, *Guardian* or *Daily Mail* reader – however we choose to travel. Developing a more sustainable system will involve making some different (and for British politicians no doubt 'difficult') choices, but in our conception a progressive realism for transport and travel – essentially a better quality, more inclusive and fairly priced system – benefits everyone, whatever their mobility and accessibility requirements.

As it transpired, some of this book was written in our respective favourite mainland-European countries of Germany and France. After many years of visiting/living in these countries we have long admired their transport systems, which include urban light railways with real scope and scale, road networks that are precisely that, rather than a collection of variable-quality routes, and towns and cities that treat the pedestrian as a priority rather than an afterthought. This is not to say that things are perfect on the other side of the Channel, and a few extra features such as selective road-user charging and (even) better cycle provision would be desirable. Nevertheless, moving towards a Continental standard of provision across the transport modes in Britain would represent a vast improvement on the current state of affairs and, moreover, should be an achievable goal for the various constituent parts of the UK governance machine. Note that passenger transport in both Germany and France is also dominated by the car at the aggregate level, and that air travel remains very popular; indeed, car ownership is higher in both countries than it is in Britain, and Frankfurt and Charles de Gaulle are among the busiest airports in Europe. The point is that at critical times and in important places, the balance between transport modes is different, and preferable, to that in the UK. For various reasons, buses, trains, trams, bikes and walking are more popular when and where they need to be, and the social and economic opportunities delivered by the transport system for everyone are consequently greater. With more effort the environmental impact can be substantially reduced, too.

The second and probably more substantial difference about this book is its structure. Rather than categorising our points by theme or mode, we have organised the text around a series of journeys, the sorts of transport experiences with which you, and we, are most familiar. This approach allows us both to explore the links between transport issues and policies as they apply to everyday activities that we all understand well, and to relate emerging themes to broader economic, social and environmental imperatives. Part of our thinking here comes from the recent trend among some authors to concentrate on the representations and experiences of travel, rather than just, as Tim Cresswell (2006) has written, the 'brute fact' of movement from A to B. Work on, for example, how rail passengers use their journey time (Lyons and Urry, 2005), and intriguingly titled pieces on the 'art and craft of train travel' (Watts, 2008), the 'affective atmospheres and the sociality of public transport' (Bissell, 2010) and the 'classy coach commute' (Jain, 2011) have focused attention squarely on the experience of travelling as never before.

At the same time, a fair proportion of this work has tended to focus on one part of a longer journey (that is, the train or coach element of a door-to-door trip), and with some notable exceptions the findings have not really been related to a broader policy agenda. In what follows, many of the journeys we feature are multi-modal, just as in real life when we're travelling from a given point of origin to our ultimate destination (we walk *and* use the car, or drive *and* take the train). They have also been chosen to reflect the life-style choices of 'Motorway Man', that particular embodiment of 'Middle England' that has become overly influential in determining the trajectory of British transport policy, at least in the last two decades or so. In our view, politicians, and by extension civil service mandarins and other policy makers, have been rather too concerned with the implementation of policies that they associate with advancing the interests of this group. This has been at the expense of better transport for everyone, including, ironically, the very occupiers of Middle England themselves.

The characters making the journeys are not real and their experiences have not been derived from extensive primary empirical work on our part; instead they emerge from a combination of some auto-ethnography and a wide range of findings published mostly by colleagues but also by ourselves in previous studies. Our characters encounter and uncover a wide array of transport, travel and mobility issues pertinent not only to their own lives but also to those of all socioeconomic groups. From their adventures emerges a critique of British transport policy that points to the need for reform of the way we think our transport system should work, the roles it should play within our society and economy, and the means by which it is delivered.

In writing this book, we owe many things (mainly a nice meal) to many people. We'd firstly like to thank Alison Shaw and Rebecca Tomlinson at Policy Press for bearing with us as we provided increasingly desperate excuses for delivering the text over a year late and at vast expense (or as this is sometimes known in UK transport parlance, 'on time and under budget'). We are also greatly indebted to Steve Bennett, David Bissell, Tom Budd, Stuart Cole, Rosie Starr, Philip Heseltine, Roger Higman, Greg Marsden and Andrew Seedhouse for reading some or all of the draft manuscript and offering extremely valuable comments from different perspectives. Jeff Kenworthy provided some crucial data and very welcome humorous and academic distractions, while Jamie Quinn provided the diagrams (only five this time!) and Nicky Harmer helped us with the research for two of the chapters. James Sidaway reminded us that the iPod playlist probably needed to include a Morrissey song or two. The book as it stands is infinitely better than previous incarnations, although of course the remaining opinions and judgements (not to mention errors) are all our own work.

Jon would in addition like to thank Martin Lanzendorf/Veit Bachmann and Matthew Tonts for arranging Visiting Professorships at, respectively, Goethe Universität Frankfurt and the University of Western Australia, where some of the research for the book was undertaken. Paul Plummer provided fantastic hospitality in Perth's splendid Western Suburbs. Sincere thanks too to Fed Caprotti, Andy Sharp and Ben Kirchmeier for ensuring these things were actually taken up in the first place, and to colleagues at First Great Western, especially Mark Hopwood and Charles Howeson, for providing the opportunity to learn how the transport industry *actually* works. Iain thanks fellow

Francophile and bonne vivante Julie Clark for her élan in identifying those elements of the text that needed most attention, and of course Andrea for her unstinting support and creating the space and time to actually get the writing done. Thanks too for Margaret's sterling work in child crowd control, which employed more Peppa Pig than is good for anyone. A big apology is, however, owed to Ruaridh and Athol, who, after hearing that we were writing about trains, expected a final product more akin to *Chuggington* or *Thomas the Tank Engine*. Maybe next time …

Finally, hearty thanks to all of our colleagues and friends in Plymouth, Glasgow and elsewhere who continue taking it upon themselves to question whether generating large carbon footprints and/or staying in hotels and apartments in various parts of mainland Europe and beyond really are inevitably entwined with the processes of thinking and trying to write about transport, travel and mobility. Well, for us they are. And at least we're honest enough to own up about it!

Enjoy your journey/Gute Reise/Bon voyage,

Jon Shaw and Iain Docherty,
July 2013

ONE

Introduction: preparing for departure

You get what you pay for; the transport debate; rhetoric and reality; Motorway Man

Heaven knows I'm miserable now

In a recent European Union (EU) study of rail passenger satisfaction (European Commission, 2011a), Britain's railways came out as just about the best in Europe. *Lonely Planet* (2009) described the revitalised St Pancras, with Barlow's magnificent train shed and Gilbert Scott's cathedralesque gothic hotel and clock tower, as 'the world's most jaw-dropping railway station'. Across London you can fast-forward through 140 years of architectural history to Richard Rogers' Terminal 5 at Heathrow, which is every bit as good as any piece of major airport infrastructure anywhere. On the roads, the UK is in the vanguard of applying technology through innovations such as the London Congestion Charge and 'managed motorways'. Britain is also home to some of the world's largest privately owned bus companies, and has pioneered the use of smart-card ticketing technology in a free-for-all bus market.

Against the backdrop of such achievements, casual observers could be forgiven for thinking that there isn't much of a debate to have about transport in Britain. Key successes in each of the major transport modes would, after all, imply that successive governments have struck a sensible and coherent balance in their approach to transport strategy and investment. Sadly, even the most cursory scratch of the surface reveals that these successes, nearly all of which are in London, are the exception rather than the rule. St Pancras is indeed glorious and justifies its boast as 'London's destination station', but it is at the end of Britain's only high speed line, HS1, which is not even 70 miles long and carries a miniscule fraction of the billion-and-a-half rail journeys made each year, since it connects London with the Channel Tunnel rather than other British cities. Beyond HS1, the domestic railway network was starved of investment for decades, has been considerably reduced in scope, is significantly overcrowded and in many cases is not an especially comfortable way to travel. And although punctuality and reliability have improved in recent years, the system costs a fortune: this is true both for passengers who pay some of the highest fares in Europe – for example, a Glasgow to Edinburgh annual season ticket costs as much as an equivalent card for *the entire* German network – and for the state, whose annual subsidy bill of some £4 billion is at least twice as big as it was before the system was broken up for privatisation in the 1990s. Tellingly, of all the other European countries that came to investigate Britain's great railway privatisation experiment, not a single one has chosen to adopt the same approach.

The story in relation to the other transport modes also becomes quickly familiar. Heathrow is the world's busiest two-runway airport (Gatwick is the busiest single-runway airport), and the absence of 'slack in the system' – it operates at more than 98% capacity – means flights are frequently subject to delays, especially in bad weather, and the environmental consequences of needlessly burning fuel as planes wait to take off or land are considerable. On the roads, the UK has fewer miles of motorway as a proportion of the whole road network than do its major European competitors, which, coupled with the fact that we use our cars more than Continentals, leads to some of the congestion that represents an annual cost to the economy of between £7 billion and £30 billion depending on the source (DETR, 1998; Eddington, 2006; *Local Transport Today*, 2012a; see Chapter Two). Congestion charging has still not been introduced beyond London, and while managed motorways have been successful in providing additional capacity, they were introduced in large part to avoid doing anything better but potentially unpopular (such as introducing another cost burden for motorists) or difficult and expensive (widening existing motorways and building new ones).

The more-or-less complete privatisation and (outside of London and Northern Ireland) wholesale deregulation of the bus network has delivered some benefits, but these have largely been to do with subsidy reduction. Such cost savings have not generally been passed on to the consumer and provincial British buses can be expensive, slow, unreliable and uncomfortable. Even though bus users are generally satisfied with the standard of service they receive, bus use has declined for many years outside of the capital. Only in London and a precious few other British cities such as Oxford, Brighton and Edinburgh does the bus represent genuinely 'public' transport. Elsewhere it has all too often become an option of last resort for those without access to a car. Meanwhile the tram, often regarded as providing a higher-quality travel experience than the bus, features little in British public transport. Despite the current very welcome expansion of systems in Birmingham, Manchester and Nottingham, this is unlikely to change in the foreseeable future, especially given the expensive debacle of Edinburgh's attempt to manage the construction of its first line. And our 'smart card' tickets may well be very smart but they will not be used to anything like their full potential. The deregulated bus industry is now so complex that the straightforward, low-tech solutions in place elsewhere for many years simply won't work in the face of our plethora of disintegrated operators and equipment suppliers. Other than in Transport for London's (TfL) regulated system, bus operators will generally not work together to offer a reasonably priced integrated ticket option. This is a great pity, given that combined ticketing across modes and providers is one of the simplest things that would make the bus and train much more attractive choices.

In short, examples of where Britain gets it right are in and of themselves impressive, but they are flashes of brilliance in a wider picture of mediocrity. While other European countries have their own headline success stories – the growth of the Train à Grande Vitesse (TGV) network and renaissance of urban tramways in France, the Inter City Express (ICE) and showpiece gateway stations such as Berlin Hauptbahnhof in Germany, the transformational cross-city rail tunnels in Sweden and the engineering flair of the *Storebælt* and Øresund fixed links in Denmark, for example – these are generally accompanied by high-quality supporting infrastructure and services.

Perhaps the fact that the British are so satisfied with their bus and railway systems is not down to the inherent quality of how transport in Britain is planned, built or operated, but instead because of low expectations of what should be provided in the first place. We can explore this view by looking a little deeper into the results of the EU's railway survey. Consider the finding that passengers in the Netherlands had the lowest satisfaction scores for 'connection with other modes of public transport' of any major nation in the survey. This is in a country widely considered to have just about the best intensively used railway in Europe, a long-standing national integrated ticketing system and world-renowned land-use planning legislation that for decades directed development explicitly to key railway nodes. This indicates to us that the Dutch, who are among the Europeans most likely to commute to work by train, demand rather more of their railways than do the British. The same survey places the UK as the major country with the highest passenger satisfaction for the length of journey time by rail, despite journey times having steadily increased across much of the network for several years for a variety of reasons (see www.railperf.org.uk). Beyond the railways, the high rates of satisfaction among bus users sit alongside the feeling among motorists that congestion is not a problem that particularly affects them (Goodwin and Lyons, 2010; Passenger Focus, 2012). According to the (now abolished) Commission for Integrated Transport (CfIT, 2001a), Britain's roads are the most congested in Europe.[1]

Here we see the makings of a self-fulfilling prophecy: the pervasive 'mustn't grumble' culture that seems to explain the apparent paradox between performance and perception of transport in Britain serves to legitimise and reproduce second-rate provision. In the four decades leading up to the early 2000s, the UK spent on average 40% less as a proportion of gross domestic product (GDP) on its transport infrastructure each year than did other leading economies in Europe

(CfIT, 2001a). This has meant that while other countries have built extensive motorway networks, developed wide-ranging electrified and increasingly significant high speed railways, and maintained or largely expanded their tram and metro systems, the UK has achieved comparatively little in each of these respects (Table 1.1).

What is more, at least some in the government seem to regard this approach to investment as having been a success. We have for many years recounted in lectures and presentations the extraordinary statement from a Treasury civil servant to one of us that, given how the UK's GDP per capita is comparable with France and (to an extent) Germany's, 'the UK was correct *not* to invest as heavily as these countries in transport infrastructure'. It could just about be argued that on one level he was right, since it is notoriously difficult to quantify the links between transport investment and economic development, especially in advanced economies (Banister and Berechman, 2001). But such a narrow-minded view takes no account of social or quality-of-life issues, nor the environmental impact of the transport system, nor, for that matter, that there are some sound theoretical reasons to explain why GDP could be higher in the absence of an outmoded and heavily congested transport system (see Crafts, 2009). To us, at least, the worldview that spending as little as possible on transport is something to be celebrated can be directly linked to the poor quality of much of our transport system on the ground. A very simple analogy can be made with the purchasing decisions of a household: buying a better-quality washing machine or water heater will cost more up front but should save money in the long run. Even if it doesn't, the benefits of higher-quality goods will be evident through reliability, ease of use, better functionality and so on, as any user of a German dishwasher (or tram system) will tell you.

While there is ample evidence across the UK's transport systems to demonstrate the old adage that 'you get what you pay for', an analysis of the relevant figures reveals the situation to be even worse that it first appears. In Britain we suffer from the double whammy of not only spending less on transport than other European countries, but also getting far worse value than we should out of what we do spend. The first ever *National Infrastructure Plan* contained the most astonishing admission:

> The UK is one of the most expensive countries in which to build infrastructure. For example, civil engineering works cost some sixty per cent more than in Germany … If we were only to reduce public sector construction costs by 15% that would result in annual savings, or additional investment, of £1 billion. (HM Treasury, 2010, p 4)

Preston (2012) cites studies that suggest the cost of building high speed rail in Britain is twice as high as in mainland Europe, and in his report on the efficiency of National Rail, Sir Roy McNulty shows that standard railway infrastructure costs 30–40% more (Department for Transport and Office for Rail Regulation, 2011). Equivalent figures for revenue spending are more difficult to calculate, but McNulty arrived at a 30% efficiency gap across railway operations as a whole. The reasons for such inflated expense are many and varied, but among them are the fragmentation of the transport sector into too many profit centres, the legal and contractual fog that results from this number of organisational interfaces, political dithering, limited procurement expertise within government and the slow speed of the planning system and its associated bureaucracy. All of these things can act as money-printing machines for private sector consultants. Given that Whitehall and the devolved administrations spend something of the order of £20 billion annually on transport across the UK, this efficiency gap is the equivalent of a lost Terminal 5, or HS1, or two Jubilee Line Extensions *every year*.

So, although the British tendency of 'muddling through' may be regarded rather fondly as having served the country well over the years, in transport we suggest that the time to celebrate the 'good enough' is over. We have fallen behind our European neighbours (and, indeed, other countries further afield) in many key areas. From the resilience and reliability of our core infrastructure and services, via the aesthetics of the urban realm, the comfort and ease of using public transport and

Table 1.1: Key transport infrastructure statistics of selected European countries

	GDP per capita, PPP (Int. $)	Population (m)	Size (km^2)	Roads (000 km)*	Motorways (000 km / % of all roads)	Rail (000 km / % electrified)	HSR (% of network / % including under construction)	Tram / light rail (track km / including under construction)
United Kingdom	35,819	63.2	243,000	417	3.6 / 0.9	16.2 / 32.6	0.7	254 / 346
France	35,845	65.1	552,000	1016	11.0 / 1.1	29.9 / 51.7	6.6 / 8.7	596 / 652
Germany	40,394	81.8	357,000	644	12.6 / 2	33.7 / 58.4	4.0 / 4.9	2768 / 2783
Italy	35,204	60.6	301,000	482	6.6 / 1.4	17.0 / 71.1	5.4	209 / 223
Netherlands	42,938	16.7	37,000	134	2.6 / 1.9	2.9/ 76.1	4.1	286 / 321

Source: Data from DfT (2012), European Rail Research and Advisory Council (2004), World Bank (2013), European Commission (2011), Office for National Statistics (2012) and UK and French tram system websites (accessed July 2013). Figures rounded up.

* Road network comparisons are difficult because these figures include unsurfaced roads to an unidentifiable extent.

the quality and productivity of the time we spend travelling on it, to the marginalisation of walking and cycling and the obesity epidemic that emerges partly as a result, there are so many aspects of transport policy in which we could, and should, be doing so much better.

Stop me if you think you've heard this one before

There is little doubt, then, that there *is* a debate to be had about transport in the UK. We have indicated that our starting point is that we should be doing better than we are, but it is not necessarily going to be easy convincing people of this if they don't think that too much is wrong in the first place. Not least, this is because transport is rarely seen as a particularly important area of concern in relation to other policy matters. Survey work by Ipsos-MORI in 2011, for example, shows that transport did not even register as a response to the question, 'What do you think is the most important issue facing Britain today?' In many ways this is unsurprising, as it competes with the standard high-profile concerns of the economy, health, education, law and order and whatever combination of Europe/immigration/gay marriage is the zeitgeist of the moment. Interestingly, though, looking back through the Ipsos-MORI archive to 1997, transport normally registers only around 2–4% of responses to the question 'What do you see as other important issues facing Britain today?'. Transport's significance generally increases only in reaction to extraordinary circumstances such as a train crash, or the fuel tax protest in 2000.

Maybe in the normal course of events people are just too concerned about other things to worry all that much about the fact that their train journey takes 10 minutes longer than it did a decade ago, or that they have no legroom in the bus, or that it takes them half an hour to drive the five miles into town on a Saturday afternoon. It is curious in this context that, despite transport's relative invisibility as a major policy issue, politicians are surprisingly wary of doing things that they judge might be unpopular with the public, and this has had massive implications on the direction of British transport policy especially in the last two decades. We return to this issue throughout the book.

If we take as our starting point that things need to improve, the next and probably most significantly contested aspect of the debate is, *how*? In the academic transport literature, the transport debate tends to take place along a continuum that links two definable camps. On the one hand, there are those who identify most with the notion of 'Predict and Provide'. This is a shorthand term that is used to characterise an approach to transport policy that favours road building (and, increasingly, aviation) as the best and most effective means of addressing a particular set of transport challenges – primarily congestion – that, its proponents argue, constrain economic growth. The term was coined to refer to the (conceptually) straightforward idea that it is possible to predict how much traffic will be on the roads at a given point in the future and then provide roads to match that level of demand accordingly. In practice the Predict and Provide camp is a broad church, with only the most evangelical few believing that in the real world it would ever be possible to completely address congestion simply by building new roads. Nevertheless, enthusiasm for road building retains support among influential elements of the transport intelligentsia, and its case is kept on the agenda through high-profile interventions by organisations such as the RAC (Royal Automobile Club) Foundation (see Banks et al, 2007).

At the other end of the spectrum are those who align themselves with the notion of 'sustainable transport', and in particular the ideas of the 'New Realism'. Predominantly associated with transport academic Phil Goodwin,[2] the New Realism was the name given to a report published in 1991 arguing that matching road space to demand, or even building enough new roads to keep congestion stable, would be impossible and, as such, policy priorities should switch to matching demand to available road space (Goodwin et al, 1991). The New Realism, which was elaborated in terms of the transport circumstances of towns and cities, did not embrace any one policy but, rather, advocated a suite of approaches such as improving public transport, promoting walking and cycling, investing in the public realm, making full use of available information and communication technologies (ICTs) and employing accessibility planning to bring services closer to where people live. More recently the idea of 'soft measures' – that is, those not involving the construction of infrastructure but instead educating people to change their travel habits – has promoted modal shift in a series of demonstration towns in England and, as such, has attracted support from many on the New Realism side of the debate. Like the Predict and Provide camp, New Realism advocates constitute a diverse bunch: in a recent publication (Docherty and Shaw, 2011a), we argued in favour of a form of New Realism that seeks a broad multi-pronged attack on the transport problem, *including* support for new road space carefully targeted at particular bottlenecks and where significant safety gains are to be had (see also Chapter Seven); others, such as Lynn Sloman and John Whitelegg, adopt an unambiguously anti-car stance in their work.

The general form of this current debate did not, of course, materialise out of thin air, and finds its roots in a series of key developments in both transport technology and our improving understanding of how this technology comes to be used. As the private car became more affordable and popular among the general population, politicians gradually realised that the existing transport system of 20,000 miles of railways and rather primitive roads would not long be fit for purpose. After a characteristic delay – Italy started building the *autostrade* in the early 1920s and Germany the *Autobahnen* in the 1930s – Britain's first stretch of motorway opened in Lancashire in 1958. At the urban level, the Buchanan Report (Ministry of Transport, 1963; formally known as *Traffic in towns*) rammed home the point that key decisions would need to be made about how to accommodate the rapidly growing number of cars, and that these decisions would have effects for generations.

In the years that followed a clear trend became discernible. A greater proportion of journeys were made by car, van and lorry than by other means (currently around 85% of mechanised trips and 65% of all trips (DfT, 2009; 2012)). Accordingly, the amount of road space increased and the amount of available public transport decreased according to demand. The social ramifications of this were relatively straightforward to understand, in that those who had access to a car would have unrivalled levels of mobility and this in turn would allow them to access all manner of services, regardless of where they were located. As settlement patterns and the locations of services decentralised, those without access to a car became increasingly disadvantaged in terms of their access to jobs, education and leisure, a situation described as long ago as the 1970s as 'the greatest social fault of the automobile' (Schaeffer and Sclar, 1975).

In addition to social polarisation, the problem of air pollution from the ever-increasing amount of road traffic had long been recognised, at least at the local level, but was often regarded as little more than an attendant nuisance of a welcome technology. After all, local pollution from transport modes was nothing new. For example, disposing of horse manure became a terrible problem in cities and was an important incentive to adopt electric traction for tramways in the late 19th century. Over time, though, it became evident not only that local air pollution was potentially dangerous to human health (famously such discoveries resulted in the removal from sale of leaded petrol), but also that developing transport trends were having a significant global impact. Increasing awareness of the effect that the carbon dioxide produced by internal combustion engines has on the Earth's climate – private cars alone are responsible for around 13–15% of Britain's carbon dioxide emissions and transport as a whole accounts for up to 32% (CfIT, 2007)[3] – brought about a serious environmental challenge to the hegemony of the private motor vehicle. But this realisation clashed with the dominant political view of the time: the private car had become a symbol of freedom, and, despite its social and environmental downsides, was first and foremost a great liberator as a result of its go anywhere, anytime qualities. It is easy to see how this transport liberation became associated with the neoliberal creed of the Thatcher and Reagan administrations of the 1980s.

For a while, what passed for a transport debate in the UK may as well have been reduced to Porsche-driving yuppies pouring disdain on 'loony lefties', environmentalists and others not able to 'cut it' in the new order of economic and social Darwinism. This was egged on by Thatcher's infamous quotes about men over the age of 26 on buses being 'failures' and the triumph of the 'car owning economy'. The credible alternative view emerged from academics and others who had started to realise not only the global-scale environmental impact of existing transport trends, but also that road building seemed to have a quite unexpected effect: rather than easing congestion, new roads could actually generate it. After theoretical and empirical testing of the so-called 'M25 effect', it was found that new roads can indeed result in significant amounts of new traffic, as journeys between different origin and destination points become easier (SACTRA, 1994). Unless additional capacity is accompanied by measures that can 'lock in' the benefits of a new stretch of road – in other words, prevent congestion returning to its previous levels – the very act of road building can become self-defeating, as available road space simply gets used up by more traffic. Given the context of the dominant 'car = freedom' narrative, a hugely significant contribution of the New Realism was that it was able to demonstrate clearly how the car is all too capable of undermining its own utility. Going anywhere at anytime is one thing, but what freedom is it to sit for hours in more traffic jams, generating more fumes, costing the economy more money in wasted time?

As these negative impacts of the car have become more and more recognised, there has been in political circles a general acceptance, at least in rhetorical terms, that the non-car modes should be taken seriously. While some new road building is inevitable, the amount that can both be aspired to and achieved is very much less than was proposed by the Conservatives in 1989, when ministers advocated the 'largest road building programme since the Romans'. In other words, politicians have settled somewhere in between the two camps of Predict and Provide and the New Realism, even if at times their reluctance to build lots of new roads has been the result of constrained resources rather than any deliberate policy choice. Have we thus reached a point where they are content to recognise the drawbacks of the car when considering its advantages, and to embrace alternative modes as capable of making positive contributions to a better and more healthy – indeed, in many ways more free – economy, society and environment?

Well ... yes and no. The positive (at the rhetorical level at least) is that there is now a cross-party consensus reflecting the most sensible position, a kind of *progressive realism* which focuses investment in the non-car modes but recognises that some (possibly large-scale) new road building will remain inevitable so long it is well targeted and genuinely locks in its benefits (Crafts, 2009; see also Chapter Seven). The problem – and here we return to a familiar theme – is that the practice has not met up to the preaching. Certainly, since New Realist-style thinking began seriously to influence the mainstream policy debate, the 1997–2010 Labour governments' much-vaunted 'decade of delivery' for transport fizzled out into nothing of note in big-picture terms (Docherty and Shaw, 2011a). HS1 was the one large-scale achievement that Labour started and finished, but that was set against the realisation of very little else. Massive investment in better railways, trams and buses was promised but never really delivered; walking and cycling were never really taken seriously, despite mounting public health evidence that they should be; and, in the light of these failures, road building once again became the default solution, albeit at comparatively low levels. The Coalition government has followed a similar path, with the caveat that those infrastructure (especially roads) projects that have survived cuts in capital spending are more likely to have been prioritised on the basis of being 'shovel ready' as opposed to any inherent economic, environmental or social benefit.

Thus the underlying transport problems of 1997 remain resilient and unresolved in 2013, notwithstanding exciting new evidence that traffic levels *might* have peaked (DfT, 2012; Le Vine and Jones, 2012; Goodwin, 2013). We have arrived back where we started: despite the political agenda changing from Predict and Provide to a more rounded rhetoric embracing elements of both road building and the New Realism, Britain's politicians have not actually committed enough resources, or found a way of securing enough value for money in what they do actually invest, to lift the UK's transport network up closer to the quality of those found in our major European partner countries.

Such a little thing makes such a big difference

Before going any further we should make clear that our objective in this book is not to paint a 'woe is me' picture of the British transport system as somehow broken beyond repair. As Sir Rod Eddington's (2006) *Independent review on transport* pointed out, the system clearly functions well enough to facilitate the 61 billion passenger and freight journeys every year that keep our economy moving and underpin our social lives. It will obviously 'keep going', at least in the interim, without radical and immediate change across the board that would be unrealistic to deliver under any government. Rather, our intention is to marshal arguments that demonstrate how, with only a measured rebalancing of priorities and without spending much more money, our transport system could be so much better than it currently is. Because such change can make life better for very many of us, it is worth raising our sights to achieve.

In the chapters that follow we explicitly challenge the status quo and suggest how we could redirect our transport priorities to achieve different outcomes that we think would help make Britain a fairer, more prosperous and greener place. The transport system as we find it in the early 21st century is the sum of decades of policy trade-offs that have privileged particular transport users undertaking particular kinds of journeys for particular purposes. This degree of path dependency suggests that long-lasting and meaningful change will be difficult to achieve (especially given the medium-term state of the public finances), but we can at least make a start. Generally speaking, enough data have been collected and enough quality analysis has been undertaken that we understand what the key transport problems are. TfL and, to a lesser extent, Transport Scotland – organisations that have been revolutionising the quality of transport in their own devolved jurisdictions in the last few years (Docherty and Shaw, 2011b) – have shown that the quality of expertise necessary for on-time and on-budget delivery of integrated transport projects can be assembled. There remain skills gaps elsewhere in the country, but it would be possible within, say, five years and certainly within a decade, to provide higher-quality and less crowded trains, to revolutionise bus travel, to reduce congestion on the roads, and to have more people walking and cycling in and between better-designed, more attractive places.

There are many reasons why ministers in recent governments have failed to get to grips with delivering their stated transport strategy (see Docherty and Shaw, 2011a). In addition to path dependency effects, politicians don't always like to authorise large amounts of expenditure on a scheme that will open years after they have left office and that they won't get the credit for opening; the civil service is famously risk averse in terms of changing policy direction;[4] the Department for Transport (DfT) and local authorities are much better set up to deliver road projects than public transport and 'soft' schemes; and, as we saw earlier in the chapter, transport is seen as less important than other policy areas and spending money on it (outside London, at least) as an extravagance to be avoided if at all possible. Added to all of this is a further British peculiarity that both fascinates us and serves as a means of teasing out the complex set of trade-offs and interplays that have dominated transport policy and its delivery in recent years: the importance to successive government ministers of 'Mondeo Man'.

Given that transport is not seen as a matter of particular concern by the public in relation to other issues such as the economy, education and health, it is intriguing to note how it has been used to define the key demographic battleground on which UK general elections have been fought since 'Mondeo Man' swung to New Labour in 1997. The *Financial Times* noted how the needs and wants of his most recent incarnation, 'Motorway Man' – a materialistic and car-dependent middle manager – were also at the centre of the closely fought 2010 campaign (Pickard, 2010). Being reasonably prosperous, Motorway Man is an intensive consumer of transport and mobility. He lives in a modern house on the edge of town near a motorway junction. He and his wife both work, travelling extensively for business purposes in addition to their daily commute. They enjoy a close-knit family life with three children who attend local state schools, and participate in a wide variety of social activities. They revel in the consumption opportunities their life-style brings, including foreign holidays as well as regular shorter leisure trips, membership of a fitness centre and almost daily indulgence in their favourite leisure activity, namely shopping. They also vote Conservative, or Labour, but perhaps after 2010 never again Liberal Democrat (!), depending on how they perceive the political parties to be treating them.

We see Motorway Man as a useful analytical and rhetorical device. It is not just that he neatly sums up the characteristics of the half a million or so people living in (suburban) marginal seats who actually make a difference to the outcomes of British general elections, but also that his kind of household – the archetype of modern 'Middle England', white, (lower) middle class and socially conformist – contains precisely the kind of family that ministers and civil servants have in their minds' eyes when making decisions about transport policy at any point in time. In other words, the multitude of individual policy trade-offs that together determine the kind of transport system we *all* experience is in large part determined according to the extent to which any given intervention will risk alienating, as we shall call them, Mr and Mrs Smith.

Because of the way Mr Smith and his family live, consume, travel and (perhaps unbeknown to them) enjoy the indulgence of prominent politicians with significant decision-making powers, we have chosen to confront the significance of Motorway Man. Rather than arrange our chapters according to the convention of addressing each transport 'mode' (car, bus, train and so on) or policy focus (economy, society, environment) in turn, we have instead adopted a structure in which each substantive chapter of the book provides a narrative focusing on a different *journey* undertaken by our own Motorway Man, Paul Smith, and/or his family. Our intention is that by describing the experiences encountered while undertaking each kind of journey, we can set out why the problems we all encounter as we travel around actually come about. We can also examine which particular policy trade-offs were made to generate this state of affairs, and, crucially, what the resulting impacts of these are not only on the Smiths but on everyone else whose transport (and education, health, employment and leisure) choices are influenced by policy makers' conceptions of them. Often we find that policy trade-offs have not been properly thought through in terms of their impacts on the wider public or particular groups; we see how politics and the impact of powerful consumer and producer interests advantage some forms of transport at the expense of others and the users who rely on them; but we also see how good transport opens up opportunities in all manner of activities, and how relatively small changes can make a big impact at a wide variety of scales.

We reiterate that in transport there really is the potential to make positive and important change. The status quo is not sacrosanct, and alternative priorities and strategies are not only possible but also desirable. Many of these alternatives revolve around the notion of rebalancing the provision of mobility so that the car becomes less dominant, and there is actually a substantial constituency of car drivers who to varying degrees would like to use their cars less than they currently do. Jillian Anable (2005) categorises them as Malcontented Motorists, Aspiring Environmentalists and Car Complacents (see also Stradling and Anable, 2008; DfT, 2011). This is massively significant in the transport debate, for it challenges the central perception of Motorway Man and many of his friends that has guided much of the thinking of policy makers scared of being seen as anti-car. As we make plain, good transport policy that involves proportionally less of a role for the car and proportionally more of a role for public transport, walking and cycling, accessibility planning and ICT, is nothing to do with waging 'war on the motorist' or promulgating some kind of dastardly socialist plot to constrain the liberty of the driver. Quite the opposite. It is about enabling all of us, drivers included, and especially those who wish to use their cars less, to get around by the means that best suit us for any given purpose. By learning from elsewhere, especially parts of continental Europe, we can achieve much better outcomes, not just in transport but also in related areas such as health, the economy and the quality of the public realm. It is the job of government to provide the leadership necessary to achieve this, not least because once he has experienced the benefits of a more balanced transport system, even Motorway Man might be more amenable to change than ministers have hitherto assumed.

Nowhere fast

Each of the next five chapters follows members of the Smith family as they make a particular kind of journey, which links to key transport issues and debates that emerge from their journey experiences. There are five members of the Smith household. Both parents, Paul and Susan, are employed, Paul in the city centre for a large consultancy firm and Susan in a suburban office in a business park. The youngest of the children, Lucy, is nine and goes to the local primary school. Her 13-year-old brother, Jack, a keen cyclist, is at the local comprehensive, and young adult Sophie, who is 17, is studying for her A Levels at the new City Technology College across town. The Smiths live in a detached house in an outer suburb of Birmingham, and own two cars.

In Chapter Two, 'The commute', we explore the complexity of how people travel to work. We address a range of issues, including the impact of congestion on people's travel behaviour, how the planning system both encourages and seeks to deal with the increasing distances between homes and workplaces, the car 'dependence' that accompanies strong urban decentralisation, and how social and technological change, such as the continuing feminisation of the workforce and the development of ICTs for remote working, might change the nature of the commute in future. The school run is the focus of Chapter Three. Despite a decade or more of policy effort to encourage walking and cycling to school, up to a quarter of car journeys in the morning peak are associated with the school run. Parents often justify the 'need' to drive their children around on the grounds of safety, but this is a complex issue, given the longer-term health risks associated with inactive life-styles, and the more immediate equity consideration that more traffic makes it more dangerous for those who do actually choose to walk and cycle. The school run also neatly exemplifies some of the unintended consequences that can emerge within transport and across public policy as a whole: the rise in car trips to school came about in part because of the policy of 'parental choice' in education, and being accustomed to being driven to school can make it more likely that young people will themselves drive earlier and more often.

In Chapter Four, 'The business trip', we follow Paul as he makes his monthly journey to his company's headquarters (HQ) in London Docklands. As he finds out, the holy grail of public transport – the seamless journey – generally remains a long way off in the UK, with coordination between and within modes often being absent; even the seemingly simple task of buying and using a train ticket can descend into a nightmare, given the bewildering array of ticket types. Some aspects of Paul's journey, especially in London, work well and demonstrate the importance of integration and sustained investment, but he has plenty of time to ponder the shortcomings of British public transport when his train is heavily delayed on the way home. Chapter Five documents the family visit to see the children's grandmother in the southern Highlands. The Smiths could make their journey to Scotland by car or train, but they fly, as it is cheapest and most convenient. This is hardly a 'green' option, but seeking to maximise a particular type of consumer choice has become so culturally ingrained in British policy making that there is very little scope to incentivise more sustainable travel. Once in Scotland, the Smiths hear tales of Paul's mother using the generous concessionary fares scheme to travel for free all over the country. Why is facilitating this kind of travel so important when other user groups, such as young people, single parents and the unemployed, might have equally valid needs that are not so generously met? Could money spent on concessionary travel be redirected towards alternative investment in making bus travel better for everyone?

Chapter Six follows the Smiths on their summer holiday. They travel on a recently opened stretch of motorway, and on arrival at Heathrow notice the sizeable Terminal 2 construction project. Sophie's not exactly concerned about the environmental impacts of these developments, despite her father's pause for thought. Once on the Riviera, the Smiths head straight into town to stock up on food and drink. Susan wonders how it is that the shops are kept supplied even in the most inaccessible of old-town locations. At this point we consider how the freight transport sector has developed to serve the needs of consumers like the Smiths, but Susan and Paul turn their attention to enjoying the local attractions. The family travels around by tram, train and on foot; some aspects of the transport system are not as good as they're used to, but they are generally impressed by the speed, comfort and efficiency that means most things 'just work'. On their way back to the UK by train via Paris, they wonder why their travel experience on the TGV was altogether nicer than they are used to on the West Coast Main Line (WCML). We discuss the UK's transport system in the context of European best practice and consider the importance of government policy direction in determining the ways in which transport is funded, organised and operated.

In the concluding chapter we draw together the key issues that cut across each of the journeys undertaken, to identify a way forward for transport policy and delivery in Britain. In essence, our argument is that while our current transport system provides many opportunities and benefits, in its current state we face economic, social and environmental costs that we do not need to impose upon ourselves, at least as much as we do. There are real, affordable and politically deliverable changes that can be made to the system in order to effect considerable quality of life improvements. We focus on the key aspects of the transport debate that need to be thrashed out, and advance our ideas about what we might do to deliver benefits quickly, within the constraints of the governance arrangements that currently exist.

Notes

[1] Recent innovations such as crowd-sourced data, including those from INRIX, Keepmoving and Tom-Tom, show different but wildly inconsistent pictures (although Keepmoving suggests that the UK has 6 of the 10 most congested cities in Europe). We cite the CfIT study, as its methodology and underpinning assumptions are fully explained.

[2] Goodwin was able to draw from a rich vein of previous work by authors such as John Adams, Mayer Hillman, Jane Jacobs, Stephen Plowden and John Roberts.

[3] Figures vary, depending on how CO_2 is allocated between sectors and whether international shipping and aviation is included.

[4] Upon taking office, David Cameron hailed the civil service as the 'Rolls Royce of the British government machine'. Two and a half years later, exasperated by what it now saw as Whitehall's truculence and intransigence, Number 10 was reported to have reconsidered its position. The transport theme to the metaphor remained, but mandarins and their staff had been recast as an 'Italian tank' on the basis that they 'only have reverse gears and move slowly backwards over all of our achievements' (Thomson, 2012, unpaginated). See also www.bbc.co.uk/news/uk-politics-19797736.

TWO

The commute

Going to work; congestion and road-user charging; transport, planning and economic development

I don't like Mondays

Paul has never much liked the start of the week. Now that Saturdays and Sundays in the Smith household are busier than ever, thanks to the increasing demands of Sophie, Jack and Lucy's social lives (Chapter Three), he likes them even less as there never seems to be any respite from the family's hectic schedule. Today is no exception, as the month end is nearing, so in between the usual round of meetings that will take up most of Paul's day, he'll somehow have to check and collate the performance figures he needs to send to his bosses in London. Like most of his colleagues in the office, Paul used to drive to work – his office is on the edge of the city centre, about eight miles from home – and although not everyone has a guaranteed parking space, it's never normally too difficult to find somewhere to leave the car. But ever since his health scare a few months ago, when the doctors implored him to get more exercise as well as give up smoking and watch his diet, Paul has taken the train into town instead. At first he found even the 10-minute walk either end of the train trip a chore, but he knew that just by taking the train to work he was building in more than the half hour's exercise per day that he'd been told to aim for (Chapter Three). Once he'd worked out how to make up his own playlist (which you can follow throughout the text!) and download podcasts onto the iPod the children bought him last Christmas, his morning and evening walks even became enjoyable. Typical, then, that today he would have to miss his normal walk because his first task was to drop the car off at the garage beside the station for its annual service.

Look out of the window in any major city in the world and what you see is strongly related to the transport technologies available to those who built it. The 'Middle England' of the Smiths is no different: its quintessential expression, that of genteel suburbia, owes its very existence to the late 19th-century railway barons who offered heavily subsidised travel to the first people to build houses around their new stations. Their expectation was that these pioneers would soon be followed by many more fare-paying passengers keen to escape the rising squalor of the industrial city, and they were proved correct. By the 1920s, some railway companies, most famously the Metropolitan, had graduated from subsidising the construction of elaborate individual villas by the wealthy to the development of whole new housing estates for the burgeoning white-collar workforce. The new communities of 'Metro-land' worked their way so deeply into the English psyche as to feature in Sir John Betjeman's poetry.[1]

And so the commuter suburb was born, transforming the historic 'foot cities' of the pre-mechanised era into the much larger 'tracked cities' built around radial tram, train and later bus lines (Docherty et al, 2008). The word 'commute' itself derives from the reduced or 'commuted' fares for regular trips to and from the city paid by those living in the American equivalents of Ruislip, Bearsden and Sutton Coldfield. The system of radial commuting from suburb to city centre, largely by train and, in London, the expanding Underground, rumbled on unremarkably, serving the politically influential, small-'c' conservative social groups that colonised Metro-land and maintained a traditional life-style focused around nuclear family life and a male breadwinner commuting 'into town'.[2] Although some blue-collar suburbs developed (for example after the Cheap Trains Act 1883), manual workers were much more likely to live nearer to work and either to walk or take the bus (see Pooley and Turnbull, 2000). Over the course of the 20th century, changing external circumstances challenged the apparent stability of the daily commute. One was the transition from 'tracked cities' to the 'rubber cities' of mass car ownership, which spurred the relocation of many workplaces from traditional, central urban locations to new, modern facilities on the edge of town, and also provided a new, flexible, quick, comfortable alternative to the train (and bus) for many commuting journeys (see Camagni et al, 2002; Hull, 2005). Added to this was the transformation of the labour market, which convulsed as a result of several interrelated trends including the explosion of service-sector jobs, a deep decline in primary and manufacturing employment and the large-scale entry of women into the workforce (see Massey, 1988; McDowell et al, 2006).

Because transport technologies have such an impact on the built form of the places in which we live and work, it is no surprise that the increasing trend towards car commuting exerted a profound set of transformations on both the transport system and urban fabric. Whereas many North American (and now Pacific Rim) cities only really grew up alongside the car – that is, they are more 'rubber' than 'tracked' – retro-fitting the necessary infrastructure to accommodate major traffic flows in historic European cities has proved to be much more problematic. In Britain, Colin Buchanan's *Traffic in towns* report (Ministry of Transport, 1963) was the starting point for a debate that has raged ever since (Chapter One). What is often forgotten about *Traffic in towns* is that it was not about the car and traffic per se; rather, it was about explaining the impact of cars and traffic in urban environments (*Traffic in urban areas* doesn't have much alliterative appeal).

One of the main reasons the report became famous, not just in the UK but also internationally, was the lavish quality of its illustrations, which brought home in no uncertain terms the scale of the changes in their physical structure that would be required of British towns and cities if they were to adapt to accommodate unrestricted use of the car. The power of the report's images – such as the most celebrated one of London's Tottenham Court Road transformed into an expressway with segregated bus lanes and stops, its pedestrians marooned on elevated concrete gangways (Figure 2.1) – depends on the almost complete distinction between the *street* and the *motorway* (Chapters Three and Six).[3] Whereas the street accommodates an almost infinitely complex and varied set of social interactions alongside its role as a traffic thoroughfare, the motorway (although strictly a technical term) is commonly understood as the kind of road dominated by fast-moving vehicles and for which pedestrians, cyclists, homes and shop fronts are all inherently ill-suited. By visualising the impact of the unfettered development of urban motorways on our neighbourhoods and towns, Buchanan expertly highlighted the stark nature of the choice facing policy makers as they deliberated over the future of transport in Britain's cities.

Figure 2.1: Tottenham Court Road transformed

Source: Ministry of Transport (1963)

Many British towns and cities at least tried to build the kind of high-capacity routes into and around their very centres that the prospect of mass car commuting suggested. Looking carefully at the map reveals those bits of the original grand plans that made it to construction. The M25 is comprised of parts of two of the four 'Ringways' originally conceived for London, and the Westway and East Cross Route either side of the Blackwall Tunnel hint at where the innermost 'Ringway 1' would have run. Leeds, Manchester and Newcastle each have a short stretch of motorway very close to the city centre that was supposed to be the first stage of a much bigger urban network (in Newcastle's case some really grandiose civil engineering was planned, including underground interchanges, a quadruple carriageway route and a bypass of a bypass) and Glasgow has half a motorway ring-road built to US rather than British design standards that includes a 10-lane bridge which, until recently, was Europe's busiest river crossing, with almost 200,000 vehicles per day (see Pooley and Turnbull, 2000).

By the late 1970s, a combination of growing protests against urban motorway building (Starkie, 1972), a change of planning policy tastes away from 'comprehensive urban redevelopment' (that is, wholesale demolition of large swathes of cities) and towards the rehabilitation and regeneration of older neighbourhoods, and the fiscal and wider policy impacts of the energy crisis killed off the grand plans for urban motorway networks in British cities (see Charlesworth, 1984).[4] What happened next was a typical British compromise. With the possibility of extensive urban motorway networks (and along with them urban rail rapid-transit networks) having largely vanished, many cities attempted to squeeze as much capacity out of their historic road networks as possible by means such as widening and the provision of some underpasses along main radial routes. This process both failed to accommodate the sheer scale of the explosion in commuting and other car journeys and ruined many local neighbourhood centres that had grown up along key roads by saturating them with traffic. The combination of worsening urban congestion and the diminution of quality of place – incidentally, an outcome almost exactly like that Buchanan had predicted, should major urban road building not in fact occur – helped alternative policy ideas, such as those underpinning the New Realism, come to prominence.

Notwithstanding the significant decentralisation of employment and services, the traditional 'radial' commute into the city centre remains an important type of journey that the British transport system has to cope with. The impressive revitalisation of many major cities in recent years means that the number of jobs in central, service-orientated locations has grown again as firms in sectors such as financial and business services seek to maximise the potential labour pool available to them (Graham, 2009; Mackinnon and Cumbers, 2011). Urban local authorities and economic development agencies focused on retaining and increasing the number of jobs in their areas are well aware of this imperative, and so the pressure to maximise the commuting catchment of major service centres remains a top policy priority. Despite heavy competition from the private car, the railway, with its historic radial structure and very high peak capacity, retains a critical role in providing transport for commuters. Every working day, 39,000 people in Glasgow, 32,000 people in Birmingham and a staggering 575,000 people in central London arrive at work having commuted there by train (Network Rail, 2011). An additional 375,000 people arrive in the centre of London by Underground (DfT, 2012).

Such is the popularity of rail commuting that many services into and out of Britain's major urban areas are significantly overcrowded in the peak hours. Some of this overcrowding could be addressed with additional rolling stock, and in several cases large infrastructure projects are now being taken forward after several years' delay to provide new capacity. The two biggest schemes, Crossrail and the Thameslink upgrade (the latter, for obvious reasons, no longer called 'Thameslink 2000'), are both in the capital and together cost more than £20 billion. When they are completed in 2019, London will have two high-capacity cross-city lines (Crossrail running east–west and Thameslink, which already exists but with limited capacity, north–south), sharing an interchange at Farringdon, and between them offering a very wide range of new journey opportunities, including, for the first time, a direct connection between Heathrow Airport, the City and Canary Wharf. Plans for a second Crossrail line, running south-west to north-east and serving the proposed High Speed 2 (HS2) terminus at Euston, are already being vigorously promoted by the London First business lobby group.[5] Quite who will pay for this £20 billion project has been glossed over, for now at least.

Other sizeable (in non-London terms) schemes, including the 'Northern Hub' package of enhancements in and around Manchester and the electrification and upgrades of the Edinburgh—Glasgow Improvement Programme (EGIP) and trans-Pennine routes, will also be completed within the current decade. For many years British Rail (BR) was starved of government investment and was forced to try to manage demand by hiking fares to the point that they would 'price off' demand, although above-inflation fare rises in recent years have been justified by ministers on the basis that the only way large-scale infrastructure investment can be afforded is if an ever-increasing proportion is funded directly through the farebox.[6] While this is leading to very welcome improvements in infrastructure (if a less welcome increase in fares), even this level of investment does little to close the gap in the quality of railway infrastructure between the major provincial conurbations and their Continental counterparts (Chapters Four and Six).

Not all British cities are fortunate enough to have that much of a rail network to start with. Middle-sized cities such as Edinburgh, Bristol and Nottingham have very few local stations, and so are almost entirely reliant on the bus as an alternative to the car for the daily commute. In some cities there have been attempts to provide light rail systems (Manchester, Croydon, Nottingham, Sheffield, Birmingham and Edinburgh) or dedicated infrastructure for bus rapid-transit schemes (Bradford, Cambridge and Crawley in West Sussex). But even where the tram has been at its most successful, the overall level of public transport provision for the commuter remains inadequate as compared with that commonplace in many of the Continental cities competing for the same jobs and inward investment (Table 2.1). Just as was the case in the early twentieth century, Paul's switch from the car to an easy commute into town on the train marks him out as one of the lucky few with a genuine choice of how to travel, and whose daily journey benefits from the attention of those who decide where our 'transport pound' is spent (Chapter Five).

Table 2.1: Indicative historic investment levels in urban transport in selected European cities

City	Annual public transport infrastructure investment per capita (€)
Vienna	464
Munich	221
Stockholm	83
Copenhagen	63
Milan	63
Manchester	32
Glasgow	23

Source: CfIT (2001a)

Chelsea morning

Although it's Paul who moans most about Mondays, Susan is probably the member of the Smith family with most to gripe about when it comes to the morning routine on any day of the week. No short walk to the station accompanied by the *Friday Night Comedy* podcast to start the week for her. A typical day for Susan begins with making sure Jack and Sophie get out of the door in time to get to school (Paul leaves by 8.00am to catch a train before they get too busy for him to find a seat), then at the very least 20 minutes in the car battling through the traffic. When they moved to this house, it had seemed ideal: a nice new development with plenty of space and a good garden for the kids, and not too far from either the local shops or Susan's office. Most importantly, the primary school where Jack was about to start was only five minutes away in the car on the way to work. But by the time Lucy was ready to start at the same school a few years later, its Ofsted reports were not so good, and Susan and Paul managed to get her a place elsewhere. With the new school, however, comes complications, because it is in the other direction from Susan's office. When she drove Jack to school, Susan used to be able to drop him off at the gates at 8.50 and still be in the office by nine. But her current morning routine means that she has to leave the house no later than 8.30 to make sure she gets to the office on time. If only there wasn't the peer pressure to be at her desk by nine, she could leave later and get to work more quickly. On the few occasions she's been running late, she's noticed that the traffic seems to evaporate precisely five minutes after everyone is expected to have logged on to the company network.

And those planners don't help either, do they? When Susan first began the drive to her office the main road out to the business park was nice and quiet, and had a 40 mph limit. Then that new supermarket was built and it needed a big roundabout that slowed everything down … To add insult to injury, the road now has a 30 mph limit and bus lanes – bus lanes! – for much of its length. When she's running late, Susan often sits frustrated in the traffic, looking at the empty red tarmac. One time the other week when she gave a colleague a lift to work, a longer than usual queue at the new roundabout prompted Susan to proclaim what she often thought to herself: 'That bus lane's empty most of the time and it's just put there by people from the council with their trendy ideas to annoy people who actually do a decent day's work and pay lots of money for their road tax.' But at least there are no parking problems: there's never any trouble finding a space, and unlike the 'exorbitant' fees that some of her friends who work in the city centre tell her they have to pay, Susan can park the Toyota RAV4 right outside her office for free.

We are all used to the idea of paying more to use services at times of particularly high demand. The concept of higher charges in the 'peak', whether for electricity, phone calls, cinema tickets or indeed the railways, is so ingrained in our psyche as to go unchallenged. Yet one of our most intensively used utilities remains stubbornly different. Every day, millions of people pour onto the roads, which in the UK remain, with very few exceptions, completely free at the point of use. And very many people set out behind the wheel at almost exactly the same time: at 8.40 in the morning, when the peak is at its highest, there will be in the order of four to five times as many people on the roads as one hour earlier, with up to one quarter of them engaged in the school run (Chapter Three).

In simple terms, we have road traffic congestion because the demand for car (and most other) travel is heavily concentrated in time and space. Lots of people go to the same destinations (work, school, evening football match) at the same time, putting huge pressure on the road network. The actual level of congestion that people experience during their everyday journeys, that is, the length of the traffic jam you see in your rear-view mirror or how late you end up for work, is a relatively complex function of the engineering performance of the road network (width of the road and its flow characteristics, length of the red phase at traffic lights and so on) plus the actual level of demand and other additional factors such as disruption caused by road works, traffic incidents and the state of the weather (Downs, 2004). Significantly, the linear addition of more vehicles to the network causes congestion to increase at a much faster rate. This is why 'gridlock' occurs as certain traffic thresholds are reached, and why in the school holidays a reduction of traffic levels of around one fifth can realise a drop in congestion of around one third.

Such is the level of congestion that we now spend a remarkable amount of time sitting in our cars going nowhere. After publishing research suggesting that Britain's roads were the most congested in Europe (Chapter One), CfIT (2002) estimated that on average we each spend something in the order of eight hours per year in congestion. While at the individual level this may not sound all that much (although remember that it is an average figure that, by definition, hides extremes), on aggregate the UK's population spends a mind-boggling 50,000 *years* stuck in traffic every 12 months. And being stuck in traffic costs money. There have been many attempts over the years to estimate the costs of congestion (Table 2.2), not only to highlight the economic waste of people being stuck in traffic rather than working (or learning or consuming or, indeed, delivering the goods that we end up consuming), but also to justify the construction of new roads and other transport infrastructure on the basis of the time and cost savings 'released' by getting traffic moving again (Chapter Four). For several years, a figure of £15–£20 billion put forward by the Confederation of British Industry (CBI) was common currency as a reasonable estimate of the costs of congestion, and although subsequent research has cut this number in half, there is no doubt that even £8–£10 billion per year is a very significant annual loss to the economy. Goodwin (2004, p 2) suggests that whatever the headline figure, 'the really costly effect of congestion is not the slightly increased average time, but the greater than average effect in particular locations and markets, and the greatly increased unreliability'.

Given the scale of the problem, actually doing something about traffic and congestion remains one of most important aspects of transport policy. Sadly, it is also one of the hardest transport policy nuts to crack. In the medium term, there are four main ways in which traffic congestion can be reduced. One, which continues to find favour with advocates of Predict and Provide, is to build new road capacity. In urban areas this is problematic, as there is often simply not the space and/or the impact on the built and natural environments will be too high. Even supposing that these issues can be resolved, or in cases where the proposed new road is intra-urban, there is the phenomenon of 'induced traffic' to contend with. We know that building new roads generates more traffic and the problem of congestion can quickly return (Chapter One). Even in the era of possible 'peak car' – the idea that falls in car use seen in several developed countries since the mid-2000s might be the beginnings of a profound adjustment of the importance of the car in our mobility system (Le Vine and Jones, 2012; Goodwin 2012; see Chapter Three) – such new roads that are constructed will need to have their benefits 'locked in' to ensure as far as possible that the boon of additional capacity is not sacrificed to further congestion only a few years into the future.

The second approach is to spread the load of demand more evenly. As we noted above, congestion is heavily concentrated in time and space, which means that strategies to ameliorate it might operate in either or both of these dimensions. The concept of spreading the commute across time is not new – many companies have successfully operated flexitime schemes for several decades now – and the continual improvement of ICTs should, at least in theory, permit more people to work from home more of the time. The slow or patchy take-up of

Table 2.2: Estimated costs of congestion to the British economy

Source	Estimated annual cost (£billions)	Comments
Confederation of British Industry, 1989	15	
BBC, 1998	19	Attributed to the industry publication *CBI News*.
The Institute of Directors, 2007	28	
The Policy Exchange (think-tank), 2008	21	
Transport Minister Norman Baker, 2010	'almost' 25	This is more than three times the Prime Minister's estimate of £7bn (see below).
Welsh Government, 2010	'around' 30	Attributed to Goodwin (2004), although incorrectly; the author makes reference to others' methodology being hypothetically extrapolated into the future.
Freight on Rail, 2011	24	Attributed to the Freight Transport Association.
British Chambers of Commerce, 2011	23.3	*Local Transport Today* editor's note: 'nice precision – ed.'.
Hitachi, 2011	22	Attributed to the government.
Friends of the Earth, 2011	19	
Automotive Council UK, 2011	'about' 12	
Transport Minister Norman Baker, 2011	11	Referring only to congestion in urban areas.
Prime Minister David Cameron, March 2012	7	
Confederation of British Industry, 2012	8	
Claire Haigh of Greener Journeys, 2012	11	Writing in the *New Statesman*.
Freight on Rail (again), undated	17	Different from its other estimate.
Passenger Transport Executives' Group (pteg), undated	'at least' 11	
House of Commons Transport Select Committee, undated	20	Attributed to the CBI.
Network Rail, undated	10	
Staffordshire County Council, undated	'around' 16	Also attributed to the CBI.

Source: Local Transport Today (2012a)

these options more generally is due to the cultures of the workplace rather than any technological or genuine operational barrier. As Susan often ponders during her morning commute, it's the peer pressure of company practices that obliges people to arrive at the office at 8.59 each day (the notion of 'presenteeism' is generated by many managers' unwittingly pseudo-Popperian belief that only work that can be directly observed actually exists). As academics, we are extremely fortunate to be in charge of our own diaries most of the time, and although this is obviously impossible to emulate in many occupations, there is no innate reason why large segments of the white-collar service economy cannot move to a more flexible work pattern (see Felstead, 2011; Fu et al, 2012).[7] The notion that employers have to 'let go' a little is important, because in order to have a meaningful effect on peak time flows, flexible working has to have sufficient leeway that commuters can completely avoid travelling in the 'traditional' rush hour.

Spreading the peak across space is more difficult, and sometimes counterproductive. Firms often attempt to reduce the impact of congestion (and other costs) on their operations by moving offices to secondary centres, but this works only where the nature of the business allows it (Chapter Four) and the provision of transport in the new location is good enough to ensure a smooth transition between sites. The decentralisation of some back-office financial services operations to outer London town centres has been a success, since the public transport network across the city is good enough to support this kind of commuting, but even here non-radial journeys to work are sometimes difficult. Elsewhere in the country employer relocations can result in the kind of 'spatial mismatch' where many workers without a car find it difficult to travel to new employment sites, given the paucity of public transport provision outside core areas (Houston, 2001).

A third means of combating congestion is to provide and promote alternatives to the car by investing in public transport, walking and cycling (see Chapter Three regarding the active modes). We have already noted that rail transport is a particularly effective way of moving large numbers of people along traditional radial routes. But achieving so-called 'modal shift', that is, the transfer of journeys from (in this case) the car to other modes, is much harder when the public transport alternative on offer is the bus rather than the train or tram. Buses have the advantage of being able to 'go anywhere' in the sense that they are not restricted to routes with tracks, and this is particularly useful in increasingly decentralised urban areas that promote a complex spatial pattern of non-radial commuting (see below). The problem is that outside of London and a (very) few other cities they tend to have become viewed as a 'last resort' means of transport, used mostly by people unfortunate enough to find themselves at the lower end of the socioeconomic hierarchy, and are not the kind of travelling environment that many car drivers would be willing to consider (see Lucas and Jones, 2012). This state of affairs has come about for various reasons, including a cultural obsession with individual motoring (Chapter Three), the impact of bus-sector privatisation and deregulation (which focused on cutting costs rather than improving the quality of services in many areas) and, sadly, a lack of political will to actually do anything about the quality of the experience of using the bus so that, in the grandiose words of a Labour government document, it would have been upgraded 'from workhorse to thoroughbred' (Chapter Four).

Although that same government envisaged 25 new light rail schemes being built in cities up and down the country, these plans were dropped because, as enthusiasm for 'doing something about traffic' waned, ministers began to view trams as representing poor value for money. This seems strange because they are recognised as being far more likely to effect modal shift – unlike the bus, they are seen by many drivers as a credible alternative to the car (see Knowles and Abrantes, 2008) – but for the time being, in the absence of lots of new trams, the bus remains the best hope for making much of the public transport system more integrated and sustainable. Some local authorities have taken a renewed interest in bus transport (transport authorities in London, Oxford, Yorkshire and the North East of England are particularly good examples), and there is *some* evidence that bus operators themselves have become better at developing their business by offering a higher-quality product (Jain, 2011; although see Chapter Four). Notwithstanding the generally poor image of the bus, particular types of service can prove popular among motorists. Key among these is Park and Ride, which usually takes people from where they have parked their car to the city centre (or another 'honey pot' destination such as a National Park centre) without stopping to pick up anyone else along the way (Meek, 2008). Partly, such services are popular because they can be cheaper and quicker than parking in town, but intriguingly the psychology of using a bus that is carrying only other car drivers – in other words, like-minded people rather than Thatcher's 'failures' (Chapter One) – is also important (see Bos et al, 2004).

Much to Susan's disgust, part of the key to making buses an attractive alternative to cars has been the idea that road space should be specifically allocated to them in the form of dedicated bus lanes. Although the concept has been around for years, the sustainable transport objectives of the Labour government gave it a new lease of life, not just to make bus journeys themselves quicker and more reliable but also to deliberately constrain the car. The likes of Susan (and Jeremy Clarkson, who made the scrapping of the bus lane on the M4 motorway into London something of a *cause célèbre* for the pro-car lobby) might think of this as a 'trendy' idea put about by interfering planners, but as soon as the problem of how best to solve congestion is conceived in terms of moving the maximum number of *people* as opposed to *vehicles* along a given corridor its rationale becomes clear (Figure 2.2). The amount of road space required to transport people in cars at the average occupancy rate for commuter journeys of 1.2 people per car is very extensive indeed. The average single-decker bus carries as many people as around 35–40 cars, and a modest three-carriage commuter train carries around 200 people, equivalent to 170 cars. These numbers make the efficiency gains available from reallocating road space to fewer, larger vehicles rather obvious.

Controversial they may be, but on their own bus lanes are actually rather modest attempts to deal with the problem of congestion in the grander scheme of things. The really big prize, which has long generated intense professional and (latterly) public debate, is the idea of charging to use the roads at the point of use. Numerous studies have shown how different types of road-user charging schemes could be very effective at

Figure 2.2: Relative capacity efficiencies of cars and buses

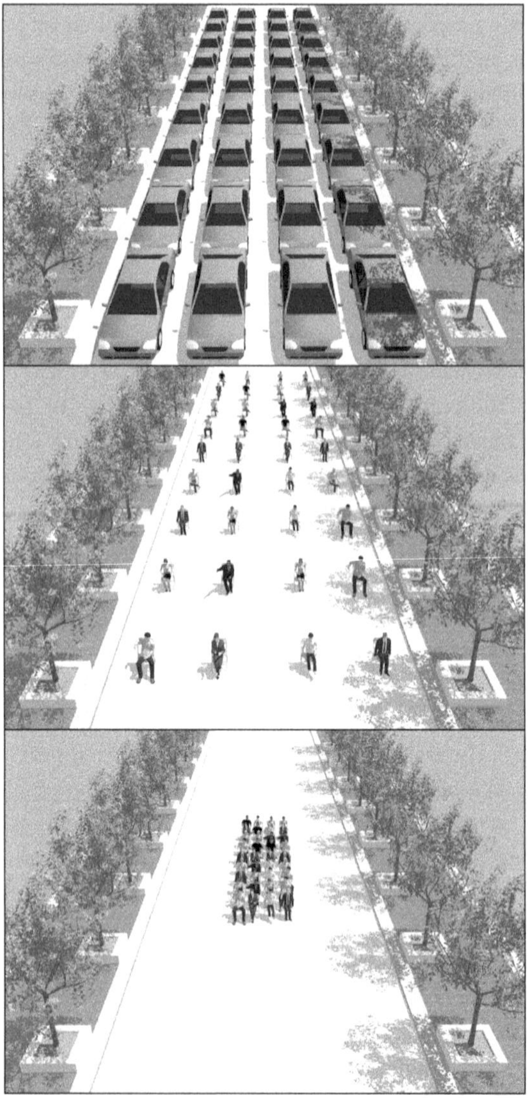

Source: Reproduced by kind permission of Fehr and Pearce Transport Consultants.

cutting congestion. CfIT (2002) reckons that a national scheme would reduce the amount of queuing traffic by up to 44%, for example, and Glaister and Graham (2005) demonstrate that reductions in road use of 9–19% could be achieved (see also DfT, 2004). Why is it, then, that roads are the exception to the rule that things should generally cost more to use when they are in greatest demand?

One reason is that although many people (Susan included) like to moan about congestion, when asked genuinely probing questions about its effects on them as individuals, it just doesn't register as *that* important a factor in people's daily lives. People may well get stressed when they're actually stuck in a jam and are late for an important appointment, but it seems that they have come to accept traffic jams as a fact of life and get on with dealing with them as they would any other mundane irritation. This is not to say that they have no awareness that congestion is at some level a 'bad thing' – perhaps because successive governments and the myriad vested interests that constitute the 'road lobby' like to talk this up in the course of defending their policies or pet schemes – but, as Goodwin and Lyons (2010, p 7) neatly summarise, their attitude seems to be, 'well, I am not bothered myself, but it must be serious because everybody else says so'. In this context, it would appear to be people's privileging of their own rather than the collective good that explains why proposals for congestion charging schemes in Manchester and Edinburgh have been struck down in referendums (Gaunt et al, 2007; *Guardian*, 2008).

There is also the reality that many people perceive road-user charging schemes as an 'extra' tax on motoring. The word 'extra' is important here, since one of the main barriers to implementing changes in policy such as a shift in how we pay for and price the use of roads is the widespread belief that they are 'already paid for'. As long ago as the 1920s, Winston Churchill argued that a direct link between 'road' taxes and 'road' expenditure was untenable when, as Chancellor of the Exchequer, he began the abolition of the original ring-fenced Road Fund, which was eventually replaced with the more anaemic-sounding Vehicle Excise Duty (VED; this remains, and is what you pay for the tax disc in your windscreen). Voicing his discontent with the roads lobby of that period in characteristic style, Churchill said, 'Motorists are to be privileged for all time to have the whole yield of the tax on motors devoted to roads? Such contentions are absurd, and constitute … an outrage upon common sense' (ipayroadtax.com, undated and unpaginated).

Unfortunately, reasoned debate about the relationship between what motorists pay to use the road network and what it actually costs to run it is all too seldom in evidence. In seeking to avoid being perceived as 'anti-car', lest Mr and Mrs Motorway Man exact revenge at the ballot box (Pickard, 2010), successive ministers have not exactly helped to advance the case for a policy that could be very effective and that they have at various times been actively considering. We in no way underestimate the political *cojones* required to deliver genuinely radical policies in the transport sphere (Docherty and Shaw, 2011a), but not confronting an issue doesn't mean it will go away, and in the case of road-user charging, failing to lead the debate has allowed some reactionary and, on occasion, frankly juvenile positions to gain credence that they simply do not deserve. In 2009, the last of Labour's (rather many) Secretaries of State for Transport, Lord Adonis, announced a *volte-face* on earlier proposals for a national road-charging scheme after 1.8 million people signed a petition on the Downing Street website protesting against the idea. Justifying his decision, Adonis said, 'I don't believe as Britain is coming out of recession and motorists are feeling under pressure, that this is the time to put road charging on the agenda.' In response, Peter Roberts, the 'Midlands Businessman' (that is, hard-core Motorway Man) who created the petition, crowed that 'It is great that the government has at last recognised road pricing is an unfair and unjust imposition on motorists, who already pay a fortune in taxes on their cars and petrol, and finally decided to scrap the idea' (*Daily Telegraph*, 2009).

Roberts' highly emotive language – unfair, unjust, imposition, a fortune in taxes – is used to position driving as an inalienable right and seems to denounce taxation on the activity as a moral outrage. He is supported in his analysis by much of the popular press, which often spins the fact that *direct* expenditure on the roads is only about one third of the £30 billion or so of income generated by road and fuel taxes annually. The *Daily Mail* (2009) claims that each British driver is being 'milked' by around £300 'too much' every year. At 55–60% of the cost of a litre of fuel, there is little doubt that the fuel tax/VAT take seems high, especially when this is considered alongside VED. But, like many good taxation horror stories, the *Daily Mail*'s is rather one sided. In this case, the calculation conveniently ignores the very significant costs associated with the 'externalities' of driving. Externalities are negative impacts that impose a cost that is not picked up by the individual(s) who cause them, but instead by society as a whole. While out of their own pockets drivers pay to buy/lease, maintain and tax their cars, and for the fuel they use and for insurance, they do not directly cover all the costs of motoring, including any congestion they play a part in causing. As we sit here writing this, for example, there is lots of congestion on the road network (it's 5.40pm) that is nothing to do with us. Yet we are still being penalised for its impact on the functioning of the economy, even if it is just that the goods we buy in the supermarket when we leave our respective offices cost more because the number of driver shifts the delivery company has to pay for is higher than it would be if more traffic moved in freer-flowing conditions (McKinnon et al (2009) estimate that 23% of delay time in road freight transport is accounted for by congestion). Once the cost of accidents, air pollution, CO_2 emissions and all manner of health-related issues, ranging from increased obesity to respiratory diseases – all paid for by the NHS, the Environment Agency, local authorities and any number of other public and private bodies (that higher price of goods again) – are factored in, then the external costs of motoring become very high indeed (Chapter Three). The Cabinet Office (2009) estimates that they add up to around £40 billion per year in urban areas alone.

We would think that Mr Roberts, as a businessman, would be very much in favour of a system of paying for road use that identifies and allocates its costs and benefits proportionately and transparently among its users. Road-user charging would recoup the costs of congestion, leaving fuel tax and VED to help pay for other externalities. While precise figures for all the different costs and benefits will probably never be attainable, we are able to work out roughly what they are, and any charging regime would clearly need to err on the side of conservatism to qualify as the art of the possible. But if the Cabinet Office's figure is anything like correct, then far from being a rip-off, driving is in fact cheap at the price, and it is society that is subsidising the motorist rather than the other way around. Churchill's logic has been turned on its head; nowadays, even if every penny of the motoring taxes that drivers pay was spent on the road network and mitigating its externalities, this still wouldn't be enough to cover the costs they impose. Perhaps some in the roads lobby should be grateful that they tend not to use public transport all that much: despite increases in vehicle running costs, by the end of the 2000s the real cost of motoring overall was not all that different than it was in 1997. Real train and bus fares increased by around 15% and 25% respectively in the same time period (DfT, 2009).

One thing for national politicians to remember is that a sizeable charging scheme has already been successfully introduced in Britain. The London Congestion Charge has now been in place for over 10 years, has reduced congestion levels by up to 15% and generates hundreds of millions of pounds for improvements in public transport, especially the bus network (Santos, 2008; TfL, 2008; White, 2008).[8] The scale of the endeavour (it costs £10 a day to enter central London), the value of the concentration of economic activity in the area it covers and the fact that very few people have to pay the charge compared to the number who benefit from it, make the capital the ideal place for a charging scheme to deliver benefits quickly. This is not to say that rolling out some kind of equivalent scheme(s) more generally across the country would not deliver important improvements, especially in other large cities. Fully 45 years after Reuben Smeed's seminal (1964) report on road pricing, and 18 years after the publication of *Transport: The new realism*, the Prime Minister's Strategy Unit conceded that 'road pricing is likely to be a highly effective way of resolving congestion in major urban areas' (Cabinet Office, 2009, p 59). It would also provide a very effective means of raising finance to help pay for road improvements that would remain necessary to bring the quality of the network up to standards that are commonplace in mainland Europe (no one should expect drivers to pay for something without getting anything tangible in return) and major public transport capacity enhancements necessary to accommodate the surge in demand for non-car modes that would arise if people decided to leave their cars at home rather than pay to use the roads at peak periods. It is about time that ministers started leading a sensible debate on the matter.

Working mother

This morning's rain showers are particularly heavy. Turning on the ignition, Susan realises she's already really quite wet just from the short dash from the front door onto the driveway and from making sure Lucy is safely in her seat. She consoles herself by thinking that she has much the best deal of all the family, given her door-to-door transport, complete with automatic climate control. 'I wonder what state Paul's in now?' she smiles, remembering that, when he'd left in his own car this morning, he'd forgotten to take the umbrella that would be very useful in town right about now. But then … select reverse and *crunch*. The car moves nowhere, and instead makes noises reminiscent of that injured animal from last night's *Springwatch*. After a few more attempts to get into gear Susan realises that no, she's going nowhere in her car today. 'How on Earth have we ended up with *both* cars needing to be in the garage on the same day?'

Susan immediately finds the number of the local taxi company in her contacts list. 'We'll send a cab as soon as possible, but it's busy this morning because of the weather,' admonishes the voice at the other end of the phone. Fortunately, the cab arrives within 10 minutes and, although the traffic is indeed worse than usual, they reach the primary school without making Lucy late. The cab then follows the rest of Susan's normal morning journey, doubling back on itself for the trip across town to the business park. Already conscious that they'd better get a move on, Susan can't believe that the driver sits in the queue of traffic rather than using the bus lane. 'Why aren't we using *that?*' she asks curtly, stabbing a finger towards the empty red tarmac. 'Not allowed to – just another stupid rule to do us in,' replies the driver.[9] After spending the remainder of the journey wondering whether hanging or flogging would be more appropriate for the council's transport planners, Susan is duly relieved of £15 as she leaves her cab. Thoroughly irritated by the start to her day, she makes her way into the office wondering who'll be first to notice her late arrival.

That afternoon, after several futile efforts to find someone who could give her a lift home at her usual time – like many women, Susan works part time so she can leave early enough each day to collect Lucy from school – she phones the taxi company again, and is promptly parted from another £15 for her return journey. A round of phone calls begins as soon as she gets home: first to Paul, whose stock sinks further on the news that his car will not be ready until tomorrow afternoon, and then to a few of her friends to see who might be able to deputise on the school run tomorrow. Fortunately, she strikes lucky with Linda, who's having a few days off work. But still, how will she get herself to the office? Even without the doubling back she'll still be forking out at least £10 for a cab to sit in the same traffic she normally battles against 'for free'. 'And how the hell do the cleaners get themselves to work? I know at least four of them don't have cars,' Susan thinks to herself. On his return home, she challenges Paul to 'use that app on your phone to work out how I can get to the office'. Sensing his wife's frustration, Paul is quick out of the starting blocks. 'According to Traveline it's a doddle,' he says, after punching in the postcode of Susan's office. 'Take the train with me one stop, then a bus to the business park.'

The profound changes in the structure and operation of the labour market we mentioned earlier in the chapter have also impacted upon the nature of the commute. Along with the shift from primary and manufacturing to service employment came the feminisation of the labour market, to the point that a majority of people now employed in Britain and many other western countries are women (see *Economist*, 2009). Of course, the distribution of work between the sexes remains nothing like equal, with women more likely to work part time, in low-paid jobs, and to combine their work with other responsibilities, especially caring for children or elderly parents (McDowell, 2004). This means that women often have very different patterns of mobility, and hence different demands on the transport system. While plenty of men maintain the traditional radial commute – it is still more likely that '*Mister* Brown goes off to town on the eight twenty-one' – Susan and millions of women like her find themselves dropping the kid(s) off at school before going to work, and picking them up afterwards, often on their way to the supermarket or to other locations such as the doctor's surgery (Dobbs, 2005; Roberts et al, 2011; Schwanen, 2011).[10]

Sometimes these journeys are rather complex exercises of 'trip chaining', that is, where trips to numerous different places are joined together rather than being made separately. Instead of leaving home and going to the school, and then returning before later going to the doctor's, before once again returning and later still going into town to pick up the dry cleaning, all of these errands are run in a single sweep. As viewed on a map, trip chaining can involve some quite elaborate route planning – double-backs and filigrees that can be extremely difficult to do on public transport. For this reason, trip chaining is often easiest to do by car: one of the enduring gender politics issues in transport is that, despite the fact that women are more likely to have to manage this kind of complex existence, they are also less likely to have access to a car, even when the household possesses one (see Dobbs, 2005; Young, 1999).

Susan's morning commute is at the height of the peak, and the fact that she is one of thousands of people competing to use the local road network at exactly the same time each day is the reason why she suffers the tragedy of the commons that congestion represents. She puts up with it because she has to, or at least because she *feels* as if she has to; until circumstances forced her hand, Susan never really gave much thought to the idea that she could fulfil her morning routine without using her car. Researchers have for some time been interested in the extent to which people feel 'reliant' or 'dependent' on their cars. There is some semantic muddle in that reliance and dependence are taken to mean different things in different studies (which, we might say, is rather typical of too much academic writing on social science phenomena), but for our purposes these terms both relate to journeys that people regard as incapable of being made by alternative modes of transport. Lucas and Jones (2009, p 117) usefully refine this point by noting that in many cases it is not actually the car itself that people become reliant or dependent upon, 'but rather what it delivers in the context of our time constrained, spatially dispersed and highly security conscious lifestyles'. This is important in understanding people's travel behaviour. Susan likes to make sure Lucy is dropped off at school to ensure she's safe and because, by today's standards at least, the journey is too long for her to make on her own at her age (Chapter Three). She can also make it to work on time and still do all her errands before Paul comes home if she takes the car.

There is some debate about just how dependent or reliant on the car people *actually* are for journeys where it is routinely used. In *Car Dependence*, a study funded by the RAC Foundation, Goodwin (1995, p 9) explains that:

> For many people, the word 'dependence' does not accurately describe their perception of how car use helps them to resolve [their journey] constraints. Rather, they see cars as providing independence, with concrete other advantages including the immediate convenience to make journeys without planning, real financial savings (and some illusionary ones), privacy from unpleasant people who might be using public transport, enjoyment of a feeling of control over choices affecting their daily lives and pleasure in performing active driving tasks.

People can usually recognise when and where they use the car solely for convenience, and where genuine alternatives are available, should they have the time or inclination to use them. A good example might be driving a quarter of a mile to the shop on a Sunday morning to pick up a paper and a pint of milk; most people could clearly walk this trip instead of taking the car. But for journeys they associate with *having* to drive, it is quite possible that reasonable alternatives have been dismissed without due consideration. Some trips are certainly what Lucas and Jones (2009) call 'objectively constrained', in that there is no online or public transport alternative available, or the purpose of the journey is such that these things are wholly impractical. Imagine, for example, taking bulky Christmas presents to an elderly relative who lives in a deep rural area nowhere near a bus route.

Other trips, though, they classify as 'subjectively constrained', in that reasonable alternatives do exist but for one reason or another are not taken up. This might just be because they are not known about, and some kind of Personalised Travel Planning (PTP) would help 'car complacents' or 'aspiring environmentalists' to leave their cars on the drive more often (Anable 2005; see Chapter One). In the Smarter Choices project in Worcester, Peterborough and Darlington, Sloman et al (2010) found that PTP can be remarkably effective at promoting modal shift (Chapter Three). Equally, it might be that alternatives are just seen as undesirable either in and of themselves, or in the context of the life-style to which car users have become accustomed. The act of having to change buses or trains is a common barrier to modal shift – the so-called 'transfer penalty' can result in the attractiveness of a public transport journey dropping by half for each change (Guo and Wilson, 2011; Vande Walle and Steenbergen, 2006) – and people often suggest that public transport journeys take too long in the context of their busy lives.

Even here, PTP has a role; all that might be required is the encouragement to see things in a slightly different way. Paul used to drive to work, but had to arrive at the office rather earlier than he does now on account of 'wasting' his time in the car as opposed to doing his emails on the train. When his doctor told him he needed to do more exercise, he briefly considered driving to the gym, before realising that he would get all he needed walking to and from the station at either end of his commute (and without the ambitious monthly membership fees to boot). Susan, too, might have more flexibility than she thinks, even if it is only on one or two days a week. Her friend Linda was able to help her out with the school run, and Paul found that the trip to her office wasn't all that bad, especially given the new bus lanes. And in any case, is it really that far for Lucy to walk safely on her own or with some of her friends?

It is also worth remembering that the number of journeys that are currently 'objectively constrained' could be substantially reduced if genuine alternatives – say, more frequent, direct and geographically widespread public transport services that operate for longer periods of the day – were made available, convenient and cheap enough. Increasing the availability of such options would be of wider societal benefit, particularly for those on low incomes who struggle to afford to keep a car running (see Gray et al, 2001), or for those without access to a car at all for whom the notion of reliance or dependence on an automobile seems a rather indulgent luxury. One of our main bugbears is when measures to reallocate resources and space from the car to public transport, especially the bus, are denounced by (allegedly) left-of-centre politicians as 'hitting the poorest' (see, for example, *Guardian*, 2009; also Oberholzer-Gee and Weck-Hannemann, 2002). Of course, such interventions actually do precisely the opposite, given that those people most deserving of support to help in accessing work, education and/or childcare are much more likely to use public transport than to have a car in the first place (see Department for Transport, 2004).

A further factor complicating journey patterns both in the commute and in regular travel is that shops, services and centres of employment have in recent decades tended to locate themselves further and further away from where we live as part of a wider rush towards decentralisation. Permissive planning policies taking advantage of the flexibility of the car have led to the colonisation of relatively cheap and easy-to-develop 'greenfield' sites around the edges of towns and cities. But this has changed the real level of *accessibility* of these outlets – in other words, the extent to which they are 'get-at-able' by the population at large (Nutley, 1979; see Farrington, 2007) – with the effect of significantly increasing the number of both objectively and subjectively constrained trips that people choose/have to make. When almost all jobs, shops and services are co-located in the city centre or in one or two large, multipurpose nodes, they are easy to reach by public transport and on foot or by bike as well as by car. When and where, however, these things are increasingly dispersed, the capacity of public transport systems to link several smaller, out-of-town retail and service sites to a city's major residential areas is greatly constrained. Walking and cycling between these places can be all but impossible, especially when they have been designed predominantly for car users.

All of this brings us back to the opening point of the chapter: look out of the window, and what you see is strongly influenced by the transport technologies available to those who planned and built the urban environment. In large part, the transport debate in Britain is now so problematic because, when you look out of the window in 2013, you'll soon realise that we are now grappling with the transport and consequent socioeconomic implications of decades of land use and development policies that have sought to graft car-friendly environments onto our historic towns and cities that are 'foot' and 'tracked' places at heart. This conundrum is given further resonance by environmental debates about how we need to (re)design places so that they become more sustainable in future. Much has been written about the 'best' form of urban structure to maximise the use of public transport and the active modes and to reduce the carbon emissions associated with transport (see, for example, Camagni and Hull, 2002; Hull, 2005). The idea that we need to make our towns and cities more compact so that activities are brought closer together is intuitively attractive, and has been highly influential in supporting the notion of 'transit orientated development' – prioritising urban growth towards high-density areas around key public transport nodes – that has been around since the first Scandinavian experiments in the 1930s and 1940s and that has influenced many US cities such as Arlington, Denver and Portland (Oregon) as they seek to reinvigorate their urban cores.

At the same time, compaction is by no means a panacea. One problem with what in the UK has become known as 'town centres first' is that it relies on a number of assumptions about how the economy functions, many of which may well be out of date, given the recent structural changes in society and the economy that we have highlighted. Take, for example, the core principle underlying the idea of compaction, that more people should live closer to their place of work in order to reduce the demand for commuting. Given the increasing churn in the labour market, the rise of part-time and portfolio working, and the 'feminisation' of the idea of work (not just that a greater proportion of the workforce are women, but that also, increasingly, men's behaviours are becoming more 'female' in their juggling of work, caring and other tasks), even if people make a decision to locate near a particular job, their proximity to a workplace is increasingly less likely to last. Added to this is the reality that many households choose to locate on the basis of a compromise between partners' commutes to different places, which themselves may change over time (Green, 1997). The traditional notion of 'self-contained' communities, in which people can access all the activities they undertake in close proximity, can be illusory (Breheny, 1995; 1997; Neuman, 2005).

A further issue is that continuing price signals from the market are hard to ignore. The high-density residential development championed by compact city advocates is only really viable in relatively few of Britain's larger, more successful cities that can accommodate both a prosperous youthful population and a growing service sector to employ them. Elsewhere, the market is still demonstrating the demand for new industry, retailing and housing in greenfield locations, especially in those places in the North that remain blighted by declining post-industrial neighbourhoods. This is why development has gradually crept along the road that Susan drives every day to her office. Even in London, with its very high densities and massive investment in mass transit modes in and around the central core, it is the suburbs that are leading jobs and population growth. We should be clear that we are not seeking to argue in support of on-going decentralisation of shops and services – it is still easier to promote walking, cycling and public transport journeys to fewer, multipurpose nodes – but the extent to which new, high-density residential development can on its own address current transport problems is very much open to question. Indeed, there is modelling work that suggests that the environmental gains to be had from compaction are not that great, and certainly are likely to be less than could be achieved from much simpler policy interventions such as road pricing (Mitchell et al, 2011).

The argument that road pricing is the most deliverable intervention (in policy, if not political terms) is further supported by the peculiarities of Britain's planning systems. Even where infrastructure improvements to the transport system are justified – perhaps because of high demand that would remain even if we introduced comprehensive road-user charging, or because outmoded infrastructure needs replacing, or because we need much greater public transport capacity to accommodate modal shift – it can be devilishly difficult to push them through the planning process. Planning in the UK has a long tradition of allowing every voice to be heard in a matter, consistent with the wider principles of the English and Scots legal systems. The obvious downside of this is that it gives NIMBYism a powerful voice, and can hold up schemes for which there is significant wider public support. As Nigel Harris from *Rail* magazine (2013, p 1) commented in relation to HS2, 'it's entirely right that someone with a pleasant, leafy view from their garden seeks to protect it, but this cannot be at the expense of the country as a whole'. Columnist David Aaronovitch voiced even more frustration in his splendidly titled piece 'Welcome to Britain, the ludicrous Land of No', in which he bemoaned 'our middle classes' depressing knack of preventing any changes that will make this country better' (Aaronovitch, 2012).

The cost of such NIMBYism can be astronomical. Take the case of the Aberdeen Western Peripheral Route (AWPR), an expressway-quality bypass for the city that has been in formal planning for almost 20 years. The Scottish Government was finally able to issue tenders to build the road after various legal actions culminated in a hearing at the UK Supreme Court in late 2012 (Supreme Court, 2012). Dismissal of the final appeal meant that the road could go ahead, but only after a near doubling of the original construction price estimates, attributed to the delays and legal costs incurred. As a result, local politicians had no hesitation in naming our erstwhile colleague and leader of the anti-AWPR group *Road Sense*, William Walton, as 'the £230 million man' (STV, 2012, unpaginated). This may be an extreme case, and one exaggerated by the political interests of various high-rolling local protagonists (including Alex Salmond, the First Minister of Scotland, whose constituency is served by the AWPR), but there is no doubt that the operation of the planning system is a major factor in explaining why it is much harder and more expensive to build transport infrastructure in the UK than elsewhere in Europe (Chapter One). Those of us in support of necessary infrastructure investment have more than a little *jalousie* towards the French, who commonly manage to plan and build major roads and public transport schemes in 7–10 years rather than the 15–20 that similar projects take in Britain. Of course cultural differences are important, with revolutionary attitudes surviving in that once a scheme has received its Declaration of Public Utility, then the state presses ahead unabashed to ensure that nothing gets in the way of the project, both literally and metaphorically. Attempting to carbon copy the French approach would be too *dirigiste* for tastes on this side of the Channel, but there have been moves none the less to try to streamline the planning of major projects to a greater or lesser degree (see Docherty and Mackie, 2010; Chapter Seven).

Reducing the time it takes to improve our transport systems is important because the gains to be had from properly designed and properly targeted schemes are real and can bring significant economic and social value. Although we are often sceptical of the more ambitious policy and political statements about the 'transformative' nature of transport investment that are beloved of some politicians (Chapter Four), we agree with Banister and Berechman's (2001) simple yet important assertion that locations with poor-quality transport are at a disadvantage when compared with those that have high-quality transport infrastructure. Lots of advice to government has reached the same conclusion, making the point that so long as they are delivered as part of a broader package of support, properly conceived transport projects can help to make the labour market function better, bring assets such as land back into productive use, and make it more likely that firms will invest in an area because it offers a good quality of life for the potential workforce (SACTRA, 1999; Eddington, 2006; House of Commons, 2011).

This final point is critical. The commute has become a grind for too many people, diminishing the quality of life that transport opportunities are supposed to support and expand (Chapter Six). Commuting may grant the 'gift of travel time' (Jain and Lyons, 2008) to a lucky few, but for the majority it is more stressful than it needs to be, and it takes time away not just from productive work, but also from family and other important social ties (Lyons and Urry, 2005; Paez and Whalen, 2010; Wener and Evans, 2011). The Cabinet Office's *Analysis of urban transport* (2009) explored why, beyond the 'usual' arguments about helping the economy and the direct impacts of congestion, reducing the impact of the commute and other journeys like it might contribute to achieving better health outcomes and improving the quality of urban environments so that general well-being is promoted more effectively. In the Smith household, our Motorway Man Paul has already learned how to substantially improve his quality of life by altering the way he travels to and from work. Many younger people are making similar choices, prioritising connectivity to their online social networks on the move rather than their parents' generation's desire to own a car as early as possible (Chapter Three). But for others, especially women like Susan with their multiple responsibilities and the complex travel patterns these generate, the transport system doesn't always help to make life simpler (Roberts et al, 2011). Glenn Lyons (2004, p 502) made the point that the 'majority of the population is female and yet arguably our transport systems have been shaped around male, middle-class, middle-aged professionals who travel without children or luggage'. In order to really 'do something about traffic', our transport policies and priorities will have to pay more attention to the needs of 'Motorway Woman' as well as 'Motorway Man'.

Notes

[1] As a plaque in London Marylebone station commemorating the centenary of his birth notes, Betjeman was a real 'friend of the railways', perhaps best known in this regard for leading the campaign to save St Pancras from demolition in the 1960s.

[2] A version of this stereotype provided the basis for *Butterflies*, *The Good Life*, *Terry and June* and a range of other highly popular sitcoms as late as the 1970s and early 1980s.

[3] Or freeway, or expressway, depending on local terminology.

[4] That said, Glasgow kept building some of its planned urban motorways right up until the five-mile long, £692 million 'completion' of the M74 in 2011.

[5] See http://londonfirst.co.uk/wp-content/uploads/2013/02/LF_CROSSRAIL2_REPORT_AW_Single_Pages.pdf.

[6] In comparison with the DfT, Scottish ministers had until recently taken a different tack by attempting to fund as much as possible of their programme of rail improvements directly, and to keep fares increases (slightly) lower. The EGIP improvements will, however, be funded on 'credit', like most schemes south of the border.

[7] We would argue that a shift in working culture away from presenteeism would have huge benefits in other areas important for overall well-being, but these ideas are for other books in this series.

[8] Congestion levels in London have since rebounded, but this is in large part a result of conscious decisions to reallocate more road space to buses and tackle the backlog of required utility upgrades and other roadworks (TfL, 2012).

[9] The decision as to whether taxis can use bus lanes (and indeed what colour to paint the bus lanes!) is down to individual local authorities, and practice varies across the country.

[10] Your male author with kids (Iain) would like to point out that this is not the case in his dual-career household (!).

THREE

The school run

Going to school; walking, cycling, safety and health; why people like their cars

Born to run

The first morning of the new school term is always pandemonium in the Smiths' household. Although Susan and Paul are both up early, they seem to have forgotten just how much earlier they need to be up than during the holidays. Of course they didn't prepare packed lunches the evening before, and getting the uniforms ready was left until the very last minute. Jack has been looking forward to seeing his classmates again, not least because he has a new bike to show off to them, and now he's 13 Paul and Susan have decided that he can cycle to school and back every day. He sees himself out rather earlier than he needs to and leaves the rest of the clan to it. Sophie, the eldest, much preferred it when her dad used to give her a lift on the way to the station, and, to her continuing chagrin, begins the new term as she did the last two, by taking the bus to the Technology College on the other side of town. Although Lucy's primary school is less than a mile from the Smiths' house, we saw in the last chapter that Susan drops her off on the way to work even though it is in the wrong direction for her commute. Susan is steeling herself for the morning rush hour. 'I much prefer it when the schools are on holiday,' she mentioned to Paul the previous evening, 'because I can have a bit more of a lie-in and the drive's never as stressful. The traffic's always much lighter when the schools are off.'

It is no surprise that a major aspect determining a household's travel patterns is the act of taking children to school. The most significant change in the nature of the journey to school over many years has been its tendency to replicate broader trends in modal share (House of Commons, 2009a). This has been to such an extent that for some people a link between driving the kids to school and 'good' parenting has become ingrained. Parents may fall victim to a 'social trap' in their 'desire to be considered as responsible parents by conforming with the practices of other parents who, for example, drive their children to school and make sure they are accompanied by adults at all times' (Carver et al, 2008, p 224). Self-help guides, such as that published by Mumsnet (undated), provide tips for 'surviving the school run', although we note that even here sheer exasperation sets in towards the end, with the admonition that 'If all else fails … Buy them a bus pass and push them out the door.'

The term 'school run' refers particularly to the practice of adults driving children to their place of education. These trips are usually made by parents driving their own children, but family friends or relatives might also be involved, sometimes with some really quite sophisticated car-pooling where three or four children might be taken to more than one school in the same car. In some respects, the term has become rather pejorative as popular coverage of the extent to which the school run generates traffic congestion and pollution has grown. These negative connotations are not just perceived by those who don't have children of school age or who don't drive their kids to school: as many as 65% of parents engaged in the school run would prefer not to be driving (DfT, undated). The effects of their not doing so would be dramatic: 32% of these same parents said they would not use their car at all in the morning peak if they did not have to do the school run.[1] Such data are not inconsistent with Anable's (2005) findings that large numbers of people would rather leave their car at home more often than they currently do (Chapter One).

The National Travel Survey (DfT, 2010) notes that the school run accounts for about 16% of traffic in the rush hour, and in urban areas this figure actually reaches 24% at the most popular school travel time of 8.40am. While for trips to school of less than a mile walking is by far the most popular mode of travel – 82% of primary school children and 9 in 10 of those at secondary school go by foot – the amount of lift-giving has been increasing quite considerably. Writing in the early 2000s, the then Secretaries of State for Education and Transport, Charles Clarke and Alistair Darling, noted that the proportion of children travelling to school by car had almost doubled in the last 20 years (DfES, 2003), and in 2010 43% of primary school pupils and 24% of secondary school pupils were driven to school. Longer journeys resulted in an even higher proportion of these 'escort' trips being by car, with 67% of primary school children and a quarter of secondary school children being driven for journeys of five miles and more. In this context it is obvious why Susan notices the difference in road conditions during the school holidays, although in part this is also because she is more flexible about her own timings, in addition to the absolute level of traffic and congestion being lower (Headicar, 2011).

Although Clarke and Darling were aware that several factors have conspired to increase the number of school run trips over recent decades (DfES, 2003), they (perhaps rather tellingly) failed to acknowledge the general context that a large part of this shift was down to the impacts of successive governments' transport and related policies. Like other journeys, the school run has become more car orientated because of the greater propensity to use cars among a wider proportion of the population, a trend which is closely linked to changing land use patterns and the relocation of activities to sites that can be easily reached only by car. It is perhaps no wonder that parents and children have become more car dependent as they build related norms and routines around its flexibility, especially when the school run is combined with a commute to an out-of-town business park of the kind Susan works at (Chapter Two).

Keen as ever not to appear 'anti-car', the Secretaries of State noted that practical constraints may mean that there are no reasonable alternatives for the school run even where parents might actively have looked for one. Especially (but not exclusively) in rural areas, where the median travel distance between home and school is about one-and-a-half times as long as in towns and cities (Burgess et al, 2006), the car may well be the only credible option because it is too far to walk or cycle, or the bus service is inconvenient or non-existent. Where buses are available they may be considered too expensive, especially by families that do not qualify for free school transport, or parents may have concerns about their son or daughter being caught up in anti-social behaviour. The issue of anti-social behaviour on public transport was incorporated into the broader 'respect' agenda of the previous Labour administrations that aimed to promote better relations between individuals in public places (see Moore, 2011). Crime Concern (2004) sought to develop a training programme to help bus drivers resolve conflicts with and between school children. 'Bus drivers see young people as a major source of stress and damage' (p 1), its report began, although it was also emphasised that any successful training programme would encourage drivers to respect school children more, as well as the other way around.

The most common reasons cited by parents for driving their children to school are concerns about safety and security. This is understandable. As the Sutton Trust (2005) points out, the school run results in 40 deaths and 900 serious injuries a year, with children from lower-income families significantly more likely to be involved in an accident (Chapter Five). Although many safety campaigns focus on tabloid-friendly issues such as overcrowding and a lack of seatbelts, parents are well-attuned to real problems such as the heightened risk of accidents associated with congestion around the school gates. All manner of dangerous driving and parking practices are reported as commonplace (DfT, undated). In a cultural and physical environment more supportive of walking, cycling and public transport, children's journeys to school would be safer if fewer people drove them there, and indeed Tolley (2008) cites research to show that the riskiness of cycling is inversely related to the level of cycle use (see below). And while fears of children facing 'stranger danger' while walking to and from school are also commonplace, mercifully it is actually extremely rare; children are around 40 times more likely to be killed in a traffic accident than murdered following abduction by a stranger (DfES, 2003).

A final, and crucially important, reason why the car is increasingly popular for trips to school is that of education policy itself. As the mantra of choice penetrates ever deeper into the mindset of politicians and civil servants, more areas of public policy are shaped by its apparently magnetic allure. Since the 1980s, Conservative and Labour governments alike have embraced the belief that the quality of schools will be enhanced by promoting competition between them. In England, for example, the Education and Inspections Act 2006 formally bestowed upon local authorities 'an enhanced strategic role as champion of pupils and parents, with a duty to promote choice, diversity and high standards for every child' (Department for Education, 2006, unpaginated). This meant more than ever that parents were not expected to send their children to a school in whose 'catchment area' they lived; rather, they would be free to choose the school that they thought best suited their sons' and daughters' needs and desires.

The government had recognised the transport implications of breaking the traditional geographical links between home and school when it launched the Travelling to School Initiative in 2003. This was designed to 'tackle a number of trends towards greater car dependency observed in school travel in recent years' by promoting 'a series of measures to increase the use of healthy and sustainable modes of transport and reduce congestion in relation to pupils' travel to and from schools in England' (Atkins, 2010, p 7). The Initiative bolstered the concept of School Travel Plans (STPs), provided funding for schools to employ school travel advisers, and introduced the opportunity to bid for small on-site and off-site capital projects. Some additional funding was also made available through complementary schemes to support walking and cycling. The role of STPs was further strengthened by the Education and Inspections Act 2006, when local authorities became duty-bound to publish a sustainable school travel strategy designed to produce health and environmental benefits. In a review of STPs, Baslington (2008) noted that some very good-quality schemes had arisen and that the Plans can be effective in addressing the school run, although a DfT-sponsored review of the Travelling to School Initiative rather bluntly concluded that STPs had not had much of an effect on average modal shares at the aggregate level (Atkins, 2010).

What is clear, though, is that an education policy predicated on competition has significant transport implications. Parents who determine that their local school is not good enough can look to send their children elsewhere. This involves making a longer journey that may be several miles in length and not necessarily easy to make by bus or train, so that there is a 'need' to join the school run. The system of school catchment areas certainly worked to the detriment of low-income groups because property prices in the vicinity of good schools increased disproportionately as better-off parents moved in to give their children direct access to a higher-quality education. Yet Burgess et al (2006) found that years of promoting parental choice had seemingly replaced one form of discrimination with another, based on the ability to travel:

> The White Paper [that preceding the 2006 Act] lead [*sic*] to an outcry that the plan involves the 'bussing' of poor children to schools in wealthy areas … But the key point is this. 'Bussing' goes on in a big way now. The difference is that this bussing occurs in people carriers, not big yellow school buses, and is not available to all. Affluent families whose nearest secondary school is of poor quality are much more likely to 'bus' their children out to schools further away than are poorer families. They have the resources to either live near better schools in the first place, or to transport them to better schools if not. (p 13)

Even making the heroic assumption that legislative requirements for free transport for low-income families have alleviated such inequalities, attempting to address shortcomings of the education system by using transport as the principal means of facilitating competition is problematic. As we have seen, the school run generates significant traffic and congestion. This is especially so in the morning peak, placing a substantial additional burden on both transport infrastructure and service provision that already are often unfit for purpose at precisely the times when people are attempting to get to work. As a major component of traffic, the school run clearly contributes to the wider negative externalities of too much car use – accidents, local air pollution and carbon emissions, for example – but, as we will go on to see, it can also play an important role in the psychology of embedding travel habits based on use of the car, habits that people often find hard to break as they get older and the attraction of driving themselves presents itself.

Fat-bottomed girls

Jack likes cycling for any number of reasons. The freedom, the fitness, the exploration, the sheer enjoyment. He loves the challenge when he's out on the hills or up in the mountains (Chapter Five), but even just the wind in his hair cheers him up no end. He also thinks it's just about the quickest way to get to and from school, given how busy the roads can be. Jumping up onto the pavement to avoid a red traffic light, he startles a woman pushing a pram coming in the other direction who shouts at him to watch where he's going. What is it with these pedestrians?! Surely he wasn't going that fast? Anyway, a quick 'up yours' puts her in her place and he's quickly on the new stretch of cycle path that runs along the main road towards town. Something catches his eye off to the right; he looks over for long enough to realise that it is a fresh wreath that has been placed along the railings on the other side of the road where someone must have been hit by a car. Jack remembers that it's still only a year since Sophie's friend Emma was knocked down by a speeding motorist on her way out to the cinema one evening. The accident made the headlines in the local papers and there was talk about the council launching a reinvigorated road safety campaign, but nothing much came of it in the end.

Turning off into the park he whizzes down the cycle path to the lake and stops to say hello to some of his friends who are having a kickaround before they wander the last couple of hundred yards up to school. Most of Jack's schoolmates are sporty. They play football in the winter and cricket in the summer, and some of them join Jack on bike rides at the weekend as well. The school runs after-hours sessions for a range of sports, but other than the football team none of Jack's mates have much to do with any of these; they spend enough time in school as it is, and 3.30 is definitely time to be out and about. Sportiness does not run in the family, though; Jack's sisters have never been outdoors types. He certainly doesn't waste time in making fun of Sophie whenever she's trying to cadge a lift off Paul. 'You'll get fat,' he warns. Just like those new kids getting out of the car by the school gates as Jack and his friends arrive a couple of minutes before morning registration. 'How can anyone want to be like that?' they wonder as they prepare for another day in front of the smartboard.

As Paul's weekend schedule would attest, it is not just on their way to school that children are ferried around. Mackett (2001) shows how nearly half of *all* children's journeys are made by car and Hillman et al's (1990) seminal study charted how the age at which children are allowed to travel unaccompanied has increased steadily over the years. But even then it is not all doom and gloom: we should not lose sight of the fact that nearly half of all Year 1–6 children still walk to school, and 7 in 10 school trips by those in Years 7–13 are either by foot (36%) or by bus (34%). Despite years of erosion, there still exists a significant base upon which to build the greater use of non-car modes for the journey to school precisely because most people have at some point been a multi-modal traveller. And at least with regard to walking, seen in the broader context of all journeys across all age groups, the trip to school remains a relative success story. Although about 80% of all trips under a mile are walked, the number of walking trips taken by UK residents has been steadily falling and the proportion of all journeys made by foot has stabilised at around a quarter. Trying to make sense of these statistics is a little difficult because of the relationship between walking and other means of transport. As Tolley (2008) notes, walking can be an 'access mode', in that people go by foot to reach a specific destination, although it is also an 'access sub-mode', where people walk to the bus stop or railway station to reach public transport services. Once they have reached their destinations, people then use walking as a 'circulation/exchange' mode to fulfil a range of non-transport activities such as going for a coffee or getting between shops. There is also, of course, the act of just 'going for a walk', where going by foot is technically categorised as a 'recreation/leisure mode'.

Similarly, cycling has been in decline across the country, but the proportion of trips to school made by bike has fallen more rapidly than cycling in general, with under 2% of all trips now cycled. This is an astonishingly low number, especially given the many advantages of getting around on two wheels (see Parkin, 2012). As Phil Jones (2005, p 827) puts it: 'The bicycle is a privileged mode of transport, in part because of its having been loaded with labels such as "sustainable" and "healthy". The bicycle can go where cars cannot and has a range far greater than is practical on foot …'. In other words, at least for short to medium-length journeys, it has a flexibility unrivalled by other transport modes, will keep you fit, causes no congestion and, once you have bought a bike, is very cheap. Yet Britons continue to find this apparently win-win opportunity 'quite resistible indeed' (Pucher and Buehler, 2008, p 495), even as some of our European neighbours are rediscovering cycling at quite a rate of knots. While in 1950 cycling rates in the UK were higher than in Germany, at around 15% of all trips, by the 2000s Germans cycled more than 10 times as much as a proportion of all trips than did the British. The prominence of cycling in Denmark and the Netherlands is even higher. And whereas in Britain cyclists are disproportionately male and of non-retirement age, in these other countries the take-up is much more demographically even.

Like walking, trips by bike are made for a variety of reasons, not just in order to reach a particular destination. Although in certain towns and cities 'access mode' cycling is comparatively high – indeed, around 18% of all journeys in York are cycled – the most significant increases in British cycling activity have been related to its function as a recreation/leisure mode. Since the 1980s the number of people using their bikes for leisure purposes has climbed steadily, and this is reflected in the view that cycling is more a healthy leisure pastime than a means of regular transport. In Scotland, home to some of the world's best mountain biking country, 54% of adults and nearly 9 in 10 children think that recreation is the main reason for owning a bike (Scottish Executive, 2005). So, while the National Cycle Network has been expanded and upgraded to a large extent, thanks to an award of lottery funding decided upon by popular vote, the cycling infrastructure in most towns and cities remains poor and underused. Gatersleben and Appleton (2007) lament that regular cyclists in Britain appear to be a rather small group who use their bikes just because they like to do so. Most people simply never contemplate cycling, although there is a constituency who could be persuaded to get on their bikes if the circumstances were right (see below).

In addition to their potential to reduce pollution and congestion, walking and cycling are more and more advocated by transport and other professionals because of the many health benefits associated with the active modes. Inactivity, it seems, is the new public health pariah. A study published in *The Lancet* in the run-up to the London Olympics in 2012 suggested that, worldwide, around a third of adults do not do enough physical activity, and that this leads to as many annual deaths as does smoking (BBC, 2012a). Although the comparison with smoking was perhaps an ill-advised attempt at headline grabbing – fewer people smoke than are inactive, and thus lighting up is much riskier to any given individual – there is a growing consensus around the unhealthy nature of an excessively sedentary life-style. Regular physical activity reduces the risk of a whole host of life-threatening ailments, including heart disease, diabetes, high blood pressure and cancer, and it also helps people to maintain healthy bones, muscles and joints and feel better in themselves; those who walk and cycle to work, for example, are reckoned to have low-stress – even 'relaxing and exciting' (Gatersleben and Uzzell, 2007, p 416) – commutes, as compared with those who drive (see also McLennan and Bennetts, 2003; Anable and Gatersleben, 2005). And while individuals can benefit greatly from regular exercise, the broader socioeconomic advantages, such as cleaner air for us all to breathe, as well as reduced cost to employers, insurance companies and the health service, are also huge. It is reckoned that dealing with obesity burdens the NHS to the tune of £5 billion a year (Department of Health, 2013). In a refreshingly frank commentary to BBC Radio 5 Live, diabetes specialist Professor Craig Currie pointed out that 'essentially, we are a nation of lazy porkers' and suggested that 'you have got to have lived on Mars if you don't realise that being fat is going to cause you a few problems' (BBC, 2013a, unpaginated).

Official advice recommends around two and a half hours of moderate exercise each week for adults. Generally speaking, people in higher-income countries are less active, but Britain is among the worst offenders. Figures vary between studies (and to an extent depend on assumptions and definitions), but up to two-thirds of British adults are failing to get enough regular exercise. This sedentary disposition correlates with the less-than-flattering statistic that the UK has the highest obesity rate in the EU. A person is officially classified as obese if they are more than 20% over a healthy weight for their size and build. Around a quarter of British men and women are reckoned to be obese, and this figure is predicted to rise to 40% by 2050 (Foresight, 2007). Millions more are 'overweight'. The fundamental cause is that more and more people are burning off fewer calories than they consume (see Davis et al, 2007). Different factors combine to lead to this situation, and key among them are poor diet, the rise of the television and computer games, an increased prevalence of desk-based jobs, and, inevitably, changing travel habits. Commentators as diverse as John Adams (1993) and P.J. O'Rourke (1987) have written (from rather different perspectives) about modern societies doing their best to eradicate the active modes, but the extent to which walking and cycling could help to address the obesity epidemic and its associated costs should not be underestimated.

A whole host of reasons is cited in the academic literature to explain why people don't walk and cycle more than they do (e.g. Pucher and Buehler, 2008; Heinen et al, 2010). The nature of the built environment is commonly referred to, with many findings suggesting that low-density development that includes out-of-town retail and service locations militates against the active modes, owing to the distances involved in getting to these places. As car ownership has increased alongside these changes in our towns and cities, people have become even less inclined to walk or take their bike because the car represents a sunk cost and, as such, may as well be used. The British climate is not especially conducive to regular bicycle use, and the lack of facilities for cyclists such as bike parks and showers at work also puts off would-be cyclists. Sometimes people just don't realise that one of the active modes might represent a viable alternative to their existing travel habits, and others just have no interest in walking or cycling. Then there are those people who simply can't be bothered or who like driving their cars too much (see below).

But another perennial barrier to fashioning a more positive public attitude towards the active modes is the perception that they are dangerous. It makes sense that parents who don't want their children to walk or cycle to school might have reservations about walking or cycling themselves. At first glance, the road safety statistics are indeed arresting. In 2011, 1,901 people were killed on Britain's roads, and around 23,000 more were seriously injured. Of those killed, 453 were pedestrians and 107 were cyclists, and fully 5,907 walkers were seriously injured, as were 3,192 bike users (House of Commons, 2012a). Yet Britain's roads are among the safest in Europe (Table 3.1), and the sustained reductions in road traffic casualties in recent decades are truly noteworthy. In his book *Transport, environment and society*, Michael Cahill (2010) lays bare the scale of the achievement:

> In 1934, 7,343 people were killed, the highest number of road deaths in Britain in the twentieth century relative to population size and the number of vehicles on the road. Around 50 per cent of these were pedestrians ... In 1934, there were around a quarter of a million cars on the roads ... If the 1934 death rate had continued then, [today] with 28 million cars, we could expect an annual death toll of 822,416.

Much of this reduction has come about through measures such as better road design and the introduction of driving tests, speed limits, pedestrian crossings, drink–driving legislation and seatbelt requirements. Further reductions, through the wider adoption of 20 mph speed limits in residential areas (most collisions can be survived at this speed), sensor technology in vehicles and 'holistic' road safety management approaches, will be achievable so long as ministers don't

Table 3.1: Estimated road traffic death rate per 100,000 of population in the EU27 and selected other countries

Country	**Fatality rate**
Austria	6.6
Belgium	8.1
Bulgaria	10.4
Cyprus	7.6
Czech Republic	7.6
Denmark	4.7
Estonia	6.5
Finland	5.1
France	6.4
Germany	4.7
Greece	12.2
Hungary	9.1
Ireland	4.7
Italy	7.2
Latvia	10.8
Lithuania	11.1
Luxembourg	6.3
Malta	3.8
Netherlands	3.9
Poland	11.8
Portugal	11.8
Romania	11.1
Slovakia	7.4
Slovenia	7.2
Spain	5.4
Sweden	3.0
United Kingdom	3.7
Australia	6.1
Canada	6.8
New Zealand	9.1
United States	11.4

Source: World Health Organization (2013)

become complacent about road safety. With recent moves towards decentralising funding and the scrapping of road safety targets, this is a worry of some parliamentarians, especially since road safety resources at the local authority level have come under pressure from competing policy areas (House of Commons, 2012a).

No transport system can ever be absolutely safe, not least because the possibility for human error is always present, and this is especially the case on the roads, where the majority of drivers are not professionals and are unlikely to have undergone more than the relatively basic training necessary to pass a driving test. (For a truly fascinating exploration of the human aspects of driving, see Tom Vanderbilt's (2008) excellent *Traffic*.) Still, public perceptions of transport and safety are rather curious. After privatisation the rail industry suffered a series of fatal crashes that were rightly subject to a great deal of media and professional scrutiny. Lawyers and some relatives of crash victims were especially vocal in calling for changes within the industry to further enhance its safety performance, although, as *Rail* magazine was moved to point out, the harsh truth is that being bereaved by a train crash does not necessarily make one an expert in railway safety. Unfortunately, some of the changes demanded would have had only a minimal impact on rail safety and, as numerous commentators at the time observed, would have had cost and operational implications that made rail transport less appealing. The irony here is that when people drive rather than take the train they are exposing themselves to far greater risk because, notwithstanding occasional accidents, the rail industry has a much better safety record than do the roads.

Road crashes, on the other hand, are perceived rather differently. Sometimes they are publicised to help make the case for a new piece of road infrastructure being promoted as capable of addressing accident blackspots (long-standing press campaigns for the dualling of a whole host of trunk roads, from the A9 and A82 in northern Scotland to the A303 in the South West of England spring to mind). More generally, crashes are mentioned matter-of-factly on radio traffic reports and scarcely attract coverage in the national news media. Although they are often less newsworthy because they are at a completely different scale than a train or plane crash, they none the less kill nearly 2,000 people a year, despite Britain's relatively enviable record on road safety. On one level, people seem implicitly comfortable with the 'invisibility' of road fatalities, given how much and how unquestioningly many of us drive our cars (and send text messages, talk on mobile phones, put make-up on or shave while doing it[2]). People's perception that the roads are too dangerous for their children to walk or cycle to school, or for a switch to bicycle commuting or a regular bike ride after work, seem to come to the fore only in circumstances *when they imagine not being in a car themselves*. The irony here is that pedestrians and cyclists would all be much safer if lots more people left their cars on the drive and walked or rode their bikes a bit more.

It is true that a disproportionate number of crash victims are pedestrians and cyclists. This statistic on its own does little to allay public fears about road safety, but international evidence suggests that we should not view the British case in isolation. The very countries where cycling rates are highest – the Netherlands, Germany and Denmark – also have proportionately the lowest numbers of cyclists killed and seriously injured. Pucher and Buehler (2008) note that between 2002 and 2005 the number of cyclists killed per 100 million kilometres cycled was 3.6 in the UK but only 1.7 in Germany, 1.5 in Denmark and 1.1 in the Netherlands. Cyclists in the Netherlands also seldom wear helmets, a mark of just how little they view cycling as a dangerous activity. It seems that there is 'safety in numbers': across countries and cities with high cycling rates, fatalities are lower than in places where there is less cycling, and fatality rates always fall as more people start to cycle. In other words, the more cycling there is, the less likely it is that cyclists will become the victims of fatal traffic accidents. The explanation is found in a combination of ambitious and well-targeted public investment and more defensive driving. As Tolley (2008, p 122) puts it, 'as the amount of cycling increases to a critical mass, traffic arrangements have to be made to accommodate it and car drivers have to adapt their behaviour to share space with cyclists, producing not only more cycling safety but more safety for motorised vehicles too'.

Some authors have attempted to calculate the effect of increased cycling in terms of life years gained through additional health benefits versus life years lost in fatal crashes. Even in Britain, where the cycling environment is hostile in comparison with that in Denmark, Germany and the Netherlands, the ratio is very positive (around 20:1). In the Netherlands it is stratospherically high (on average 3–14 months gained, compared with 5–9 days lost), and de Hartog et al (2010, p 1109) rather understatedly conclude that 'the estimated health benefits of cycling were substantially larger than the risks' (see also British Medical Association, 1992). As the built environment becomes more cycling and pedestrian friendly, this has further positive effects in relation to the quality, as well as the length, of life. 'Liveable streets' tend to promote more social interaction, reduce the fear of crime and offer a generally pleasant environment for people to enjoy. This can have economic benefits as well. Carmen Hass-Klau (1993) found that in almost all cases pedestrianisation increases the turnover of businesses situated along newly carless streets. None of this would have been a surprise to Jane Jacobs (1961), who back in the 1960s was writing in her classic *The death and life of great American cities* that walking is the essential ingredient that distinguishes streets – with their richness of social and economic exchange – from mere roads (Chapter Two). Reimagining our urban roads back into streets might even mean that it is once again possible to see children playing in them for real, rather than in an aged photograph.

The challenge for policy, then, is to promote the widespread uptake of walking and cycling in the UK. That we have a long way to go has been recognised even by the Prime Minister. Speaking in connection with a cycling campaign orchestrated by a national newspaper, David Cameron, a keen cyclist himself, said that '[a]nyone who has got on a bicycle – particularly in one of our busier cities – knows you are taking your life into your hands every time you do so, and so we do need to do more to try and make cycling safer' (Burgess, 2012, unpaginated). The problem is that, at the national level at least, successive governments have failed to demonstrate the leadership necessary to raise the profile of walking and cycling above its currently moribund state. The UK government published a cycling strategy in 1996 and *Walking and cycling: An action plan* appeared in 2004. The devolved governments produced similar statements, with the Scottish Government going so far as to ringfence a modest increase in financial support for the active modes. But, as is often the case, it is London that leads the way. Not only has TfL implemented a comprehensive bike hire scheme based on the Lyon and Paris models, but late in 2012, Mayor Boris Johnson reacted to some high-profile cycling fatalities by committing nearly £1 billion to cycling improvements over a 10-year period designed to increase safety for the capital's growing number of bike users (*Local Transport Today*, 2012b).

Outside of London, and to a lesser extent Scotland, there is little sense of policy coherence, and the amount of money available tends to be rather small. Cycling Demonstration Towns and Cycling Towns received some term-limited funding, and training initiatives such as Bikeability have been supported to the tune of £11 million in a year. Perhaps the most significant government initiative has been Smarter Choices, which was designed to reshape the behaviour of residents in Worcester, Peterborough and Darlington. Up to half of the £15 million funding was spent on 'personal travel planning' – making individuals aware of ways of making their journeys by means other than the car where possible – and other 'soft' measures such as travel awareness campaigns and public transport marketing were deployed. Although largely devoid of capital expenditure, the scheme was a success: walking increased by around 10% and cycling by up to 30%, both against a backdrop of decline in comparable towns elsewhere (Sloman et al, 2010). Sadly, little has been done to build on this success by rolling out Smarter Choices across the country or moving the policy approach into the mainstream, and the approval of capital investment in small schemes to promote walking and cycling remains minimal (Chapter Four). As with transport policy more generally, it is not that the government has done nothing; it is more that the task at hand is somewhat more onerous than ministers want to recognise.

There is a considerable body of knowledge about the kinds of things that need to be done to promote walking and cycling (see Forsyth and Southworth, 2008; Pucher and Buehler, 2008; Tight et al, 2011; International Transport Forum, 2012). The clear message is that any plan of attack must be wide ranging, multifaceted, sustained and well resourced; its policies should be internally consistent and mutually reinforcing; and its implementation must be coordinated (see Ogilvie et al, 2004 for a rather negative review of smaller interventions). In the case of cycling, transport and spatial planners need to provide an extensive network of separate bike lanes (especially along or to avoid busy routes and junctions), traffic-calming measures, bike parking and integration with public transport, traffic education and training, and regular promotional events. It helps, too, if policy makers have a good appreciation not only of what measures they might introduce but also of how these will be experienced by walkers and cyclists themselves. Rachel Aldred (2010) talks of producing 'cycling citizens', and cultural geographers, among others, have sought to investigate what walkers and cyclists actually feel and encounter en route (see Middleton, 2010; Jones, 2012). The point is that the better the experience can be made, the more likely it is that people will want to try it. Part of the challenge, interestingly, is to address perceptions of existing cyclists that are held by those who don't currently use a bike much themselves. Daley and Rissel (2010) found that although cycling was regarded by some as being green, healthy and fun, cyclists were often seen in much more negative terms. Echoing the views of the lady whom Jack startled on the pavement on his way to school, some people see cyclists as 'risk takers' and 'law breakers' and are upset by the behaviour of those who run red lights,[3] ride on pavements and generally threaten the safety of others as well as themselves (see also House of Commons, 2009b). Others commented on what they see as the low social status of cycling compared to motoring, but then these may be the kind of drivers that will never be persuaded to leave their cars at home.

At the same time, it is not enough for a local authority transport department to pursue an active modes revolution on its own. Davis and Annett (2013) make the point that joint working with healthcare authorities and providers can be especially productive. Both parties have a professional interest in securing behaviour change, and the message that walking or cycling more can make a real difference to your health and well-being is a powerful one, as Paul realised in Chapter Two. Equally, it will take more than a change of priority by transport planners to deliver the kind of safe and attractive pedestrian environments that represent genuinely liveable streets; to do so requires a coordinated effort across several domains of public policy, from urban design and spatial planning to economic development. Given the high proportion of all UK journeys under five miles in length, the potential for promoting an active modes revolution is enormous (Banister and Gallent, 1998): walking or cycling a greater proportion of those journeys that are currently made by car could make a huge difference to pollution and congestion, especially if policy is able to focus on those journeys such as short school run or commuting trips that can be especially problematic, in addressing the *local* congestion or environmental problems that tend to worry people the most. Even swapping the 8am trip for the papers on a Sunday from car to bike or foot is worthwhile for individuals and society alike. Although these trips are unlikely to hold up anyone else or emit huge quantities of CO_2, each one made by an active mode makes a positive contribution, however small, to improving the health of those who make them, and to reducing the societal cost of our collective indolence.

Driving in my car

Sophie leaves the house in a sulk, rather later than Jack, wondering why she ever signed up to go to the Technology College on the other side of town. It wasn't too bad when she used to be able to cadge a lift into town with Paul when he parked at the station every day, as then she had to get only one bus across to the campus. Secretly, she takes to heart Jack's taunts about getting fat, and has done so even more since Neil (a rather self-regarding and status-driven bloke at the College) started to take an interest in her. It really is too far to walk … still, travelling on the bus is such a faff! Sometimes it's the other passengers – although it can be quite funny when they get on one particular driver's nerves to the point of creating a standoff – but more than anything it just takes so long to get anywhere. Two buses and the best part of an hour to go about three miles, as the crow flies.

There's also the credibility thing. Sophie is 18 on her next birthday. When Paul and Susan were her age Mrs Thatcher said that buses were for losers, and how true is that! Sophie doesn't want to be a loser. She's not exactly sure yet what she is actually going to do, but whatever it is it will not involve being a loser like those chavs on the number 23. (Like many young adults of her age, Sophie has yet to realise quite the extent to which she's going to have to put in the hard yards at university, and the amount of debt she's going to have to accrue along the way, to reach the same level of professional standing as Paul and Susan, but that's a story for a different book.) 'I'm going to have a Mini like my aunt's got,' she tells her friend on the first of the morning's two bus journeys. 'My test is coming up in a month and six days' time – not that I'm counting – and mum and dad have said they'll buy me a car. Then I'm never getting the bus to school again.' Sophie's friend nods and can't help but feel a bit envious because there's no way her parents could afford to buy her any sort of car, never mind a Mini, but at the same time she kind of likes the fact that using public transport allows her to catch up with stuff on her smartphone. 'And imagine,' Sophie finishes with a flourish, 'the look on Neil's face when I pull up next to his car – you know, the Corsa VXR? – in a flash new one of my own. I'll *totally* have arrived.' Sophie's friend works on retaining a supportive expression as she updates her Facebook status: 'Some people on the bus are soooooo lame.'

Why do many young people like Sophie look forward so much to being able to drive? Sometimes it seems like acquiring a driving licence is a rite of passage into adulthood, and one which the car industry assiduously promotes in its marketing and brand-awareness campaigns. And then why, once they have a licence, do people tend to drive cars more and more, leaving behind the other modes of transport that they may previously have been happy to use? In part the answer to such questions is rather obvious and instrumental in nature.

Drivers regularly point out that they use the car because it is quick and convenient. We also saw in Chapter One how, especially for the Conservatives in the 1980s, cars were about more than instrumental qualities such as flexibility and speed; they became symbols of ideology and progress, an important part of the Thatcherite social revolution based on freedom, choice and private wealth accumulation. Thatcher herself was indeed disparaging about public transport. In addition to her comment about men over the age of 26 on the bus being failures, she also reportedly said to the Board of British Rail that if 'any of you were any good, you wouldn't be here'. Heavily subsidised and in many cases a state monopoly, public transport was producer-led and viewed as hopelessly out of touch with an economic model based on the desires of the consumer newly let off the leash. If the car allows people to go anywhere they want at a time of their choosing, public transport manifestly doesn't. Walking and cycling share these anytime, anywhere characteristics for short and medium-length journeys, but are seen as being slower than driving, fail to convey economic status and often involve expending more energy than many people are these days comfortable with doing.

Of course, the car can be flexible and convenient only if you have access to one, but Thatcher really did succeed in making sure that individualism sank into the national psyche, and so the feeling of liberation and empowerment associated with driving is important in explaining why people like to get behind the wheel more in Britain than elsewhere in Europe. Indeed, it is now well understood that the popularity of the automobile is not just to do with its instrumental qualities, but also with what researchers call its 'symbolic' or 'affective' value; in short, the way it makes people *feel* (see Lucas et al, 2011). Drivers often say they like cars because they make them feel in control. For some aspects, such as internal temperature, choice of music, choice of company and so on, this is undoubtedly true, but sooner or later something will expose the limitations of the driver's assumptions. In unfortunate cases this will be an accident – caused either by the driver in question (who naturally is in control of his/her car) or by somebody else (who presumably was also in control of their car) – but more frequently it is likely to be congestion. As we saw in Chapter Two, congestion is generally the manifestation of too many people trying to travel to/from the same places at the same time. Thus the collective action of individual drivers, each desperate to be 'in control' of their own journey, ends up turning Thatcher's 'great car economy' into the 'great democracy of the traffic jam'. On top of all this is the double irony that many people in the jam have to travel at set times and between places that can only practicably be reached by car, and so probably have little choice about being on the road during busy periods in the first place.

Nevertheless, once people have developed the habit of taking the car this militates against the active consideration of alternatives, because routinised behaviour can all too easily become automatic (Oullette and Wood, 1998). And feeling good about something – it is not uncommon for authors to associate cars with feelings of arousal (!) – hardly promotes critical reflection on an entrenched practice. Indeed, some drivers derive status and/or identity from their cars: in essence, the better the car, the better they feel both in an absolute sense and in relation to others when driving it, or thinking or talking about it (Ellaway et al, 2004). The car is a projection of image, a trophy, an extension of the private realm of the home that is the Englishman's castle. Public transport, in this context, becomes the equivalent of a block of council flats; you have to share it with some dreadful human beings, to paraphrase erstwhile Tory transport minister Steve Norris. Clearly there are marked differences in taste with regard to what represents a good car and what does not. While for certain socioeconomic groups a manifestation of status might be a top-of-the-range BMW or Audi (with plenty of room for the golf clubs), for others it will be Neil's souped-up Vauxhall Corsa complete with ludicrously bass-heavy sound system and blue LED lights that illuminate the road.[4] Falconer and Kingham (2007) investigated boy racer culture and found that although the 'hooning' behaviour associated with such characters is generally seen as undesirable, the drivers themselves were not seeking to subvert established social norms. In boy racer subcultures, as well as more generally, car ownership was regarded as socially powerful. The better (that is, the more pimped-up) the car, the higher the prestige, but more broadly the car was regarded as providing the glue that holds social networks together, just as it is for the most respectable of suburban communities (Chapter Five).

Falconer and Kingham's work is important because it flags up the need to understand the symbolic and affective motivations for driving and particular driving behaviours, especially if the aim is to persuade some people to drive less, or differently. We have seen that there are those who would like to use their cars less, and initiatives such as a combination of Smarter Choices and the provision of better alternatives may well be enough to at least begin the process of behaviour change. For those who might be willing to explore alternatives, it is important to figure out how to align these with the positive feelings associated with car use. Although Anable and Gatersleben (2005) found that instrumental factors such as convenience tend to trump affective considerations for British work trips, Linda Steg (2005, p 147) found the opposite in the Netherlands: car use was 'most strongly related to symbolic and affective motives, and not to instrumental motives'. This was especially true among particular groups such as frequent drivers, men and the young. It is worth reflecting on this finding for a moment: driving to and from work was explained more by the way cars make people feel than by their convenience and flexibility. Such affective factors are also important in leisure travel (Anable and Gatersleben, 2005).

Of course, people do not develop their feelings towards cars in a vacuum. There is evidence to suggest that children who are driven around a lot by their parents become accustomed to car use and effectively just morph into the next generation of drivers. The same can happen to children who are not necessarily 'spoiled' by excessive lift-giving but who see their parents drive a great deal and come to associate adulthood with driving to reach places. There are also far broader processes of socialisation that familiarise children with the dominance, and hence 'normality', of car travel. Partly these will come from peers or the families of peers, but they also result from generalised representations of transport and travel that pervade society.

John Urry (2000) has written that the idea of the car is embedded in social and economic life to the extent that it has to be seen in relation to almost all human activity; indeed, he describes it as 'quasi-private' transport, since, although it is privately owned, so few technologies impact so much on the public sphere. Kingham and Donohoe (2002) found that children were aware of makes and types of car at as young as four years of age, and Baslington (2009, p 305) refers to the social emphasis on cars that has an intellectual impact that is 'detectable in the perceptions and attitudes of many children'. Her theory suggests that children learn about travel modes in the same way as other aspects of culture through 'agents of socialisation' such as the family, school, media and peer groups. Carrabine and Longhurst (2002) describe the anticipation of using a car felt by teenagers approaching driving age.

Roger Mackett (2002, p 29) was concerned that as children become more dependent on the car, their limited experience with other modes would have 'significant adverse impacts on policies aimed at reducing car use'. Sounding a grave warning that 'the situation was likely to worsen', he prophesised that 'car ownership will increase further, with a greater increase in households with children than those without. Car use by children is likely to increase considerably. This is a very worrying trend.' In a similar vein, Meaton and Kingham (1997, p 12) concluded with some alarm that:

> the origins of the car culture so pervasive in adult society are nurtured at the very early stages of a child's development. Car culture, as a result, is almost seamlessly perpetuated between generations, and it appears likely that the next generation will be even more wedded to their cars than previous ones. To break the cycle of admiration, aspiration and consequent addiction, it will be necessary to devise a complete package of innovative campaigns targeted at all sections of society.

At the same time, other studies show that by no means all young people are enamoured of the car. A DfT (2007) investigation into young adults' travel found that attitudes towards automobiles ranged from enthusiasm to downright scepticism. Early work on 'peak car' is throwing up some intriguing propositions, especially that young men in the United States, Europe and Australia are becoming less dependent on car travel (Delbosc and Currie, 2012; see also Le Vine and Jones, 2012; Kuhnimhof et al, 2012; Goodwin, 2013). There is relatively little research into why this is the case, although, as Goodwin (2012) points out, the phenomenon seems to pre-date the current recession. At least in part it could be a result of the huge rises in the cost of car insurance for young males over recent years, and there are other possible causes, such as growing environmental awareness among young people and the associated suggestion that the car is increasingly seen as 'uncool' in some quarters.

Perhaps the most tantalising possibility is that the relationship between physical and virtual accessibility really is beginning to generate profound change in how, when and where we travel. A survey by Gartner Research in the United States found that 46% of 18- to 24-year-olds would choose internet access over access to a car if forced to decide between them (Read, 2012). When physical accessibility is required, the advent of smartphone technology means that people can be online as they travel, so long as there's a good enough phone signal and reasonable public transport (or lift-giving) services are available. The reduction in popularity of the private car among young people is perhaps one of the reasons why the notion of 'peak car' has emerged in OECD (Organisation for Economic Cooperation and Development) countries, and, in the context of our overall argument, the emerging potential to strike a better balance between the different transport modes is certainly most welcome indeed. Consolidating these early movements into an identifiable and sustainable trend will be the role of transport and related policy in the coming years, and in this sense Meaton and Kingham (1997) are right to argue that any 'package of innovative campaigns' designed to promote alternatives to the car would do well to target school children and teenagers as well as their parents. Whatever the generation, a key trick is going to be to make all of the Smiths and many more like them *feel* much better about walking, cycling and using public transport.

Notes

[1] Which, as we will see shortly, can often be translated as 'if we didn't live so far from our choice of school'.

[2] All actions that we've witnessed people doing while driving ourselves in recent years. Again, see Vanderbilt's *Traffic*.

[3] The Prime Minister, who has declared in Parliament that he doesn't break the law, has been photographed cycling the wrong way up a one-way street and straight through a red light. See also: http://www.bbc.co.uk/news/magazine-22614569.

[4] Should you feel so inclined: http://www.halfords.com/webapp/wcs/stores/servlet/product_storeId_10001_catalogId_10151_productId_787897_langId_-1_categoryId_272452.

FOUR

The business trip

Transport and ICTs; privatisation, deregulation and integration; appraising investment; disruption, reliability and recovery

OK computer

Paul hopes that the weather forecast will offer some respite from the economic doom and gloom dominating *News at Ten*, but he is to be disappointed. It is going to pour down in the morning, so his monthly trip to the company HQ in London Docklands will have to start with his raincoat and umbrella. Unimpressed with the idea of his usual walk to the station in a near-monsoon, he determines to get the bus and quickly checks the timetable online; Paul only ever uses the bus to get to the station when the weather is really bad and he can never remember the times. Better safe than sorry, because tomorrow one of the directors from the US is coming over specially, and Paul really doesn't want anything to go wrong. Although he quite likes the chance to get down to the buzz of London every few weeks, he often wonders why, in the days of video conferencing and Skype, his company still spends a load of money sending people from all over the place to sit around the same table for a few hours. But as his boss, John, once neatly summarised, face-to-face communication remains important in the digital age because 'I need to see the whites of your eyes when you give me bad figures, dude'.

In the late 1990s, it was fashionable to write about 'the death of distance', following Frances Cairncross's (1997) seminal book of the same name. The promise of the digital revolution was such for some theorists that a lively debate appeared about how cities – with all their attendant problems of congestion, high prices and, in many cases, resilient social and environmental decay – would before long empty out (see Graham, 1998). People would be able to do just about everything online, from working to learning to shopping and even accessing healthcare. Certainly some business sectors are in the process of being transformed by online competition. Home delivery services have captured huge market shares (Amazon now accounts for a quarter of all book sales in the UK, for example (*Retail Gazette*, 2011)), and we have witnessed the almost complete demise of the record shop as the combination of Amazon and other online retailers, plus Apple's iPod, iTunes and other downloading services make physical discs increasingly redundant for films and music.

But the overall economic and social picture is quite different. It is true that the internet further opens up the potential for footloose working and associated 'amenity migration'. People can run their businesses from places they want to live in rather than having to remain proximate to an office or, indeed, their primary market, and some rural development agencies still see high speed broadband as some kind of wonder drug capable of transforming their economic prospects (see Dini et al, 2012). Yet in the excitement of the digital revolution it is sometimes forgotten that there is quite a large number of people who remain offline at home because they can't afford or don't want to be connected to the internet. For those on the wrong side of the so-called 'digital divide', ICTs have little direct impact on their own travel behaviour, except perhaps where journeys are made to the library or a friend's house in order to access the web if they cannot do so at work (for discussions of the digital divide in a transport context see Kenyon et al, 2002; Velaga et al, 2012). Even for those who are online, a lot of journeys, such as the morning commute and the school run, are made by people who have to be in certain places at certain times, and thus cannot be substituted by virtual mobility (Chapters Two and Three).

In other circumstances, however, evidence suggests that increasing digital connectivity has the capacity to complement or even enhance physical mobility as well as to reduce it (Mokhtarian and Tal, 2013). For one thing, ICTs can be used to make existing journeys easier. Real-time information for users of both road and public transport networks allows last-minute decisions to be made about route or mode choice in the event of known traffic jams or service disruptions. Picking up on the capacity of ICTs to change the ways in which journeys are made, as well as more broadly on the ways in which we now tend to organise our lives, some authors highlight the 'fusion' between transport and communication technologies (see Kwan, 2007; Schwanen, 2008; Schwanen and Kwan, 2008). The increasing use of mobile and, latterly, smartphones has allowed people to better accommodate uncertainties in scheduling by softening their plans and refining existing arrangements on the move (Line et al, 2011). Kwan (2007) refers to 'mid-course readjustment', where a last-minute change of plan is communicated to those on their way to a previously arranged destination that has now been superseded: 'this place is far too busy; let's go to the Coal Hole and tell Luke we've left Covent Garden'. She also talks of 'interactive coordination', where plans are firmed up on the move. Let us suppose your authors have loosely agreed to meet 'in town this evening' but only actually get around to deciding on the Betjeman Arms at St Pancras after we realise at some point during our respective journeys that Jon's train gets into Paddington half an hour before Iain's gets into Euston. What is more, as online working on the move becomes more and more prevalent, the already existing potential for place functionality to be blurred is amplified. The office could always be anywhere, even without ICT connectivity, because it is not a requirement to be online to work on a train or a plane. Now, though, it is possible to be in contact with the office and the work computer anywhere, anytime, so long as the internet connection is good enough (Lyons et al, 2008). This is easy to get used to and potentially awkward to be deprived of, as Paul discovers in the next part of his journey to London.

Rather like the Pony Express, the telegraph and telephone before them, Facebook, Skype and other social media make it easier for people to keep in touch. But much more than earlier technologies, the internet also has the potential to promote new journey opportunities, particularly among better-off socioeconomic groups. For regular internet users, especially those with relatively high disposable incomes, it is far easier to book flights, hotels, holidays and the like than in the days when travel agents were the dominant means of doing such things (Chapter Five). Reflecting on our own experience writing this book, on at least five occasions a two-minute website transaction was enough to book travel to and from Plymouth/Glasgow once emails firming up visit dates had been exchanged. Only 15 years before, making the necessary arrangements for a trip by plane or train would have taken very much longer and might have necessitated a trip all of its own to the travel agent (many of which have now closed down) or railway station (in some of which the ticket offices have closed down). And even where people do choose to access services online instead of making a journey, this does not necessarily remove an element of mobility from the transaction. Internet banking may well cut out the need for a trip to the high street, but online shopping still has to be delivered (Edwards et al, 2009). For some packaged items this means additional loads for the Royal Mail and for couriers, but groceries tend to be dropped at people's homes by the supermarkets themselves. The proportion of all journeys accounted for by light vans (so-called 'white vans') has increased considerably in the recent past (DfT, 2012), and internet-related delivery runs partly explain this (Browne et al, 2007; see Chapter Six).

Thus, while there is great potential for ICTs to weaken the link between mobility and accessibility, the extent to which in the future they actually will is anybody's guess. Maybe some people will find that Skyping once a week reduces the need to visit friends or loved ones by a couple of trips a year, or business people will find that ever more meetings can be held using videoconferencing facilities. But others will not. There are those for whom Skype only increases the desire to be together, and for whom nothing can really replace the handshake in a business deal. Indeed, in the business world the importance of larger cities as centres of interaction has been reasserted in the context of their so-called 'agglomeration economies'. These are the economic benefits that accrue from having very large numbers of people and firms in close proximity; the potential to generate and the act of sharing ideas are thought to reinforce the centrality of such places as hubs of exchange and innovation (Morgan, 2004). Although some former industrial towns and cities have fared rather badly as communications technologies and 'the knowledge economy' have taken hold, other, usually larger, service centres have done very well indeed. London's performance through the 1990s and 2000s, when it re-established itself as a 'world city' of real global scale and presence, is an excellent case in point (Buck et al, 2002).

People of Paul's generation who grew up watching *Tomorrow's World* might tell you that most of the more fanciful ideas about the likely impact of technological innovations on existing behaviour patterns tend to be greatly exaggerated (see, for example, Rietveld and Vickerman, 2003; Disdier and Head, 2006), although it is at least possible that some combination of trends could lead to something like the death of distance in years to come. It is almost certain that internet access and use will increase in the future as tech-savvy generations replace those who are older and less technologically literate. People will also use new technology in novel and unpredictable ways, and indeed the most profound technological changes of the next few years may themselves turn out to be completely surprising. But for the time being at least, in the absence of such 'unknown unknowns', 'tele-presence' technologies are nowhere near good enough to recreate the visceral and emotional elements of communicating that we get from being physically together. Humans are social beings, and non-verbal interaction remains crucial to the nature and context of conversational situations. The need for such 'co-presence', to quote John Urry (2007) once more, suggests that social and business networks will remain to some degree dependent on real, as well as virtual, mobility.

London calling

Paul sets his alarm for 6.00 and plans to be at the bus stop for 7.00 to catch the 7.05 down to the local commuter station. It's only about a mile, and his train is not until 7.27, but Paul has plenty of preparatory work to do on the train, so he builds in as much slack as he can for a stress-free morning's journey. Of course, as things turned out he didn't hear the alarm clock straightaway, but he was still out of the house by ten to seven and just rounding the corner to the bus stop no more than six or seven minutes later. But hang on: aren't those the tail-lights of a bus disappearing into the distance? Paul knows from years of experience that trains don't depart ahead of timetable and assumes buses must be the same, but another bus doesn't show up until just after 7.15 and now he's getting nervous about catching his train. Without really thinking he flashes his train season ticket at the bus driver, who looks quizzically back. 'That's your train ticket, sir; you need a Swiftcard, but then I'm not sure if you can use that on the train. Anyway, if you're going to the station, that'll be £1.70.' It's only just over a mile! Paul fumbles around in his pocket, holding up the bus in the process, and grudgingly hands over the money. He doesn't remember it being like this in London; 'doesn't everyone just "tap in" with an Oyster card down there for everything? Seems so much quicker!' He finally arrives at the platform at 7.32, and although the local trains are every 10 minutes he is flustered enough to forget that he needs to pick up his London ticket from the machine. It's only as they trundle past the grammar school that he suddenly remembers. Never mind, he'll still have time to get them between trains at New Street.

Sadly, while Paul's train was on time at Four Oaks, it spends a long time limping into Birmingham and by the time he has negotiated the crush on the escalator up to the concourse he's running short of time. He gets out the company credit card and stabs the booking reference into the FastTicket machine, which seems infuriatingly slow (and why do they always seem to be different depending on the station you go to?). By the time Paul gets to the departure board he's only got a minute left to get the London train, and given the weather he has to descend to the platform rather more gingerly than he would like. When he reaches the train, the inevitable has happened: the doors have just closed, the member of platform staff offers an apologetic shake of the head, and the Pendolino eases off into the tunnel. For the second time this morning, Paul's journey experience is summed up by a set of disappearing red tail-lights. Thankfully, the next London train is only 20 minutes away and so he has time for a quick coffee and a leisurely amble back to the platform.

This time, he secures a very comfortable first-class seat and, despite the rather stressful start to his day, he feels better immediately and reminds himself how travelling by train can be rather agreeable after all.

A few minutes into the journey, Paul is in full swing polishing his short PowerPoint presentation when the train manager comes round to make his ticket inspection. Paul smiles and offers his ticket without really taking his eyes of the screen, but when he hears 'excuse me, sir,' he looks up with a start.

> 'I'm afraid this is a fixed price ticket that was valid for the previous train,' the train manager explains. 'To travel on this train you need to buy a new ticket, sir.'
>
> 'Oh! I didn't know that, sorry. How much is that then?'
>
> 'A first class single from Birmingham to London on this train is £271, sir.'
>
> 'Really? Well what about second, then?'
>
> 'A *standard* class single is £158, sir.'

After a second or two to recover from the shock, Paul realises he may well have to pay for the replacement ticket himself, and decides to head to the other end of the train. Unlike first class, this is very busy indeed and hardly any of the seats have proper tables. Paul eventually finds an empty 'airline' seat with rather limited legroom and sits down, but there's no room to spread his papers out and for some reason the WiFi has stopped working. Remembering that last night he forgot to download the figures he needs, he has to give up on his presentation. Looking out of the window, he reflects on the likely false economy of his company's recent decision to prevent its employees travelling in first class from next month; how was he going to be able to get anything like as much work done in these cramped conditions in the future?

One of the most striking aspects of the British transport sector is the extent to which it has been privatised and deregulated since the early 1980s. There is no major economy in the world whose domestic transport public provision is more reliant upon private industry for, in Peter White's (2009) words, its planning, management and operation. The enthusiasm of successive governments for privatisation is linked to an international trend of pursuing ideas associated with the neoliberal intellectual movement. Writers such as Friedrich Hayek (1960) and Milton Friedman (1980) inspired the administrations of Margaret Thatcher and Ronald Reagan to pioneer a radical shift from the largely centrist politics of the post-war era in which the state assumed a significant role in the affairs of society. A new, 'hard' right alternative was championed, in which the virtues of the free market were advocated in the broader philosophical context of supporting human liberty. Rather than over-involving itself in the society it governs, the duty of the state would much more be to promote the effective functioning of the market as the best means of allocating goods and services.

As far back as the mid-1970s the Conservative Party (Fowler, 1978, cited in Shaw, 2000a, p 3) was publishing leaflets rejecting 'the idea that transport ought to be regarded primarily as a social service to which the taxpayer must be forced to contribute huge and continuing subsidies ... The best way to ensure the public interest', the document continued, 'is to promote free competition between the providers and free choice between the users.' Once elected in 1979, the Conservatives set about getting rid of state-owned companies and deregulating markets. Some undertakings were sold outright – British Airways (BA), the National Freight Consortium (NFC), Associated British Ports (ABP), the British Airports Authority – while others were commercialised, split into smaller concerns and sold off to a range of bidders. The National and Scottish Bus Companies (NBC and SBC) and British Rail (BR) fell into this category.[1] At the same time, the transport market in general was liberalised in an attempt to secure 'free competition between the providers' – in other words, competition between bus companies and other bus companies, rail companies and other rail companies, and between bus companies and rail companies. The question of whether this would be at all productive was vigorously debated (see Banister, 1985; Beesley and Glaister, 1985; Gwilliam et al, 1985), but many in the transport sector already knew the answer; Herbert Morrison had identified 'wasteful competition' between transport operators as the key barrier to progress as long ago as the 1930s. Public transport's main competition is of course the car, not other public transport.

In much of mainland Europe, a key aim of public transport policy is to provide a high-quality alternative to the car for as many journeys as reasonably possible (Chapter Six). In Britain, the way the system is set up makes it difficult for transport companies and authorities to focus on this goal. When the NBC and SBC were privatised in the 1980s, the concurrent deregulation of the bus market made it all but impossible for an integrated network of bus services, fares and ticketing options to exist. Companies could introduce and withdraw from routes subject only to a notice period of 42 days (this has now increased to 56) and passengers accustomed to having city-wide travelcards could no longer use their tickets on buses other than those to whose drivers they had paid their fares. Organised integration with the railways was lost at the same time. This explains why Paul could not use his season ticket when catching the bus to the station.

In London, bus operations escaped full-scale deregulation in favour of a system of competitive tendering. The newly formed London Regional Transport (LRT) would determine fares, service quality, frequency and integration across the network and invite bidders to run services. This allowed inter-operable ticketing to be retained and the Travelcard, which included the tube and rail services within the Greater London area, survived. This has now morphed into the Oyster Card. It is astonishing to think that it is not standard practice to provide readily available, multimodal, inter-operator tickets in any of mainland Britain's major provincial cities; this would be unthinkable in other European countries because it makes using public transport so much more difficult and unappealing.[2] Some inter-operator bus tickets have started to emerge (in Bath and York, for example), but their cost tends to be more than single-operator equivalents. The basic problem is that bus companies see inter-operator tickets as commercially unattractive, since they will receive only a share of the revenue, but the tragedy is that since privatisation the market for fare-paying passengers outside of London has been in general and quite steep decline. Patronage in the 20 years from 1985 fell by around 20% across Great Britain as a whole, and in provincial cities by almost a half. The bus companies effectively compete with each other for a larger share of a declining market, rather than working out how to appeal more to car users. London now accounts for around half of all bus journeys, some 2.3 billion, made in England every year (TfL, 2012).

Ironically, competition between bus operators also declined to the point that market dominance by a single company had emerged in most locations by 2004 and, not surprisingly in the absence of regulation, fares went up sharply (Knowles and Abrantes, 2008). In London, where the competition was 'off the road' and where much greater stability of service patterns remained, cost savings were also achieved but patronage grew by around 60% between 1999 and 2012 and fares were kept relatively low. Since 2000 buses have been made a policy priority by Mayors Ken Livingstone and Boris Johnson, and LRT's successor body, TfL, sets operators extremely high and exacting standards in its tenders (see White, 2008). All of this comes at a price, with subsidies rising to more than £600 million per year, but TfL has taken the view that you get what you pay for. In the rest of the country, policy may have been 'markedly successful in improving the efficiency of Britain's transport industries in the narrow sense of reducing unit costs', but governments 'chose to take virtually all the benefit in the form of reduced public expenditure' (Glaister et al, 2006, p 269). London-style regulation is now possible outside of the capital through Bus Quality Contracts, and although the authorities in West Yorkshire and Tyne and Wear are seeking to introduce these, none has yet been put into place. Generally, this is because local councils have insufficient political will to improve bus infrastructure where it involves reallocating road space away from cars, little desire to upset their local bus companies by interfering with their existing operations and a lack of in-house expertise capable of actually fashioning and managing a fully integrated transport network.

BR was sold off in the most extraordinarily complicated privatisation ever undertaken in the UK (Shaw, 2000b). Only one element of the company, the infrastructure, was to retain its monopoly status, whereas passenger and freight rail services, rolling stock, maintenance activities and ancillary services were all split between nearly 100 different companies in a bid to ensure competition within the industry. Rather like in the bus sector, much of this competition has vanished because it was unnecessary or unworkable, especially in the maintenance and renewal sectors, where the infrastructure owner Network Rail has taken these activities back in-house. Some on-rail competition does take place at the margins where the operating areas of the 20 franchised Train Operating Companies (TOCs) overlap, and there is off-rail competition for the franchises every 7–15 years, depending on government policy. Competition in the freight sector, where seven businesses were sold outright, has developed more effectively.

There is heated debate as to whether or not rail privatisation has been a success (see Shaoul 2004; 2006; Wolmar, 2005; Jupe, 2010; Inside Government, 2013). The headline points are that, at 1.5 billion per year, passenger journeys have increased to their highest levels since the 1920s, when a much larger network was in existence. Freight kilometres have risen by more than 40%, to levels last seen in the 1970s. Equally, passenger rail subsidy trebled to a high of around £6 billion per annum (it is now around £4 billion), when a key aim of selling off BR was to reduce the call of the railways on the public purse. In some ways, though, the point about subsidy is a bit of a red herring. Christian Wolmar (2005) rightly identifies the 'transaction costs' bound up with the need to negotiate so many contractual interfaces between companies in the fragmented industry structure, but much of the additional money is accounted for by the need to make good decades of underinvestment in BR and its predecessors. This is especially unfortunate, given the industry's cost structure and current difficulties in securing value for money from infrastructure investment (Chapter One).

In the context of the 30–40% 'efficiency gap' in UK rail spending (DfT and Office of Rail Regulation, 2011) there is an obvious need to bring down the cost of running the railway. But since politicians of both major parties are responsible for creating and perpetuating the current structure of the industry, and for starving the railway of investment throughout much of the 20th century, shrill and insistent calls in Parliament for subsidy reduction ring a little hollow. Acknowledging the scale of, and guaranteeing funding for, the work that still needs to be done while applying gentle pressure to refine working practices and orchestrating some structural reform of the industry would be a better approach. It is probably fair to say that the current government is halfway there. On the one hand, it has committed to significant (but long overdue) enhancements such as electrification and a second high speed line (HS2) in the context of on-going unit-cost savings by Network Rail. On the other hand, its franchising policy is in disarray, following high-profile blunders, and this is likely to compromise any advances made in the efficiency of procuring large-scale infrastructure projects (Laidlaw, 2012; National Audit Office, 2012; Brown, 2013). Moreover, the DfT's current policy of reducing subsidy to only 25% of the total cost of running the railway will entail further price rises for passengers who have already endured a decade of above-inflation fare increases. This is very much a return to the bad old days of BR's attempts to 'price off' demand in the 1980s, on the instruction of Treasury mandarins who did not wish to pay for capacity enhancements.

The extent to which the increase in patronage is due to privatisation is hard to estimate. There are many more train services operating now than before privatisation and the train fleet is newer, although it is again starting to age in the absence of recent train orders. Indeed, the limited availability of rolling stock is causing serious problems of overcrowding in pinch-points across the network, and we would suggest that much of the new and refurbished rolling stock that has entered service since the late 1990s does not guarantee a comfortable journey even if it is not heavily loaded: carriages are often cramped and legroom is poor, and ride quality is frequently bumpy at best. It is certain that a long period of economic growth until 2008 provided natural buoyancy for passenger numbers (see Preston, 2008), but then patronage has continued to rise strongly in the economic downturn despite the overall cost of motoring having risen far less than train (and bus) travel in real terms (Chapter Two). We also saw in Chapter Two that people don't appear to be all that bothered by road congestion, at least as it affects them individually (Goodwin and Lyons, 2010). In this sense it is likely that the activities of the TOCs do indeed account for a fair proportion of the growth in patronage since privatisation. Sales of discounted advance tickets are especially strong and Le Vine and Jones (2012) have identified a discernible uplift in business travel on the train, no doubt associated with the potential for productive travel time use. But it is a reasonable bet that BR would also have witnessed burgeoning passenger numbers had it received the same amount of money that has been thrown at the private-sector railway. It might have secured better value for money for large-scale upgrades, as well.

Although many of the TOCs are owned by bus companies (Stagecoach, First, Arriva, Go Ahead), integration between bus and rail services remains hit and miss. Even when the trains and buses serving a station are owned by the same company, coordinated timetables are by no means guaranteed, and although it is possible to add connecting bus and tube tickets to rail ticket purchases, the process of actually buying the right rail ticket in the first place can be confusing enough.[3] The practice of 'commercialising' the price and range of tickets available was started in the 1980s, as BR reacted to constant pressure from the Treasury to increase revenue in order to reduce its subsidy requirement. The TOCs have taken the art of ticket pricing to a new level, borrowing strategies used elsewhere, particularly among the airlines, and the sheer complexity of today's fares structure is one of the most frequently made criticisms of the privatised railway. While they are obliged to accept a certain number of traditional 'walk on' fares that are valid across the national network and can be purchased until departure (simple singles, returns and season tickets), the TOCs are at liberty to set the prices for 'advance purchase' tickets which are valid only on their own services. Most TOCs now operate some form of yield management, where pricing of advance purchase tickets is determined using detailed data on the number of passengers on each train, and how many are likely to book ahead as opposed to walk on with an open ticket. This produces a sliding scale of ticket prices with a few very cheap headline deals, and a larger number of mid-price tickets.

It is undeniable that the opportunities for yield pricing seized upon by the TOCs have led to significant innovation and the introduction of some very cheap off-peak fares. Time it right and you can travel from London to Edinburgh for as little as £17 each way, for example. A consequence of this is that there has been an explosion in the number of fares that are available, each with its own particular conditions of use. Take Paul's journey from Birmingham to London: at the time of writing we could find a staggering *84* single ticket options available (not to mention returns), some of which can be used on any train and others that are specific to the three competing operators, Virgin Trains, London Midland and Chiltern Railways (CR). Not only can this make the railway difficult to understand for irregular travellers, but also, as Paul found out to his cost, buying an advance purchase ticket substantially reduces the flexibility of the rail network (the industry used to pride itself in *not* being like the airlines precisely on the basis that you could simply buy a ticket and walk onto the train). The financial penalties for missing your train can be significant: boarding a train other than that on which your ticket is valid will mean you are 'liable for the full single fare to your intended destination'. This can be extremely expensive.[4]

Pricing policy on the railway is arguably now out of control. Informed travellers will be aware of the contortions required to play and beat the railway at its own game, such as buying three tickets (Glasgow–Perth, Perth–Dundee and Dundee–Aberdeen), rather than one, because it costs less.[5] The Scottish Government has recently cut a deal with ScotRail to eliminate these anomalies at an annual cost of around £3 million in additional subsidy. Although travellers in England and Wales are now promised better information about split ticket options, the DfT has not chosen to follow the Scottish Government's lead and attempts to play the system are still not tolerated. For many years, regular commuters to Gatwick would buy a return ticket to Three Bridges, the first station beyond the airport from London, to avoid the premium fares charged to the airport itself. (Premium fares, we should point out, that are little more than the fleecing of a captive audience largely composed of overseas visitors and domestic business travellers, like Paul, who were spending the company's money rather than their own.) To prevent this, TOCs now actively enforce the rule in the National Conditions of Carriage – which in any sensible system would be wholly unnecessary – that forbids getting off a train before your ticketed destination.

Coming up with an appropriate fares system for the railways or public transport more generally is notoriously difficult, involving all sorts of trade-offs, such as balancing the differential revenue yields of calculating fares on the basis of distance travelled versus demand for particular routes, the spread of demand across time of day (British travellers are used to the notion of peak and off-peak, but the potential exists to have more time categories such as 'shoulder' pricing either side of the peaks themselves), flexibility or otherwise and so on. But then other European operators seem to have managed to make the final systems they come up with less bewildering. Some maintain a model close to the traditional 'per-kilometre' system, with tickets priced according to the distance travelled. Cheap advance fares are still possible under simpler systems – for example, Deutsche Bahn's full fare/25% discount/50% discount structure is both effective and very easy to understand – and indeed network-wide discount programmes like the BahnCard can be developed. BahnCards are generally bought for a year, provide a 25%, 50% or 100% discount on the full fare for any journey and are available for first and second class travel. In effect, you pay an amount up front to retain full flexibility but guarantee advance purchase fares. An equivalent in Britain is not possible because the variance in the prices for any given journey is just too much.

The proportionate difference in price between standard and first class fares is also an important component of railway pricing policy. In Britain we have reached the stage where even the most senior members of government are vilified for travelling in first class, feeding the view that it is simply gauche to do so even when working. Admittedly the political circumstances of the moment – a hangover from a vicious row over expenses and privileges combined with the fallout from a member of the government reportedly having referred to a policeman as a 'pleb' – caused Chancellor of the Exchequer George Osborne rather more political embarrassment than usual when he found himself in a similar ticketing situation to Paul (BBC, 2012b), but something of a popular witch-hunt against the use of first class has emerged. Many public and private sector employees are now permitted to travel only in standard class, by dint of a rather ill-thought-out blanket ban that means employers are deliberately giving away the increased productivity they would gain from staff travelling in a more conducive working environment. Perhaps if standard class were more comfortable the issue would not arise. Again drawing on the German example, Deutsche Bahn has provided levels of on-board comfort unrecognisable in the British context, especially on its long-distance services.[6] This makes first class travel all but unnecessary unless extreme levels of quiet or privacy are required, although of course this would be problematic in terms of a privatised TOC's bottom line.

Going underground

Things are looking up for Paul as he walks down the escalator from the main concourse at Euston. Given that he's a regular traveller to London, he has an Oyster Card and as he holds it against the reader on the gate he looks across at the ticket machine queue and thinks how much better this is than fishing for change like he had to earlier in the morning. In no time at all he's on the Northern Line. There's a choice of different routes to Docklands and sometimes he changes onto the Docklands Light Railway (DLR), but today he jumps onto the Jubilee Line Extension (JLE) at London Bridge on his way to Canary Wharf. With its space-age architecture and platform screen doors, the JLE still feels very new 14 years after opening and quite unlike most of the rest of the Tube, although the new trains on the Northern Line and the general state of the stations are also much better than they were only a few years ago. Indeed, he doesn't understand why people moan about the Tube these days. 'They should try living and working in other cities like Birmingham where there is nothing like it, and the buses aren't as good either,' he thinks to himself.

As Paul emerges from Canary Wharf station the rain finally stops. The journey from Euston took only 24 minutes and, despite the inauspicious start to his trip, he's arrived at his company HQ on time, if not fully prepared. He makes his way to the meeting room to find that his colleague Jacqueline from Glasgow has taken a direct flight to London City and beaten him there, and that Philippe from Paris has also just arrived via the Eurostar. Over coffee, and after the inevitable chit-chat about the weather, the conversation turns to their journey experiences that morning. Jacqueline had no problems at all other than a rather bumpy landing through the rain, and Philippe wonders for how much longer his Eurostar is going to flash through Stratford International station without stopping (Stratford is close to Docklands and is connected to Canary Wharf by the JLE). He is, though, forced to agree with Paul that St Pancras International is a much, much better gateway to the country than any French station. The conversation is still in full flow when their boss, John, walks in, half an hour late: he's come straight off the plane from New York, and he is quick to bemoan the state of transport in Britain: 'Y'all had it easy: I've just had to crawl all the way across London from Heathrow in the rush hour. Terminal 5 is all very well, but £20 on the Heathrow Express to be dumped on wrong side of town? That's a rip off. And I don't know why this Crossrail thing has taken so long? It should have been done years ago. I mean, Heathrow's on completely the opposite side of London from Docklands and the City … don't these planners understand business? I thought you Europeans were supposed to do transit!'

We have noted several times that London stands apart from the rest of the British transport system, but never is this more obvious than when comparing getting around in the capital with doing the same elsewhere in the country. If journeys outside of London involve fragmented public transport systems, wasteful competition between bus and rail companies and inconvenient or impenetrable ticketing options, the situation in London could not be more different. A single ticket, and a smart card at that, gets you on the buses, the Underground, the new Overground lines and all suburban trains (not to mention the Emirates Air Line cable car!); you can prepare for your journey by topping-up your credit online; there is a choice of routes from A to B; and the bus network is planned and regulated.

Then there's the infrastructure. The critique of the over-dominance of London is well made across many aspects of economic and social life in the UK (Amin et al, 2003), but in transport it is staggering. Compared to Paul's home region of the West Midlands, transport spending in London is *three times* greater per head of population (Table 4.1). Alongside a mayor who is genuinely interested in transport and a highly competent transport authority in possession of appropriate powers to regulate its network (Chapter Seven), this is why the bus service is dense and frequent, some of the local railways are being transformed into the kind of regional metro service commonplace across Europe and the capacity of the Tube is still increasing, thanks to a programme of comprehensive renewal. The DLR has seen several extensions and capacity enhancements, and the new St Pancras station has been opened, with its connections to HS1. By 2019, Thameslink will, finally, have been rebuilt and hugely expanded, and Crossrail, also significantly delayed, will have been completed as well. Even in the context of all of this investment, it is notable that symbolism remains important: the same roundel logo has represented London's public transport for decades, and the buses are all still painted the traditional red colour (rather than some new, garish concoction of pink and purple). Such things give the impression of a stable, reliable system.

Interestingly, the extent to which Crossrail actually represents a good investment is debated, not least by economists who have subjected the scheme to many cost-benefit analyses (CBAs). Whatever John might think about his experience in getting from Heathrow to Canary Wharf, such is Crossrail's cost (around £16 billion) that its 'benefit:cost ratio', or BCR, hovers perilously close to the 1.5 threshold under which the Department for Transport would regard it as 'poor' value for money. As this is London, special assumptions about the value of time have been made to capture the 'wider economic benefits' of the project – those agglomeration economies again – that push the BCR figure up to a far more acceptable 2.5.[7]

Table 4.1: Transport spending per head of population (£) in the English regions and devolved jurisdictions

	2006/07	2009/10	2010/11
North East	229	265	255
North West	279	354	337
Yorks. and Humber	238	285	276
East Midlands	228	256	235
West Midlands	262	273	242
East	236	278	328
London	609	721	774
South East	277	263	239
South West	244	217	212
England	306	343	344
Scotland	529	562	536
Wales	300	384	400
Northern Ireland	222	310	360
UK average	322	363	363

Source: HM Treasury (2012)

CBA (or CoBA, as it began its life) was adopted in Britain for the evaluation of roads projects in the 1960s. The basic idea of CBA is to determine whether or not any given scheme will provide value for money, by comparing its cost of construction and maintenance over a given period (usually 30 years) with the monetary value of the benefits it is likely to realise. The output of any given appraisal is expressed as a BCR. It is obvious that this number is deceptively simple and its originators (in the transport sphere the likes of Michael Beesley and Sir Christopher Foster), we are sure, would not claim that the technique is perfect. While it is *relatively* straightforward, if not exactly uncontentious, to estimate the cost of building and maintaining a scheme (although see Flyvberg et al, 2003) and by how much the direct operating costs of vehicles might change, it is more problematic to account for costs and benefits that have no intrinsic monetary value. How much is a shorter journey time worth to any given individual? What about to the economy as a whole? How much is saving a life worth? What is the benefit of removing lorries from a village centre? What about the cost of destroying wildlife habitat? Estimations are often derived from empirical studies that have worked out what people would be willing to pay for such things. A life saved, for example, is valued on the basis of what people are willing to pay to reduce the risk of death (Glaister et al, 2006). But willingness-to-pay studies are by no means flawless. For one thing, they give very different answers to alternative methodologies (for example, willingness-to-accept-compensation studies), and they can also privilege the view of the wealthy, who can afford to pay more. This is to say nothing of the ultimately rather meaningless nature of any answer to a question such as 'How much would you be willing to pay to reduce the risk of death?' Where it is impossible (or requires even more ridiculous questions) to attempt quantification, then qualitative judgements are made as to the cost or benefit of a particular impact.

The more widespread consideration of qualitative elements to transport appraisal is a relatively recent innovation introduced in the 1990s as part of the Labour government's New Approach to Appraisal (NATA). It is to be applauded because it forces policy makers to recognise that in many cases: (a) it is futile even to try to ascribe a monetary value to certain things and (b) they are often trying to compare apples with oranges when attempting to reach a decision about the relative merits of a particular scheme. Whether or not recognising the value of qualitative analyses makes the appraisal process any more or less robust is open to question, however. Modern appraisal techniques may well have become quite sophisticated, but the predominant variable in transport CBAs remains the value of time saved as a result of a new scheme's completion. This is because the DfT assumes that the time we spend travelling is completely 'lost', on the basis that the very act of travelling makes it impossible to do anything else that might be economically beneficial. It is easy to see in this light why roads projects often generate very strong BCRs compared to other schemes: when scaled up to the level of traffic on major routes, even time savings as small as a minute or two per driver or passenger on a new bypass can add up to a seemingly enormous, if at the individual level pretty trifling, economic benefit.

In the context of building new infrastructure in the 1960s the idea that 'travel time = wasted time' was probably reasonable before mobile phones, and the idea of people using transport other than as a means to an end was poorly understood. Now we know that people use their travel time for all sorts of activities and travel for all sorts of reasons (Laurier, 2004; Lyons and Urry, 2005; Hall, 2008; Jain and Lyons, 2008). Look around any inter-city train and you will see people like Paul attempting to work on his PowerPoint presentation, while others do all manner of things from catching up on social emails and text messages, making telephone calls (especially in the Quiet Coach!), enjoying the journey experience with friends and family or simply making use of the time to rest (see Bissell, 2010). And the act of 'going for a drive', enjoying heritage railways or walking and cycling for fun (Chapter Three) provides evidence aplenty that people make journeys precisely for the sake of making journeys – so-called 'undirected travel' (Mokhtarian and Handy, 2009). All of these activities are clearly important to the individuals concerned: certainly for us a train journey really is one of the few opportunities we get to actually read, reflect, discuss and write together without the inevitable distractions of the office. But to the economists in the DfT they are still worth nothing at all. (We assume that consulting companies working for the government concur and are quite happy not to charge for the time spent by their professional staff working on the train.)

A key problem is that politicians like simple numbers to bandy around when talking about particular transport projects, and BCRs thus retain credibility in the British government machine. For a favoured scheme, the trick is being able to produce a BCR agreeably above 1.5. Numerous 'pet' schemes of politicians have experienced uplifts in their BCRs as new studies have been commissioned to address mistakes in existing analyses (that is, use different assumptions). The Borders rail line in Scotland is a good example (see Docherty et al, 2007), as also, to a certain extent, is Crossrail, but the most recent is the controversy over HS2, the first phase of which should speed Paul from Birmingham to London in 49 minutes by 2026. Provided that other public transport spending is not compromised, there is a very positive case for a network of high speed railways across Great Britain, of which HS2 is a logical first step (see Preston, 2012 for a critical and not entirely positive review of the main issues). Increased speed is certainly one advantage – even though people pursue a wide range of activities on the move there is no sense in wasting time unnecessarily – and a second, very significant, benefit is the additional railway capacity the new line will provide. The WCML is almost full, despite its recent modernisation (see below).

But the case for such a network of high speed lines is rather weakened by having to rely upon some very dubious claims indeed in order to produce a simple number which then can be used to sell the project to a highly cynical press (and public). In support of HS2, the government has had to perpetuate the notion that passengers will do nothing meaningful with their time while travelling between England's first and second cities. For 125 miles, people will be in complete stasis, but because that stasis will last for 35 fewer minutes than on the existing route, the sums will somehow add up. Even if ministers have not helped themselves by presenting the scheme in isolation rather than as part of a wider, planned network (this would have resulted in a better BCR), some anti-HS2 groups have done well at undermining the formal business case for the project. Goodwin (2010) has shown how the case for a whole host of transport schemes can suddenly become more favourable when the underlying assumptions are changed.

Whether or not Goodwin intended to undermine CBA as a process for appraising transport projects – parts of his paper could certainly be interpreted in this manner – a better way of deciding between infrastructure schemes might simply be to determine which interventions are most likely to achieve the stated aims of transport policy (Metz, 2008). Achieving value for money in this context is much more to do with expert project procurement than it is about overly complicated appraisal procedures that are open to manipulation. The approach advocated by Metz is already used in other Whitehall departments and *should* at least provide an element of transparency and credibility to debates skewed by the perception of 'dodgy' BCR figures (we refrain here from commenting on the competence of negotiators in other government departments, but there is no doubt that it would have to improve somewhat in the DfT; see Chapter Seven). Perhaps the current Secretary of State for Transport, Patrick McLoughlin, agrees. Reacting to a National Audit Office report that 'called' the DfT on its preposterous numerical contortionism, he admitted that, actually, 'economic modelling is just the start of the story. If we only relied on modelling, we would not have built the M1, parts of the M25 or the (Tube's) Jubilee line extension to Canary Wharf' (*Guardian*, 2013a, unpaginated).

As an aside, one misfortune associated with ministers' preference for focusing on large-scale road and (now) rail projects is their tendency to overlook decidedly unsexy but very important local schemes that can make a real difference to the everyday lives of huge numbers of people. Junction safety improvements for pedestrians and cyclists, repairing local pavements, building cycle paths and implementing traffic-calming schemes generally have a much harder time being justified, despite making up a vanishingly small proportion of the overall transport budget. The irony is that these small local projects often display BCRs that are 10 or even *20* times better than standard road and rail projects (see Goodwin, 2010 for a thorough exploration of these issues). While Britain is woefully lacking in decent pavements and cycle tracks, we should also remember that its major transport infrastructure is some way short of the quality and extent enjoyed by comparable European economies; the country has lacked the kind of big infrastructure projects represented by Crossrail and Thameslink, and ministers need to pursue HS2, the Northern Hub and other mass people-moving schemes along with a range of smaller schemes, as well as complementary measures such as road-user charging, if genuine progress is to be made in arresting congestion and all of its associated externalities. We return to these issues in Chapter Seven.

The wires are down

Paul is not alone in his ability to wing it in presentations, and so the meeting comes to an early end shortly after lunchtime. As everyone prepares to say their goodbyes, the conversation turns to the journey home: John is staying in London over the weekend to meet some clients; Jacqueline, who flies almost as much as John, jealously guards her gold Executive Club card and has already used her flexible ticket to switch to an earlier flight, since she is eager to surprise the kids by picking them up from school later; and Philippe plans to stay at St Pancras for a while to do some shopping and have a glass of champagne or three before the Eurostar. Paul also harbours thoughts of an early return home, until he remembers that, as for his outward trip, he has a fixed-price ticket valid only on the 17.23, and so he now has almost three hours to kill before leaving Euston. Or two-and-a-half, because he doesn't want to repeat this morning's expensive mistake.

Finally getting to take his seat after a pleasant stroll around central London, Paul relaxes with a glass of red wine on the train back to New Street. Sitting in his pre-booked First Class seat complete with power socket and free WiFi (it seems to be working again now), Paul decides to catch up on email since he'd kept his phone off during his walk around town. He gets through more than 50 messages before he realises the train has ground to a halt. Then comes the first announcement to say that there is a problem with the train in front, followed by the next one a few minutes later, which causes hearts to sink: 'Ladies and gentlemen, I'm sorry but it seems that the train in front has brought down the overhead wires. We're not sure at this point how long we'll be delayed, but it could be some time. I'll keep you updated as best I can, and of course we are very sorry for the delay and the inconvenience this may cause you.'

Somehow expecting that nothing was going to be straightforward today, Paul shrugs his shoulders and continues the battle against his email backlog. After several false starts and a wait of around 45 minutes, the train starts to move forward again. Very soon he realises that something unusual is going on: the ride was less straight and smooth than normal and, just as he's thinking that he doesn't recognise the view from the window, he sees that the train was passing through Northampton station, away from its normal route. A final announcement confirms that the train has been diverted, and will arrive in Birmingham around an hour late. 'At least we're moving,' Paul thinks to himself as he decides to call it a day with his email and starts browsing the web instead.

We described earlier in the chapter how the railways' sell-off was fearsomely complex, and that the legacy of decades of underinvestment has left the railways in a poor state of repair and starved of capacity. Trying to put these things right in the context of a fragmented railway industry and policy hysteria is proving a long and expensive task, and the WCML, on which Paul depends to get to and from London, is a good case in point. Matters are not helped by the line's complex history: actually, the very word 'line' is something of a misnomer, as the WCML is the sum of a collection of routes that diverge from and converge with a core railway running from London to Crewe and on to Scotland. These were originally built by different companies with little reference to one another, and often followed famously curvaceous alignments so that the properties of the privileged elite could be avoided (there is a parallel here with the NIMBYs who oppose HS2 in the Chilterns and Warwickshire). This is hardly the most auspicious basis for a modern high speed railway of the 21st century.

The public perception of any high speed railway is often shaped by the notion that premium end-to-end express services are its dominant business, but in reality the role of trunk routes in Britain tends to be much more complex. On the WCML, for instance, substantial sections of the line around London, the West Midlands, the North West and Strathclyde are integral parts of heavily used local commuter networks whose slower, stopping services reduce capacity for inter-city express trains. A host of regional services also use short sections of the line and, to compound matters, the route carries in excess of 40% of all British rail freight, traffic that tends to be heavy, slow and to exert lots of wear and tear on the infrastructure. All of this makes planning the core north–south train service extremely difficult. The European approach to dealing with this level of operational complexity has been to try to accommodate different kinds of trains on different routes and infrastructure. The separation of suburban and long-distance trains began in Berlin as early as the 1910s, leading to the S-Bahn rail networks that serve all of Germany's major cities. Even the idea of the high speed railway owes a great deal of its existence to the separation of different kinds of rail traffic. The original Paris to Lyon TGV line was designed as much to create additional capacity by removing long-distance passenger trains from the 'classic' line to the south-east, which could then accommodate even more freight, as it was by the need for speed.

By contrast, decades of underinvestment on this side of the Channel have prevented the adoption of these well-developed solutions on the British railway network. While some piecemeal investment has taken place, the failure to follow through on an overarching vision for developing the railways has simply added further complexity, and at times resulted in some blatantly perverse outcomes. The WCML was electrified in two stages in the 1960s and 1970s, but further attempts to improve the quality of its services proved abortive. The Advanced Passenger Train experiment of the 1980s pioneered the tilting train technology on which the WCML and many other railways around the world now rely, but this was abandoned, due to lack of government support. The InterCity 250 programme of the 1990s, which would have applied the lessons learned from the German experience of upgrading existing routes for better performance and higher speeds through a combination of cutting-edge rolling-stock design and carefully targeted infrastructure improvements, was also shelved. By the 1990s the WCML was in such a state that there was no option other than to rebuild the line. The route's upgrade was to be the flagship project of privatisation, designed to show what the industry could achieve once freed from the yoke of the state. Sadly, the 'WCML Route Modernisation' project turned out to be protracted, enormously disruptive and hideously over budget. At around £10 billion, it ended up costing *five times* the original estimate and still isn't properly finished (large-scale projects continue to disrupt train services).

Although some extra track was built (in the Trent Valley) to separate fast, long-distance services and slower, stopping local trains, the project hinged on the idea that a clever form of signalling, which worked by measuring and managing the distance in between trains, would squeeze more capacity out of the existing route.[8] Perhaps predictably, given how it had already failed on the operationally far-simpler Jubilee Line Extension, the technology couldn't be made to work and the project had to be downgraded and redesigned. The TOCs were paid hundreds of millions of pounds in compensation both for the disruption caused when the works finally went ahead and because the potential for more and faster trains – and hence more passenger revenue – that they were promised could not be delivered. Indeed, the WCML is already again close to full capacity fewer than five years after its upgrade was 'completed'. At great expense the WCML Route Modernisation project has produced something that Deutsche Bahn or SNCF would be likely to recognise as a functioning 1970s trunk route, rather than the 'world class railway for the 21st century' hailed by British ministers.

The tale of the WCML demonstrates another feature of British transport policy, namely, that time after time, governments have failed to engineer enough redundancy – what Goodwin (1992) refers to as a 'quality margin' – into the transport system. Key transport infrastructure such Heathrow, Gatwick, much of the motorway and railway networks and countless junctions on non-trunk roads, is working at or over capacity and there is very little if any slack to cope when things go even slightly wrong. The mindset has developed over the years among those who write the cheques for investment in British transport systems (that is, our old friends the mandarins in the Treasury and DfT) that slack in the system is a waste of money. In planned operational conditions, a quality margin is not necessary because the predicted number of cars is using a road, or all the trains and planes using stations and airports are running on time. Planned operational conditions are by no means guaranteed, however, especially where the underpinning network has been heavily underinvested in. Many stretches of the road network operate wildly in excess of capacity (although, as we argued in Chapter Two, at least some of the answer here is to charge motorists to use them), and the railways are little different. Indeed matters here were made worse by rationalisation following *The reshaping of British Railways*, otherwise known as the Beeching Report (British Railways Board, 1963), which led to many secondary lines between cities being torn up on cost grounds. In the South East of England's airports the lack of runway capacity, owing to politicians' dithering, is severe (Chapter Six). Britain would be a laughing stock except that the knock-on effects to other countries' air networks caused by every foggy or windy day at Heathrow are so profoundly annoying across the Continent. The airport's own apparent inability to clear what other European airports would regard as the most insignificant of snow flurries doesn't help matters.

The effects of bad weather on transport operations were brought home spectacularly in 2012, the wettest year on record in England and the second wettest in the UK as a whole (Met Office, 2013). Flooding was commonplace and Network Rail discovered to its horror that a large number of problems occurred in places never before regarded as vulnerable. In the broader context of climate change, Ryley and Chapman (2012) make the point that those responsible for transport networks and operations will have to adapt to more frequent and severe bad weather events (see also Institution of Civil Engineers, 2009; Jaroszweski et al, 2010). Clearly, this means auditing and potentially altering existing assumptions and engineering practices, but it also means that more of a quality margin is required. In the South West of England, for example, landslips and overtopping events along the coastal stretch of railway between Dawlish and Teignmouth would not be such an issue if the route between Exeter and Plymouth via Okehampton (or even that between Exeter and Newton Abbot) had not been closed (see Clifton, 2012). While our transport system may indeed operate efficiently for some or much of the time, this is only at the expense of episodic and catastrophic inefficiency when things go wrong. Goodwin's (2004, p 2; see Chapter Two) point about the really costly impact of congestion being the 'greater than average effect in particular locations and markets, and the greatly increased unreliability' is worth reiterating in this context.

Paul was rather lucky on his journey home from London because the loop through Northampton is one of the few examples of a viable diversionary route available on any major line anywhere in the country. Had the train in front brought the wires down a little further north, then the situation would have been quite different, because nearly all of the other potential diversionary routes remain diesel only. The slow and piecemeal way in which successive governments chose to electrify the railway network has always been problematic, but privatisation actually exacerbated the situation. For the first decade of rail franchising, there was virtually no incentive to extend electrification at all: the now-defunct infrastructure owner Railtrack considered overhead wiring to be an irritating additional 'interface' that made its core objective of reducing engineering costs more difficult. Incredibly, the company actively considered de-electrifying the northern stretches of both the East and West Coast main lines in the 1990s to simplify its operations. Meanwhile rolling stock companies were reluctant to buy new electric trains in case they were subsequently unable to lease them out to future TOCs once the initial round of franchises had expired. The concern was that, given the limited extent of electrification across the country, future franchisees might decide to run diesel-only fleets to enhance their flexibility (Virgin had decided to do exactly this when it took over the original CrossCountry franchise, for example). Such was the strength of these concerns that the standard justifications for electrification – reduced journey times, cheaper running costs, improved reliability, reduced emissions and the so-called 'sparks effect' of increasing passenger numbers in response to the better travelling environment – were ignored. Thankfully the Coalition government's recent commitment to a sizeable electrification programme is based on realising these very benefits and has consigned Railtrack's perverse logic to its rightful place in the dustbin of history.

The fragmentation of the industry compounded the long-standing problem that transport policies on the ground never seem to join up to deliver on a larger strategic vision. Certainly, outside of TfL's jurisdiction, individual transport policy decisions often appear to be made in almost complete isolation from each other. This is why Paul couldn't use his season ticket on the bus, why HS2 has been appraised on its own as opposed to as part of a wider suite of high speed lines, why Heathrow is full and why the railway 'network' remains more accurately a collection of different lines, often with variable engineering standards, that makes simple inter-operability (such as diverting an electric train around an obstruction) far more difficult than it should be. In the broader scheme of things, even interventions like the £10 billion WCML Route Modernisation project amount to little more than a 'make do and mend' approach to transport policy. In a situation where it is the transport problems rather than the system's operations that are resilient, make do and mend simply isn't good enough.

Notes

[1] Northern Ireland's buses and railways remained in public ownership.

[2] This is not only because it makes ticketing less convenient but also because it slows down bus services quite considerably. In London the high proportion of tickets bought off-bus means that average boarding times are around two seconds per passenger (White, 2008). In provincial towns and cities they are very much longer.

[3] TfL Travelcards and PlusBus tickets for outside of London can be added with one click before payment details are entered on railway ticketing websites. PlusBus is very good value for money, but the lack of integration in local bus networks is evidenced by the warning that PlusBus tickets are accepted only by 'participating operators'. A separate check of the PlusBus website is required before you can be sure that your ticket will be valid on the service you actually want to use. One of the services from Plymouth city centre to Jon's house (the 7D) is excluded, for example.

[4] A walk-up 'anytime' single from Manchester to London is £154; from London to Plymouth it is £131.50.

[5] There is even an App available, Tickety-split, that will work out the cheapest combinations of split journeys for you!

[6] Chiltern Railways' new 'mainline' services come close, and interestingly CR is owned by Deutsche Bahn, but then again so is CrossCountry, whose exceptionally cramped, smelly and uncomfortable Voyagers are the most unsuited trains for a long distance journey either of us has ever used anywhere in northern Europe.

[7] See www.crossrail.co.uk/assets/download/857.

[8] This is so-called moving block signalling. Conventional signalling works by allowing only one train at a time in any given signalling 'block' (the distance between signals).

FIVE

The family visit

Transport, travel and social inclusion; promoting and constraining choice; transport subsidy and opportunity cost

Mamma mia

Over dinner one evening, Susan suggests to Paul that it's about time they go to Scotland to see his mother again. Time's flown, apparently: it was fully a year since the family went to Pitlochry, and Paul has been oblivious to the hints Mrs Smith has been dropping in their recent conversations. Perhaps it's because, Mrs Smith having learned to use Skype, Paul has it in his mind that he 'sees' her once a week now. It's not that Paul doesn't want to go to Scotland. He fondly remembers being taken there as a child to visit his grandparents, and since Mrs Smith moved there with his late father 20 years ago, Paul has come to really appreciate the sense of peace and tranquillity he gets while walking around by the banks of the Tay. Susan likes catching up with Mrs Smith too, and Jack loves to mountain bike on actual mountains as much as he can. There's also been something of a sense of duty about the Smiths' trips to the Southern Highlands since Paul's father died. He has noticed that his mother, who doesn't drive, talks frequently about how one of her friends up the street whose family also lives a long way away has become very much more dependent on her as she gets more and more frail with age.

We have discussed in earlier chapters how increased car use is a result of numerous factors, from the decentralisation of activities to the desire to project a particular image of success. But regular access to a car is by no means universal. Overwhelmingly it is the case that better-off households such as the Smiths' are likely to have the best access to car transport. Interestingly, over the past 30 years the proportion of households in the top two income quintiles owning no cars has remained more or less steady. The gentrification of inner cities and city centres has no doubt offset the general trend towards increasing car ownership; among those people moving into such renovated areas are a number who choose not to buy cars on account of being close to almost all of the professional and leisure destinations they require (Clark, 2010). At the same time, more than half of those in the top income quintile and 40% of those in the second now possess two or more cars.

In the lowest income quintile, the situation couldn't be more different: the number of households with no cars has declined significantly but still remains at more than half. Those that do own cars often find themselves in what the RAC Foundation (2013) calls 'motoring poverty', spending up to 27% of their disposable income on buying and running a vehicle. The equivalent for the best-off car-owning households is 12%. Stradling and Anable (2008, p 184) make the stark observation that people from the predominantly better-off households with car access 'travel more often, further and for longer durations thereby increasing the number and variety of destinations to which they have access'. As a result, they are far more likely to be socially included – that is, to be able to access the things they need in order to participate fully in society – than are those people in lower-income households (see Farrington and Farrington, 2005; Lucas, 2013).

While the poorest members of society make fewer journeys overall than those in the highest socioeconomic groups, other factors such as gender and disability can compound lack of access to a car in terms of their effect on individual mobility. Women suffer disproportionately for a host of reasons, including domestic/caring responsibilities and the fear or perceived fear of walking or using public transport, especially after dark (see Pain, 1997). This can result in potentially necessary trips being foregone even where they are technically quite possible. Innovations such as 'Design for All' are removing many of the needless barriers to mobility faced by the disabled that have to do with the physical layout of infrastructure (high kerbs, lack of lifts and the like), but for obvious reasons carless mobility remains a challenge for many depending on the nature of their impairment. And in any event, relative wealth does not automatically reduce the 'mobility gap' between those who possess cars and those who do not, because car access is rarely shared equally among all the members of a household. To all intents and purposes a one-car household becomes a no-car household once one member of the family is using the vehicle, and in some cases the effects are quite restricting. Where the man in a household uses the car to get to work (as he is more likely to do), women and children can face particular accessibility challenges, especially in areas where public transport is poor.

The ability to secure a high level of mobility is by no means the only determinant of social inclusion, as a vast array of social science literature on educational attainment, class, gender, ethnicity and so on will attest. Still, a welter of studies highlights the on-going significance of the car in helping people to realise available opportunities (Hine, 2008). In the 2000s the government's Social Exclusion Unit (2003) investigated the specific links between transport and social exclusion. From its report can be derived a rather predictable, though nevertheless depressing, narrative of disadvantage. In essence, members of households without a car travel less than half the distance to work and around a quarter of the distance to go shopping, as compared with those in households with one or more cars. In a world of spatially dispersed jobs and services, the ability to travel less distance constrains choice, and the range of employment possibilities, goods and services easily available to those in lower-income households is rather less than those available to people who are better off.

In relation to the labour market, particular problems can develop when companies that employ large numbers of people from lower socioeconomic groups are not already in, or move away from, easily accessible locations. In the absence of dependable public transport connections, a 'spatial mismatch' (Chapter Two) can emerge between where members of a workforce live and where they work. Those people not easily able to make the journey to a site of employment find it much more difficult to secure and/or retain jobs. With regard to shopping, buying goods in local stores tends to be more expensive than in supermarkets that usually require a car to get to, and even where public transport is a viable alternative, average fares are among the very highest in Europe (the Social Exclusion Unit found that only in Denmark and Sweden are they higher). The final insult is that those least likely to own a car pay the highest social price for car dependence: if you live in a deprived area, there is a higher chance you will be killed or seriously injured in a road traffic accident. This is because you are more likely to be a pedestrian for all or a significant part of your journey and, as a result, are more vulnerable than if you were driving or riding in a car. Of course, major improvements in road safety for walkers and cyclists will occur once these activities become far more popular across society as a whole (Chapter Three). For the time being it seems that the poor are already, if involuntarily, doing their bit, but there is not enough support from others who routinely insist on using their cars for journeys they could easily make by other modes (Chapter Two).

Members of carless households are also generally less able to travel far to visit friends, and because social networks have dispersed in the same way as the provision of goods and services some people encounter difficulties in maintaining them. We saw in the last chapter that people like to be 'co-present' and, as such, retain the desire to travel between places where other people in their social networks are located, no matter the 'virtual' alternatives (Urry, 2007). Problems can arise when people rely on the car to retain their social networks, especially if these networks provide a support as well as a social function. Paul's mother's friend is a case in point. Because she is frail, she seldom leaves the house, and since her sister, who could drive, died, her opportunities to make trips have become very few and far between. Mrs Smith's friend is not alone, and her experience highlights the importance of informal lift-giving relative to public transport in providing mobility for those who don't drive. Indeed, in rural England and Scotland the most common form of transport for people without a car is the car (CfIT, 2001b; Scottish Executive, 2004). What happens if a person's regular lifts suddenly become less reliable or even unavailable?

Older people, especially older women, are among the groups most severely affected by the removal of a source of lift-giving. Although the gap has closed in recent years, across the generations men are more likely to have a driving licence than women. It is also the case in some relationships that even where the woman possesses a driving licence, because the man does the driving the woman effectively becomes a non-driver. Either way, if the man dies before the woman (which is statistically likely), or once a decision to stop driving has been taken – although evidence suggests that older people are generally extremely reluctant to do this, not least because it is seen as giving up freedom (Rosenbloom, 2011) – the woman can lose the principal source of her lift and suddenly becomes reliant on the goodwill of others to retain her mobility. So long as friends and family are close by, trips to the shops or to social occasions can still be provided, but this is less likely to be the case when affected individuals find themselves short of people they can rely on to ferry them around.

Mrs Smith's friend is lucky because she has someone to look after her and do her shopping at the small local supermarket (albeit rather than at the much bigger and cheaper ones in Perth). But in some rural towns and villages, especially those that are desirable as second-home or commuter locations, social networks can break down if incomers fail to develop connections within the community, and/or gradually displace those long-standing residents who enjoyed closer ties (Gray et al, 2006). Over time the previous, close-knit community is eroded in favour of a far looser association of people whose professional and social networks are located beyond the place in question, generally a car ride away. As community ties weaken, then the likelihood of long-standing residents and incomers alike being able to obtain lifts may diminish. It is at this point that 'non-traditional' approaches come more and more into play: voluntary schemes such as community transport become important, and local authorities sometimes provide Demand Responsive Transport (DRT, a kind of 'ring and ride' service that may or may not feed into regular service bus routes; see Brake et al, 2004) or taxi voucher schemes.

The future of such schemes depends upon the availability of volunteers and/or local authority funding, and neither can be guaranteed. More broadly, the issue of providing transport for older people is not going to disappear; in fact, it will increase in significance and complexity over the coming decades as the population ages (TRACY, 2012). Although more old people will have cars and more of both sexes will have driving licences, there will remain those who don't drive and it is likely that the expectations of those who remain active will be higher in terms of their mobility requirements (Rosenbloom, 2011). At the same time, an increase in the number of, say, over-85s could result in the need for community transport and other voluntary schemes to expand considerably when decisions are finally taken to give up driving. Paul and his family's visits to Pitlochry have therefore taken on an additional dimension in the last couple of years. As well as serving a purely social function, they have become kind of 'scoping trips' to judge the extent to which Mrs Smith will actually be able to fend for herself as she gets older and less able to get around.

Making your mind up

At about 350 miles each way, a one-off journey to Pitlochry should not be that much of a big deal in itself for the Smiths, given the amount they all travel, but this particular trip has become rather tedious because of the number of times they make it. This perception is not helped by the fact that the last time they drove they got caught up in a two-hour jam close to Manchester on the way home. As a result, Paul is keen to avoid driving, and suggests to Susan when she's online that she has a quick look to see how much it would cost to fly or take the train. Susan remembers that she recently had an email advertising cheap flights to Scotland, so clicks on the link. 'Look, it's only £29 to Edinburgh,' she says and quickly types in the family's details. Five adult travellers actually works out to more than £500 once various additional charges have been factored in (it's actually £58 return, and then £26 for each person to take a bag and £8 to pay with a credit card, but what galls her most is trying to figure out how to avoid being charged £13 per person for an *automatic* seat selection).

The train is even worse: seven hours each way and £620 for the family as a whole, as all the cheap tickets appear to have gone. In any case, Paul dismisses the train idea: 'Thinking about it, I go on the train every day to work, and don't you remember that the luggage racks were too small and I had to sit with my case on my knees the last time we tried it? And the fact I had so little legroom made it really uncomfortable.' When they see that a very cheap car hire package is available at Edinburgh airport, the deal is sealed and a few clicks later the booking confirmations are printed.

Once in the air a few weeks later, Paul and Susan catch up on some reading. Paul spots a piece in the in-flight magazine about the green credentials of the airline: recycling wherever possible of course, but most intriguingly self-certifying its fleet as 'environmentally friendly'. He wonders if he is still correct in his previous assumption that flying was the 'dirtiest' way to travel. Susan is sure that it is, but admits there was no incentive to go a greener way, given how the plane was over £100 cheaper, will be a lot quicker, and can be easily combined with a rental car that gives them so much more flexibility at the other end. After landing, the family picks up their rental car and has a jam-free journey from Edinburgh up the M90 and A9 to Pitlochry. They think back to previous car and train trips from Birmingham, and as the open spaces of Perthshire unfold around them, they all agree that they would be fools to not to make this trip by plane every time.

Paul and Susan are not alone in having chosen to fly for a journey they would previously have made by other means. In the 2000s, the market for air travel grew by around 35%, until the economic downturn began to impact on the sector (DfT, 2012). Domestic passenger numbers have now returned to their 2000 levels, although international passenger numbers are still around 20% higher than they were at the beginning of the millennium. In part this is to do with the deregulation of the European aviation market between 1988 and 1997 and the subsequent innovations of the 'low cost' carriers such as easyJet, Ryanair, Jet2 and Flybe (the 'low cost' moniker refers to the business models assumed by an airline in relation to its cost base, rather than necessarily to the fares paid by passengers). It is interesting to note that the long-term growth rate of passenger numbers of around 5–6% per year did not actually increase following the advent of the low-cost carriers (CAA, 2006). Other factors such as steadily rising incomes and the development of cheap package holidays using charter flights accounted for the aviation sector's expansion in previous decades, but it is safe to assume that the low-cost airlines have played their part in continuing the momentum by exerting competitive pressure that forced established carriers to change their existing practices.

The low-cost carriers (also referred to as 'no-frills' or 'budget' airlines) base themselves to varying degrees on the business model developed by Southwest Airlines in the US. Doganis (2001) estimated that by stripping out a lot of the service features traditionally associated with flying, a typical low-cost carrier could operate at 40–50% of the unit cost of an established or 'legacy' airline, although throughout the 2000s these companies have themselves implemented aggressive cost-cutting strategies. The low-cost carriers' impact on the domestic and European aviation sector is not to be underestimated. Between them they now offer around 30% of all available seats on intra-European air services (Ryanair and easyJet between them account for nearly 10 million seats a year; Table 5.1) and have pioneered a network of domestic and short-haul international routes that would have been unthinkable in the 1980s, including many niche (or at least what would previously have been thought of as niche) services on routes such as Exeter–Belfast and Newcastle–Newquay. Although such routes are relatively common they remain surprisingly peripheral to the low-cost carriers' core business of serving major cities and tourist destinations (Dobruszkes, 2013). Indeed, despite Ryanair's doing its best to promote the perception of low-cost carriers flying from 'nowhere to nowhere' – Glasgow Prestwick, Frankfurt Hahn, Hamburg Lübeck and so on – generally speaking they fly to secondary destinations only in the context of multi-airport systems in a metropolitan area (Stansted rather than Heathrow, say). Such developments in the aviation sector have, not surprisingly, been welcomed by the government. For a start, they are seen as being

Table 5.1: Main airlines operating intra-European air services, January 2012

	Seats		Flights		Seat kilometres	
	Millions	Rank	Thousands	Rank	Billions	Rank
Ryanair	5.87	1	31.07	3	6.47	1
Lufthansa	5.07	2	42.09	1	3.38	3
easyJet	4.33	3	27.17	4	4.15	2
Air France	3.47	4	34.72	2	2.34	4
SAS	2.45	5	18.30	5	1.59	7
British Airways	2.27	6	16.13	7	1.98	5
Alitalia	1.89	7	13.20	8	1.25	11
Air Berlin	1.85	8	11.82	10	1.79	6
Iberia	1.80	9	17.71	6	1.50	9
Norwegian	1.69	10	9.40	14	1.53	8

Source: Dobruzskes (2013)

good for economic growth, on the basis that more routes and greater competition between airlines improves connectivity between places. Oxford Economic Forecasting (OEF, 2006) has estimated that the aviation industry directly contributes more than £11 billion to the British economy and directly and indirectly generates around half a million jobs. Keen to ensure that such benefits could be spread around the country as much as possible, the devolved administrations in Scotland, Wales and Northern Ireland each for a time encouraged the development of new routes to and from their jurisdictions by introducing subsidies in the form of Route Development Funds (RDFs) (Shaw et al, 2009). Early official reviews of the RDFs claimed that they had been successful in generating economic benefits and developing a broad spectrum of air routes (Scottish Enterprise, 2004; Department of Enterprise, Trade and Investment, 2006). It was predicted in Scotland, for example, that an initial investment of £7 million would bring £300 million of economic benefits and 700 tourism-related jobs. By 2007 the Scottish RDFs supported 36 routes from seven airports.

But connectivity works in two directions and economic activity can just as easily flow out of a region as into it (Graham and Shaw, 2008). At the national level, the UK's 'tourist deficit' – the difference between what British people spend abroad and visitors spend here – runs at over £20 billion, and Friends of the Earth Scotland (2006) reckoned the net impact of aviation to the Scottish economy in 2004 to be a cost of £1.4 billion. In this light the economic benefits of the aviation sector are less clear cut, although speaking to the Transport Select Committee in 2009, then Transport Minister Lord Adonis did not seem too bothered. He contended that because the tourist deficit is 'not a measure of the impact of aviation on the contribution of the tourism industry to the value of the UK economy, [i]t would not be meaningful to compare estimates of the tourism deficit directly with the £11 billion value added figure' (House of Commons, 2009c, p 14). It has to be said that it is far from clear whether Adonis's argument is all that meaningful either.

Also of importance to politicians is that the benefits of air travel are in theory made available to many more people. Quoted in the same report as Adonis, the pressure group Flying Matters referred to the so-called 'democratisation effect' of the low-cost carriers when it suggested that '[a] revolution has taken place in flying since the 1960s. Today, flying is no longer the preserve of a privileged elite.' It is indeed true that there are more people from lower socioeconomic groups flying now than in previous decades, but then there has been a significant increase in the number of people flying from all income groups. The most noteworthy trend 'is of middle and higher income and socio-economic groups flying more often than in the past, and often on shorter trips' (CAA, 2006, p 5). In other words, the likes of Paul, Susan and their family are making trips within Britain and Europe that they previously would not have made, or would have made by a different mode of transport. Many of these are work-related (the CAA cites evidence that business travellers have benefited from low-cost airlines rather more than have leisure travellers at the aggregate level), but others are for leisure, including city breaks, semi-frequent return trips to second homes and the same kind of 'visiting friends and relatives' jaunts as the Smiths' to Pitlochry.

Never mind, then, that the economic benefits of aviation are far from certain, and that in reality much of the patronage growth has come from the middle classes flying more often. Like the privatisation of the bus and rail industries was supposed to do, the development of the low-cost airline sector has promoted *choice*. Many politicians, especially when in government, have become transfixed by the notion of choice. It is now so fundamental to ministers' conception of how society should be organised that it often goes unchallenged in any meaningful sense. In previous chapters we have touched upon how choice finds itself a key organising principle in other significant policy areas such as education, as well as in transport. And as we have seen, the relationship between choice in transport and in other policy sectors is interesting because decisions about the latter have profound impacts in terms of where we go, when we go and how we get there. The more schools, hospitals, supermarkets or leisure opportunities people can choose between, and the further away from their homes they are located, the further they are likely to travel (see Metz, 2008).

Having retreated from the initial view that there was a *Consensus for change* (Labour Party, 1996), the 1997–2010 Labour governments rather abandoned the idea that transport 'policy' could be about intervening to change the share of mobility accommodated by each mode (Docherty and Shaw, 2011a). Towards the end of its term of office, Labour's policy had become one of 'modal agnosticism', a seemingly clever phrase coined by former Transport Minister Tom Harris but in fact one tantamount to admitting that the government had no transport policy at all.[1] The narrative shift from promoting 'sustainable' transport, to 'integrated' transport and then 'choice' can be readily discerned in Labour's copious transport policy statements from 1997 to 2010. On one level, this can be read as an increasing aversion to actively changing the status quo, should this constrain choice by artificially privileging one mode over and above another. But in relation to the first principles of the transport debate, Harris couldn't have missed the point more completely if he'd tried. The pursuit of policies to improve public transport systems, enhance walking and cycling opportunities and promote accessibility planning cannot constrain choice. As, ironically, Labour had recognised in *Consensus for change*, such a course of action can only *increase* choice, because the result will be that people have more options available to them when travelling to and from their destinations (of choice). Conversely, the pursuit of policies that have eroded the quality and availability of the non-car modes over several decades has had the net effect for many of taking choice away. Generally speaking, and especially in semi-urban and rural areas, as more people have bought and used cars, the quality and frequency of bus services have been undermined and local shops have closed, it has, over the years, become more difficult to live without a car (Chapter Two).

Returning to Paul and Susan's choice to fly rather than take the train or drive to Pitlochry, while this journey is much longer than most of their usual trips it was also influenced by their everyday experiences of different transport modes. Both of what might have been genuine alternatives, the car and the train, were in the end ruled out because previous encounters led to their being viewed as too expensive, too slow, too familiar, too much hassle and/or not comfortable enough for a 700-mile round trip. Neither Paul nor Susan would know that Britain's roads are the most congested in Europe, but their travel behaviour and journey choice on this occasion were directly impacted upon by their perception of the *likelihood* of experiencing congestion at some point in their planned journey. When people are forced to factor in the possibility of being charged directly for the use of a stretch of road, they may think twice about using it. This is why the M6 Toll has relatively light traffic volumes – it is used by only just over half of the expected 79,000 vehicles per day – and why the London Congestion Charge is often judged a success. Across much of the rest of the country there is little incentive for people to choose to avoid sitting in/causing traffic jams, other than the traffic jams themselves, but we know from Chapter Two that this is not much of a deterrent, given how most people tend not to think of congestion as something that affects them all that much. Paul is an exception.

Congestion charging might prompt some drivers to decide not to make a journey they had thought about, or to go somewhere else instead (a different supermarket outside the charging cordon, for example), while others may travel at a less congested time so as to secure an off-peak discount. But even if only 10–15% switched modes, this would have huge implications for public transport. The bus industry outside of London has largely been managed for decline, and would need substantial improvement and expansion before it could accommodate such a large number of additional passengers comfortably and efficiently. The impact on the railways would be even worse, since the network is already running close to capacity, and the scope for trains to absorb much in the way of additional patronage is very limited, especially at peak times and on key flows.[2] The lack of domestic high speed rail, which as we saw in Chapter Four is often about new capacity as well as raw speed, also restricts the extent to which trains can compete with the airlines, at least on key routes to and from London, Birmingham, Manchester and Glasgow/Edinburgh. Rail has a 46% share of the air/rail market on Britain's 10 busiest airline routes, and although this has risen from 29% in the mid-2000s (partly to do with railcard use by the over-60s and the availability of cheap advance-purchase tickets) it still compares unfavourably with routes such as London–Paris, Paris–Lyon and Frankfurt–Cologne (Steer Davies Gleave, 2006; Association of Train Operating Companies, 2013).[3] Trains can compete more effectively with airlines over long-distance trips when the duration of the rail journey decreases (Dobruszkes, 2011), and journey times between all of Britain's major cities would fall dramatically with high speed rail links. Numbers aside, longer and more trains on any route, not just high speed rail, also allow more passenger comfort, and indeed if Paul had been travelling on an ICE in Germany, then he would have had no concerns about legroom or luggage space even if the train had been completely full.

Then there is the issue that the transport choices we all make carry with them particular, and in many cases highly significant, environmental impacts. It is usually asserted that planes are the most 'dirty' means of transport, and while indeed this is often the case it should not be taken for granted (Table 5.2). Engine size and type of fuel used can influence the environmental impact of a transport mode quite considerably, but also of great significance is load factor (the number of people actually in a vehicle, relative to the number people it can carry). One of the reasons why cars are particularly environmentally unfriendly is because in Britain they have an average occupancy of 1.6, although for commuting and business journeys it is only 1.2 (DfT, 2010). This is inefficient by any measure, and is especially problematic in the case of a large car with a big engine. Improvements in technology, including hybrid and electric vehicles, will be ever more significant in reducing emissions (see King, 2008; House of Commons, 2012b), but travel behaviour change is also crucial: if two or more people are in the car, then assuming that the second person is making a journey he or she would otherwise have made by a separate car, the fuel efficiency increases hugely, especially for a work-related or business journey. The impact on congestion is not inconsiderable either, which is why commuters who car share can qualify for special perks such as guaranteed parking spaces or the use of High Occupancy Vehicle lanes.

If carrying three people, the greenhouse gas (GHG) emissions of a small car at around 0.07 kilograms per passenger kilometre are roughly the same as for an averagely loaded train. Trains themselves vary in impact, from diesel Sprinters 'carting fresh air around the country' (to quote Tom Harris's former boss, Alistair Darling (BBC, 2004, unpaginated)) to fully loaded electric Underground sets moving hundreds of people at a time. The environmental performance of high speed rail, often spoken of favourably by advocates of 'sustainable transport', is not necessarily as good as conventional rail because very fast trains require more power and the construction of brand new lines (Preston, 2012). Interestingly, too, the GHG emissions of well-loaded aeroplanes are less than is sometimes assumed. A long business journey in a large car will generate more emissions than the equivalent flight, for example, although, because planes fly at high altitude, their emissions have additional environmental impacts. It is worth mentioning here

Table 5.2: Estimated total GHG (CO_2e) emissions from different vehicle types

Vehicle	Total GHGs, kg per km	Vehicle	Total GHGs, kg per passenger km
Small petrol car (<1.4l)	0.198	Local bus, not London	0.149
Medium petrol car (1.4l–2.0l)	0.249	Local bus in London	0.100
Large petrol car (>2.0l)	0.357		
		National rail	0.067
Small diesel car (<1.7l)	0.028	Tram/light rail	0.076
Medium diesel car (1.7l–2.0l)	0.035	London Underground	0.081
Large diesel car (>2.0l)	0.047		
		Domestic flight	0.201
Medium hybrid petrol car	0.139		
Large hybrid petrol car	0.248	Short haul int'l flight, Euro Traveller	0.109
		Short haul int'l flight, Club Europe	0.164
Medium LPG car	0.213		
Large LPG car	0.306	Long haul int'l flight, World Traveller	0.095
		Long haul int'l flight, World Traveller Plus	0.153
Medium CNG car	0.196	Long haul int'l flight, Club World	0.278
Large CNG car	0.281	Long haul int'l flight, First	0.383

Note: Figures for cars are per vehicle kilometre, whereas figures for public transport are per person kilometre, assuming average load factors. When comparing between modes, the figures for cars are equivalent to person kilometres if there is one person in the car.
Source: AEA (2012)

that aviation fuel remains untaxed and this effectively subsidises the cost of plane tickets. In this context the airlines' recent gripes about the introduction and subsequent increase of Air Passenger Duty should be taken with a pinch of salt, although they are right that a levy designed to promote planes flying as full as possible, a 'plane tax' as opposed to what is effectively today a 'passenger tax', would be preferable from an environmental point of view.

While a technological 'fix' continues to hold promise for the longer term, for now, reducing the environmental impact of the vehicle and aircraft fleets will largely depend on behaviour change capable of both maximising the load factor of each of the respective transport modes and shifting demand towards the more fuel- and emissions-efficient modes. As it stands, UK transport policy is nowhere near capable of doing this, and indeed it is impossible to conceive of any realistic scenario in which the notion of 'modal agnosticism' would be able to promote the kind of changes in travel behaviour necessary to bring about real and significant reductions in pollution and congestion. In his review on the economics of climate change, Sir Nicholas Stern (2006) suggested that efforts to reduce transport emissions could be delayed until after other 'quick wins' have been secured in the domestic and energy sectors, but several authors have questioned the wisdom of such thinking (see Anable and Shaw, 2007; CfIT, 2007). The Climate Change Act (2008) requires that total UK CO_2 emissions fall to 80% below 1990 levels by 2050, and if this target is to be met – remember that transport accounts for up to 32% of current emissions – then action is needed sooner rather than later. Attempting to change current mobility trends to the extent that transport-related CO_2 emissions fall appreciably will take years, and the longer the task is left unaddressed, the higher the risk that the requirements of the Act will not be achieved. Moreover, the additional CO_2 released into the atmosphere between now and 2050 as a result of unhurried action is not inconsequential (Figure 5.1).

People make their current transport choices on the basis of a status quo that shapes what they come to expect. The problem is that the status quo all too often fails to provide enough choice, and locks people

Figure 5.1: Different emissions scenarios from transport until 2050

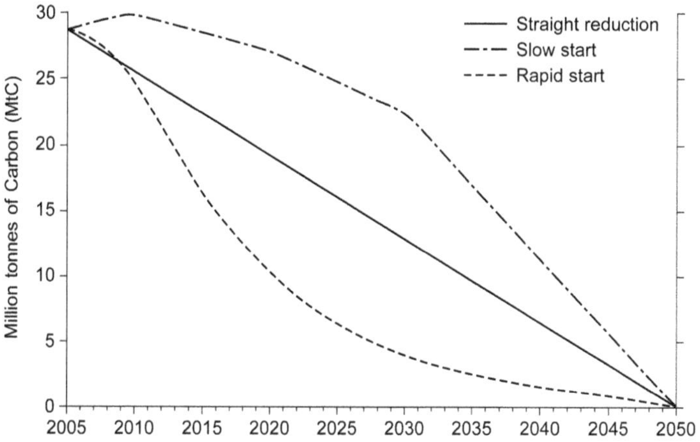

Note the very high overall emissions under the 'slow start' case.
Source: After Anable and Shaw (2007) and with kind permission of Keith Buchan..

into particular options that, when scaled up, make things worse rather than better overall. Paul and Susan chose what they did because it suited them; their choice might have been different if something else had suited them better. By the same token, millions of other people making everyday transport decisions choose the car because it suits them best, and their *choices* might be different if something else suited *them* better. In transport as much as in other policy sectors we can harness the idea of choice to positive effect, but we have to be clear about what we mean by choice. Venerating the car to such an extent that realistic transport alternatives to facilitate patterns of daily life are increasingly fewer and further between is not a sensible policy approach. And while there are many benefits to air travel, it should not simply become the default mode for longer journeys when realistic alternatives could be made available. The per passenger-kilometre emissions of the aviation sector may not be as bad as is commonly thought, but if the 5–6% growth rate of recent decades continues into the future, then it is reckoned that flying alone could generate 25% or more of the UK's *total* CO_2 output permitted by the Climate Change Act in 2050 (CfIT,

2007). Put simply, past and present transport policies have constrained choice by failing to support the provision of wider-ranging, higher-quality, better-value alternatives to the car, the aeroplane and indeed the journey itself.

We have been clear that making transport better does indeed mean providing more choice. Contrary to what politicians might like to believe, this is neither as simple as stepping back and letting the market determine the outcome (as with roads and aviation), nor as complex as reshaping public services to ape 'free' market conditions (as in the bus and rail industries). Even in the most neoliberal of states public services will exist precisely because sometimes markets fail. There will always be political influence over the relative merits of modes as they appear to travellers, and infrastructure will always require public funding. What is needed is *genuine* choice: at the very least the different transport modes should be able to play to their respective strengths on a reasonably level playing field. There would be clear benefits if we walked or cycled more short trips, and used buses, coaches and railways for more quick, comfortable and efficient journeys on urban (and other) corridors and inter-city routes (DRT and community/voluntary transport can fill in the gaps in some cases). ICTs will play an increasingly important role, but are unlikely ever to replace the need for mobility (Chapter Four). All of this still leaves key roles for the aeroplane and, especially, the car which, if some kind of different charging or taxation scheme were in force, would benefit from less congested and polluted roads and airports, and be better for everyone as a result.

Daytripper

The next three days go very quickly indeed for the Smith family. After spending the Friday afternoon and evening catching up, they decide to take the whole of Saturday to enjoy what they hope will be the first of the year's good weather. Sadly, inevitably, by Sunday the skies have already darkened and Mrs Smith suggests going for lunch in a nice pub she used to go to with her husband. Paul thinks this is a splendid idea, but his heart sinks when he realises that the pub is in Blair Atholl and that his mother wants everyone to go on the bus to get there. 'It's ever so good', she beams, 'and best of all it's completely free for me! If you pay for the rest of the family's fares, I'll buy the lunch.' Paul realises that at least he'll be able to see the scenery better, and so chooses not to raise objections. When they arrive Susan orders a bottle of wine and Paul also twigs that he can actually have a glass or two, as he doesn't have to drive. After far too much food and a stroll to walk some of it off, the family takes the bus back down the A9.

It turns out that Mrs Smith is doing just fine, for the moment at least, and is able both to help out her infirm friend up the road and enjoy the benefits of her free bus pass. She tells Paul that she makes the trip into Perth at least once a week, and often finds that there are other pensioners to talk to on the bus. Occasionally she arranges with friends from church or the social club 'just to go for a ride' – she's already been up to Inverness and down to Edinburgh twice since Easter. 'I'd like to see Albert and Glenys a bit more, but they live out of town and there's only one bus a week that goes there', she says, and she's heard of some people in more isolated areas where there's no bus service at all. 'It's not much use giving someone free bus travel if there are no buses for them to use!' When finally she waves off the family on Monday afternoon, Jack just having made it back in time from a final blast up and down Bheinn a' Ghlo, Paul realises that he hasn't even picked up the car keys since he put them on the mantelpiece three days ago. He wonders when the last time was that he didn't think about driving for that long.

In addition to using the buses for necessary tasks such as shopping, Mrs Smith and her friends now see them as a kind of mobile social club and from time to time make the journey itself, rather than any given destination, the centrepiece of their activities. The main reason they do this is because, upon the introduction of national concessionary fares schemes in the 2000s, bus travel for Mrs Smith's social circle – as well as everyone over 60 and all disabled people – became free of charge.[4] Concessionary travel is a key plank of transport policy in each of the four devolved jurisdictions of Scotland, Wales, Northern Ireland

and London, and the DfT administers the English scheme on behalf of the UK government. The schemes were introduced primarily as a means of tackling social exclusion by ensuring 'that bus travel … remains within the means of those on limited incomes and those who have mobility difficulties' (DfT, 2006, unpaginated). Ministers claimed that the English scheme alone would reduce the cost of travel for approximately 11 million people aged over 60, as well as help more than half of pensioner households who do not have a car to travel without hindrance in their local area (Butcher, 2009). Pass holders in London can obtain free bus travel elsewhere in England and vice versa, but this is the exception rather than the rule; in the other cases passes are valid only in the jurisdiction of issue.

Exact details of the schemes vary from jurisdiction to jurisdiction, but one thing they all have in common is that they are very expensive. UK-wide, the concessionary fares schemes has been subsidised to the tune of around £1 billion per year (Mrs Smith's card is one of the 1.6 million currently in use in Scotland). We saw in Chapter Four that when such a large amount of money is spent on a transport scheme, it is usually subjected to a CBA to determine whether or not it represents good value for money. For capital schemes a BCR of 1.5:1 or higher is normally required.[5] Interestingly, in the case of the English Concessionary Fares scheme, which is by far the largest of the five in operation, the government decided not to reveal its views on the matter. For reasons known only to ministers and civil servants, a BCR was never published. We of course raised concerns in relation to CBA as a means of transport scheme evaluation in Chapter Four, but our point here relates to consistency. Ministers are usually obsessed with making public the BCR of any given transport investment, if only because it provides a simple number around which an argument for or against the scheme in question can be constructed. Perhaps the timing of the announcement, just weeks before Tony Blair's historic third-term win at the 2005 general election, was influenced by ministers' desire to secure the 'grey vote' and there was insufficient opportunity to carry out a detailed CBA in the circumstances. Or perhaps this was just coincidence. It is not for us to speculate.

There is no doubt that the Concessionary Fares scheme has had a number of positive outcomes. Since its introduction, there has been an upturn in bus patronage and the long-term steady decline in the number of bus journeys being made in the English shires has been arrested. Moreover, some of this growth has been the result of modal shift. Passenger Focus (2009) reports that in England around 35% of concessionary trips used to be made by car, and Rye and Mykura (2006) found that take-up of the free bus pass is highest among those who own a car. Socially, Mrs Smith and many like her have benefited from the Concessionary Fares schemes. More than 25% of concessionary trips are seen by users as fulfilling a social purpose, and tales of 'bus bingo' – where individuals or groups of pass holders go to a bus stop or station and board the first bus to turn up – and of buses being used as 'common rooms' are being recounted in academic and other literature (see Andrews et al, 2012). Indeed, people who use the bus pass tend to regard it as having improved their quality of life.

But the generally parlous state of the public finances has refocused attention on whether providing free bus travel for the elderly is an effective use of hundreds of millions of pounds a year, and it is worth at least considering what else the annual cost of the scheme might buy. Perhaps greater overall benefit would be derived from a differently targeted scheme, such as one that provided free travel to job interviews for the unemployed, or travel to work for those on low incomes or for lone parents. Or maybe bringing into operation reduced-fare (as opposed to free) schemes could realise savings that could be redirected into capital investment – new bus fleets and infrastructure to provide regular, comfortable, punctual and reliable services – for the benefit of everyone, including concessionary fare pass holders. By our calculations,[6] various changes, such as introducing a 50p flat fare, could free up more than £500 million annually for such investment (Chapter Seven). This would be unprecedented in the UK and would bring about nothing short of a revolution in the quality of bus travel and the amount of available capacity in the bus sector. In such circumstances the likes of Paul, who appreciated the benefits of a relaxing trip back to Pitlochry on the bus as opposed to driving, might be tempted to use the bus far more often than just for the occasional trip to the railway station on the way to London. Such behaviour change among even 5–10% of drivers, especially during peak hours, would have a very much greater effect on modal shift than the current Concessionary Fares scheme could ever achieve.

The debate over whether or how far concessionary fares should be funded from general taxation is just one aspect of the broader question of 'Who benefits from transport subsidy?' Subsidy, at its most basic level, is a means of securing a given outcome or set of outcomes that would not otherwise be provided by the market. Concessionary fares to promote social inclusion for the over-60s would not be provided (to the same extent) by the goodwill of the bus operators alone. Large sections of the railway network that are deemed to provide a social service would close if money were not given to the TOCs and Network Rail to keep them running. No new Tube line would ever be built and so on. At the same time, the budgets of the DfT and its devolved equivalents are finite, and thus there are clear opportunity costs involved in spending money on one mode or scheme rather than another. Concessionary fares schemes come at the cost of better bus services for everyone. Upgrading Reading station, to take another example, means that the £850 million being spent increasing the Great Western Main Line's capacity at that location cannot now be spent on anything else. Where expenditure on public transport is concerned, because, like Motorway Man, the over-60s and the middle classes who commute by train are important political constituencies, their needs tend to be afforded more attention by government than are others'.

There is sometimes confusion between the terms 'subsidy' and 'investment'. While technically these are separate things, the waters have been muddied by political rhetoric that has led to some policy makers and commentators automatically assuming that investment is 'good' and is ideologically permissible (even if, in the UK, rather difficult and expensive) and subsidy is 'bad' and to be reduced wherever possible. The underlying idea is that we invest in success but we subsidise failure; the state must pay to prop up something that is not capable of functioning without its support. This is an alluringly simple and, especially for supporters of Predict and Provide, very convenient conceptualisation, not least because in a world where road building is promoted on the back of a sympathetic CBA regime, a new motorway or bypass almost always appears to represent excellent value for money, as compared with a new railway line or bus network (Chapter Four). Of course, the 'real' cost of motoring is likely to be far higher than the supporters of Predict and Provide like to think, and public transport schemes have substantial difficult-to-monetise benefits, such as enhancing social inclusion (Chapter Two). In other words, it is only the market *as currently constituted* that leads to outcomes where spending money on one (road) scheme is seen as investment, whereas outlays on another (equally worthy but bus or rail) scheme are deemed as subsidy. Different underlying assumptions would lead to different conclusions: a policy approach based on providing genuine choice, as discussed earlier in the chapter, might result in the return on a given road scheme being lower and that on any given public transport scheme being rather higher (Goodwin, 2010). Transport is not unique in this sense – there is an on-going debate about whether we should spend public money on the arts, for example[7] – but for the purposes of our discussion here it might be better to think simply of transport 'expenditure' than of subsidy or investment.

The key point is that arguments about the merits of one outlay versus another need to be seen in the broader context of what we actually want the transport system to *do*. When we spend money on our transport system, we are contributing towards something that helps to enable the functioning of the economy and society. We have already seen that different transport modes have different strengths, and part of the point about providing genuine choice in the transport system is that each should be able to maximise its economic and social contribution while minimising its environmental impact. This implies a greater emphasis on walking and cycling, more public transport use and less of a role for private vehicles and domestic aviation. In turn, at least in the short to medium term, this means increased – not to mention better targeted and more efficient – expenditure on buses, trains and facilities for pedestrians and cyclists, and *proportionally* less on roads and airports.

In other European countries there is more of a culture of supporting and using public transport than in the UK, which feeds through directly into policy making (Gray et al, 2013). In large cities especially, the modal split between cars and other modes is different from that in Britain (Table 5.3) and this is generally accommodated by public

Table 5.3: Percentage of passenger journeys by different modes in major European cities, 2005: non-motorised (walking, cycling); public (bus, tram, train); private (car, taxi)

	Non-motorised	Public	Private
London	25.2	30.3	44.5
Manchester	24.2	9.6	66.2
GB overall	24.5	10.0	65.5
Berlin	38.6	20.6	40.8
Bern	34.5	21.8	43.6
Brussels	26.9	15.5	57.6
Copenhagen	38.3	9.8	51.9
Dusseldorf	38.2	22.4	39.4
Frankfurt	42.9	23.1	34.0
Geneva	41.0	14.0	45.0
Graz	33.4	19.3	47.3
Hamburg	39.0	15.9	44.1
Helsinki	34.4	26.6	39.1
Madrid	29.2	35.0	35.8
Munich	39.0	22.0	39.0
Oslo	28.7	15.7	55.6
Stockholm	34.5	21.8	43.6
Stuttgart	32.0	23.8	44.2
Vienna	31.0	34.0	35.0
Zurich	51.9	18.5	29.6

Source: Figures rounded up from DfT (2012), and personal communication with Professor Jeff Kenworthy. There are some problems of comparability in that city boundary definitions are different, some being more tightly conscribed than others.

transport systems that are more extensive, have greater capacity and are better quality than their British equivalents (Chapter Six). Even this level of availability of alternatives to the car and the van/lorry does not mean that traffic congestion does not exist and that considerably more couldn't be done to get the transport system functioning more efficiently. There is an obvious case for congestion charging in some large cities (such as Paris, although here the mayor has chosen to focus on the reallocation of road space to pedestrians and cyclists on major boulevards rather than on pricing), and the charging systems in operation on some countries' strategic road networks could be extended and increased in sophistication in order to address exceptionally heavy traffic flows at certain times in certain places. We return to the issue of transport expenditure in Chapter Seven.

Despite the apparent political pressures (Docherty and Shaw, 2011a), it is possible to actually 'do something about traffic', and at least to start to create a better balance in the provision of mobility between the modes. Road pricing or other additional taxes on the car can be justified where non-priced or 'free-for-all' behaviour produces identifiably negative outcomes. Additional expenditure on the active modes and public transport can be justified where their additional uptake results in identifiably positive outcomes. In other words, where clear objectives for transport policy are set based on a solid understanding of how best the transport system can support the achievement of economic growth, social inclusion and environmental improvements, a particular mix of subsidies, investments and charges that work with each other to promote the most efficient means of moving us all around will emerge. Policy will be transparent, properly take account of opportunity costs and in the end provide more genuine choice for all travellers, including the Smiths.

Notes

[1] Harris was no doubt experienced in coming up with seemingly clever phrases, having been a PR executive in the transport sector before becoming an MP.

[2] The next time a train enthusiast tells you that the railways are the solution to the congestion problem, remind him or her that a 5% shift of passengers from road to rail would require the railway network to roughly *double* in capacity.

[3] Britain's 10 busiest airline routes are: London to Edinburgh, Glasgow, Aberdeen, Manchester, Newcastle and Inverness; Bristol–Edinburgh, Birmingham–Edinburgh, Bristol–Glasgow and Birmingham–Glasgow.

[4] The DfT has changed the qualifying age in England to the current retirement age for women. This is increasing in stages to parity with that of men, which at present is 65.

[5] It is worth bearing in mind that concessionary fares expenditure is on-going, and so is the equivalent to a (very) major railway electrification scheme every 12 months or Crossrail every 15 or so years.

[6] In relation to the flat fare: the amount currently paid to bus operators for individual concessionary fare journeys differs depending on where in the country the journey is made, but 70p–85p per journey is a reasonable estimate based on discussions with staff involved with the process. Overall annual expenditure has fallen from the high of £1 billion, but this still implies more than a billion journeys made every year. With 50p per journey paid by the traveller, the subsidy drops to 20p–35p per journey. If the number of journeys drops to reflect the re-introduction of a charge, then the government's overall contribution falls further because fewer journeys need to be subsidised.

[7] It is customary for us to mention the incomparable *Yes Minister* at least once in each of our books, and so here we point to the episode entitled 'The Middle Class Rip-Off', which explores the subsidy–investment debate. After explaining to Jim Hacker that he can't intervene to save his local football team from receivership, Sir Humphrey finds himself animatedly justifying munificent public subsidy for the opera and art galleries.

SIX

The summer holiday

Transport and the environment; shopping and freight; celebrating mobility

It's the end of the world as we know it

All of the children are excited about the family holiday, even though it would not be cool for Jack to admit it and Sophie's been telling all her friends that she'd rather be going on a party trip to Malia. Paul and Susan are burned out and need the break, and they also realise, given that Sophie will be 18 next year, that this will probably be the last time that they all get to go on this kind of holiday together. They've never been to the south of France as a whole family: Paul and Susan came here twice before the children arrived and loved it, but for the last 20 years the lure of the Spanish and Greek Islands, and latterly of Florida, has won out. They like the guarantee of two weeks' unbroken sunshine and some decent temperatures after a British washout, but can't be troubled with long flights any more. In any event, Jack's been keen to try out the Alpine mountain biking tracks for a while now; Susan, Sophie and Lucy have got their sights fixed firmly on the beach and the shops; and Paul has secured permission to 'poke around at the market on Monday across the border in Italy' (although Susan might disapprove of the bottle of Sangiovese and several Limoncellos with which he intends washing down a vast lunch in Ventimiglia).

They arrive at Heathrow in plenty of time and, gazing out of the window of Terminal 5, Paul can see the tops of several tall cranes where Terminal 2 used to be. 'Blimey!' he exclaims, 'I thought Heathrow wasn't being expanded? Wouldn't another runway mean a whole load of extra noise? I think they'd have to completely flatten a village just up the road to get the extra space they need at the airport.' Sophie looks up from her plate. 'It's progress, dad,' she explains. 'Remember those fields we used to walk in when I was little that got bulldozed through for the new motorway? It was a shame back then, but it was useful this morning when we got here so quickly, wasn't it?'

We have already discussed the problems associated with the lack of operational resilience in the British transport system, and the planning difficulties that can arise in the (usually delayed and less common than would be desirable) event that a large-scale infrastructure project is built (Chapters Two, Four and Five). It is no surprise that Paul was confused when he saw the cranes at Heathrow. The debate about how or whether to expand airport capacity in the South East of England has been raging for decades and is unlikely to be resolved in the short term. The redevelopment work currently under way is replacing outdated passenger handling facilities rather than building a new runway. Paul was looking at the new Terminal 2, which together with the about-to-commence replacement for Terminal 1 will be capable of handling the same number of passengers (30–35 million annually) as Terminal 5.

London has the busiest airport system in the world (in 2012 some 135 million passengers – see Airports Council International, 2013), but after years of indecision by Labour, David Cameron's Coalition government kicked the can further down the road by setting up a Commission of Inquiry chaired by a former head of the CBI, Sir Howard Davies. Although interim recommendations are due in 2013, the full report will not be delivered until 2015, after the next UK general election (BBC, 2013b). This effectively absolves the current government of the need to make any politically unpopular decisions: many tens of thousands of people (that is, voters in important constituencies) are affected by aircraft noise in the South East of England, even if many of these same people fly a lot. Second runways at Gatwick[1] and Stansted are certainly possible recommendations of Davies's review (indeed, Labour supported the expansion of Stansted and even, eventually, Heathrow, before the Coalition intervened), but in reality they will do little to address what is seen as the biggest problem, namely that most airlines want to expand their operations at Heathrow because it is the only genuine hub airport in the system. While Gatwick and Stansted serve mainly point-to-point markets, around a third (34.6%) of Heathrow's passengers 'interline', or change between flights on their way to other destinations (Heathrow Airport, undated).

The aviation industry is clear that airport capacity expansion is necessary, and it is supported by several high-profile analyses that seek to demonstrate the economic importance of air transport to the British economy (OEF, 2006; House of Commons, 2009c; 2013; see Chapter Five). In relation to the on-going provision of a world-class hub facility, two options are most commonly discussed. The first is the construction of additional runway capacity at Heathrow. The benefits of this approach are that there would be no need to move the existing airfield and its supporting infrastructure, which includes the best public transport connections of any UK airport and a very sizeable local labour pool, but Heathrow is in a pretty dreadful location that requires planes to approach it directly over central London and several heavily populated suburbs.[2] The second option is a completely new, four-runway airport in the Thames estuary. This is politically convenient because relatively few people would live under the flight paths, but at around £60 billion it would be extremely expensive, not to mention that it is on the wrong side of London for easy access from most of Great Britain and that it is environmentally problematic because of the presence of large bird populations. The current Mayor of London's enthusiastic support for the new airport on reclaimed land in the Thames has earned this potential development the nickname of 'Boris Island'.

There can be little doubt that there is a need for further runway capacity in the South East of England. By international standards it is curious that Stansted and Gatwick only have one runway apiece, since airports with their amount of traffic in other developed countries would usually possess two. A third, full-length runway at Heathrow would also not be unreasonable in this context (see House of Commons, 2013). But there is less of a need to spend £60 billion on a showpiece facility in the Thames estuary, because the economic case that has been advanced in favour of such lavish provision is questionable at best (out of interest, the difference between what it would cost to expand Heathrow and to build Boris Island would provide the funding for two more high speed rail lines). Perhaps the strongest case for new runway capacity in the South East of England is on operational and environmental, rather than purely economic, grounds.

In relation to our discussion in Chapter Four about the need for UK transport infrastructure to incorporate an improved quality margin (Goodwin, 1992), the operational case for expansion is easily understood. A case for more runway capacity for environmental reasons might seem strange, given our analysis of 'choice' in the transport sector in Chapter Five. It shouldn't be forgotten that at current growth rates aviation could account for more than 25% of the UK's total CO_2 impact by 2050 (CfIT, 2007; Potter et al, 2013). But at this point it is worth revisiting one of the most significant questions in the debate about runway expansion in and around London, namely *why* is it necessary to expand Heathrow, Gatwick and Stansted at all? The 'traditional' answer – that is, the economic case – is that London's airport system is losing ground to competitors across the Channel such as Paris Charles de Gaulle, Amsterdam Schiphol and Frankfurt, each of which has more runways than does Heathrow. Other hubs further afield, such as Dubai, are expanding at an astonishing pace, at least by European standards. This means that Britons flying from 'regional' airports such as Newcastle, Manchester, Edinburgh and Belfast have a greater choice of carriers when travelling to long-haul destinations (Air France, KLM, Lufthansa, Emirates and so on), as they no longer need to change planes at Heathrow. More significant from London's point of view is that if Heathrow's position as a hub airport continues to be eroded, its range of international destinations will further contract in relation to its competitors'. This is at a time when opportunities for economically important connections between the capital and emerging nodes in the likes of India and China are presenting themselves as never before. Such a relative loss of connectivity would thus impact on London's status as a world city and, arguably, on the UK's economy more broadly (BBC, 2013b).

At the same time the economic assumptions underpinning analyses of aviation's contribution to the British economy are open to question (Chapter Five). Key reports cited by those making the economic case for expansion generally refer to *net* benefits and say little about the extent to which airlines facilitate spending by British people abroad. Interestingly, too, London's very status as a world city might be another factor that undermines rather than supports the argument for airport expansion purely on economic grounds. There are many reasons why people want/need to visit London, and that more than likely will make them want/need to continue to visit in the future, and for these people it is indeed important to provide a warm welcome to the country in the form of world-class airport facilities and onward surface connections. But there is far less need to provide airport facilities at Heathrow for the millions of people a year who have no intention of either staying in London or flying on from there to another UK destination. British Airways, who would undoubtedly be the biggest loser in any reduced focus on interlining passengers, may disagree, but David Cameron was right at least to question the case for building new runway capacity to benefit those whose primary contribution to the UK economy is to buy an 'airside' cup of coffee (*Evening Standard*, 2008).

In the short term, capacity at Heathrow can be expanded by the more efficient use of slots. 'Mixed mode' operation, where runways are used for take-offs and landings simultaneously, is being trialled. Airlines could be required to fly fewer services with larger aircraft to heavily serviced 'commuter' destinations such as Manchester, Glasgow, Edinburgh, Aberdeen, Paris and Frankfurt, although reducing the frequency of flights to British destinations would generate staunch opposition from the Scottish and Northern Irish administrations and business communities who are understandably keen to safeguard slots into the UK's premier hub airport.[3] Larger aircraft could also be used to grow certain markets, a strategy currently being pursued by BA with the addition of 12 Airbus 380s to its fleet. Moreover, the airline's recent acquisition of bmi provides it with more slots, and thus the opportunity to recast its international network to service new long-haul destinations. In the longer term, assuming it is properly linked to Heathrow and HS1, HS2 will effectively remove the need for flights to and from Manchester, Leeds, Newcastle, Paris and Brussels (witness how Deutsche Bahn works closely with Lufthansa on connections to German cities from Frankfurt, for example), and by our calculations this would free up more than 85 of Heathrow's take-off and landing slots each weekday.

Should a new runway be built, this would theoretically provide 40–50% more slots. But what if the airport were limited to an increase in the number of aircraft movements to 80% of its expanded capacity? Similarly at Gatwick and Stansted, new runways could be used to increase capacity by only up to 50%, rather than the 90–100% uplift technically possible. This would force the airports and their client airlines into more efficient working practices, and guarantee a comfortable margin of operational resilience currently absent from all three of London's major airports. In the context of the on-going need for high-quality global air connections, such an approach would also secure environmental benefits by reducing the quarter of a million or so of tons of CO_2 emitted by aircraft waiting to land at London's airports every year.

Under such scenarios, considerable economic benefit would still result from the additional capacity in London's airport system, but the aviation industry, its passengers and the government would all need to increase their commitment to promoting more resilient and efficient aviation. Higher landing charges, and perhaps some government subsidy if necessary, would pay for some of the additional capacity, but could also compensate residents affected by increased levels of overflying across a wider area.[4] For the same reasons of congestion and pollution, unfettered flying is no more an option than is unfettered driving, and stringently enforced limits on aircraft movements would 'lock in' the benefits of new runway infrastructure, having a comparable effect to road-user charging designed to prevent induced traffic (Chapter Two). The environmental price of aviation policy's degenerating into another form of Predict and Provide is far too high to contemplate.

Residents of West London, Crawley and Bishop's Stortford will clearly have their own views about the provision of new runway capacity for London's three main airports, and their situation reminds us that transport activity has environmental impacts other than CO_2 emissions. Such is the ubiquity of discourses these days surrounding the need for decarbonisation that it is sometimes easy to forget that the negative effects of transport stretch beyond their contribution to climate change. One major concern of those who live in areas close to proposed major transport development is the land take associated with new infrastructure projects. New runways at Heathrow and Gatwick would involve the demolition of many existing properties and expose more householders to transport-related noise, and the construction of HS2 is sparking fierce debate over similar issues (*Rail*, 2013).

Railways and roads are different from runways in that they can stretch for very long distances between origin and destination points, and in so doing create significant problems of severance in relation both to wildlife and human communities along tens or even hundreds of route miles. Famous pitched battles were fought in the 1990s between government security staff and environmental protestors to clear the way for the construction of the A34 Newbury Bypass and the extension of the M3 to Southampton through Twyford Down, with the activist 'Swampy' becoming the hero/villain of the piece for his stand in support of habitat protection. Although both roads ended up being built, Swampy and his acolytes' peaceful if disruptive and, for the government, expensive actions played a role in persuading ministers to cut back the road-building programme (Shaw and Walton, 2001). With regard to the severance effect of busy transport infrastructure on human communities, Appleyard and Lintell's (1969) classic study of a neighbourhood in San Francisco shows how differences in traffic volumes can determine the extent to which people socialise. The authors found that people who lived along lightly trafficked roads had many more friends and acquaintances along their street than did people who lived on much busier roads, and cross-street socialising was all but wiped out on the busiest of thoroughfares. Their findings were corroborated in a recent study in Bristol (Hart and Parkhurst, 2011).

In both cases mitigation measures can be taken to minimise the impact of new or existing infrastructure. On occasion these are relatively small scale, a good example being the 'bat bridges' installed when constructing the Dobwalls bypass in Cornwall.[5] On other occasions they are much larger, such as tunnelling projects to conceal new stretches of road (for example, the new dual carriageway section of the A3 at Devil's Punchbowl in Surrey) or railway (a significant proportion of HS2 will go through tunnels to address both environmental and NIMBY concerns). Since the 2000s quite wide-ranging and sophisticated legal/regulatory measures have been in existence to ensure that developers pay proper heed to environmental protection when new infrastructure projects are being designed and built. Emerging from the far narrower and for this reason heavily criticised process of Environmental Impact Assessment (Thérival and Partidário, 1996), Strategic Environmental Assessment demands the high-level evaluation of plans and programmes. In practice this creates a procedural framework for evaluating the cumulative impacts of transport plans and potential alternative strategies (Potter and Bailey, 2008). Environmental concerns were also given more prominence following the introduction of NATA (Chapter Four) and further safeguards such as related EU Directives can be invoked in the face of unwanted (by certain groups) transport projects. The extent to which environmental issues are trumped by economic arguments for transport development is frequently subject to question, however (Chapter Four).

Part of the assessment of any new piece of transport infrastructure will of course take account of its operation once completed. Indeed, both new and existing transport activities have the potential to affect people's health in ways additional to those impacts associated with inactivity discussed in Chapter Three. Exposure to transport noise, for example, can result in stress-related conditions and disturbed sleep patterns (see Griefahn et al, 2006; Clark and Stansfeld, 2007; Jones and Rhodes, 2009). But perhaps more widely understood is the impact of transport activities on local air quality. Internal combustion engines produce various harmful pollutants which are known to be capable of damaging human health in a range of different ways. Among these pollutants are carbon monoxide, nitrogen oxides, sulphur dioxide, ozone, volatile organic compounds and particulate matter. Some people, particularly the frail and those who already have respiratory conditions, are disproportionately vulnerable to the effects of bad air quality, and recent estimates have shown that in London alone the number of people who die prematurely each year as a result of air pollution may total as many as 4,000. In the whole of the UK the figure could be as high as 50,000 (House of Commons, 2010a; *Guardian*, 2010). As former Mayor of London Ken Livingstone was keen to emphasise in an interview with the BBC in early 2013, many of these deaths are alarmingly premature, by up to 11 or more years.

Such figures persist against the backdrop of significant reductions in major air pollutants in recent years, and in overall terms air quality in the UK is thought to be better now than at any time since the Industrial Revolution (NAEI, 2013). These improvements, especially in recent decades, are due to a combination of better technology and tighter (especially EU) regulatory controls, and of course the two are closely linked. The NAEI reports that carbon monoxide emissions in 2009 were 75% down on their 1990 levels (which it attributes largely to the introduction of catalytic converters in cars); sulphur was reduced by 89% (because of low-sulphur fuels); and nitrous oxide emissions were down by 60% (also as a result of EU vehicle emissions standards). These developments are clearly very welcome indeed, not least in the context of rising traffic levels in much of the two decades since 1990, but levels of nitrous oxide and particulate emissions remain too high, and around 60% of British local authorities have implemented Air Quality Management Areas (AQMAs) in attempts to address this. Mathematical models suggest that the levels of most pollutants will continue to fall, but nitrous oxides, particulates and ozone will remain problematic and air quality in London is unlikely to meet required standards until 2025 (Potter et al, 2013). Boris Johnson has recently proposed an ultra-low emissions zone in London, but, to the consternation of environmental and health groups, this would not take effect until 2020 (BBC, 2013c). It is not often that we have found aspects of the capital's transport policy to criticise, but the absence of tougher air quality regulations – London's is among the worst air quality in Europe – serves to provide an additional reminder of the need to effect modal shift for local environmental reasons as well as for economic (Chapters Two and Four), social (Chapters Three and Five) and climate change (Chapter Five) imperatives.

Convoy

The children have been promised that after lunch they can go and look around the shops in Terminal 5. There's a veritable array of 'opportunities to make my wallet lighter', as Paul puts it, although much to his embarrassment it's he who makes the first purchase when he remembers that he's left his sunglasses in the kitchen drawer. 'Well … it's not as if I've … had cause to leave them lying around, given the weather we've had', he stutters in the face of Susan's raised eyebrow. In the end, the damage is not all that bad (although Susan doesn't seem to think the prices are all that much different from elsewhere) and Sophie's armload of magazines isn't going to break the family bank. They go to their gate, board on time and sit patiently through the taxi and 15-minute plane jam at the eastern end of the airfield as they wait for take-off clearance. From his window seat on the left-hand side of the plane, Paul gets a lot of time to study the brand new terminal whose cranes he had spotted from Terminal 5 a couple of hours earlier.

Remembering how relaxed he felt not having to drive around anywhere in Pitlochry, Paul has insisted that he doesn't want to hire a car in France. After they touch down in Nice, the family jumps on a bus to the centre of town (the city's second tram line, that promises to whisk them in from the airport, is set to open in 2017) and wander the couple of hundred yards to the holiday home they have rented. The bus comes in along the Promenade des Anglais right next to the sea, and even Jack fancies a quick dip in the late afternoon sunshine, but Paul and Susan are keen to get all of the chores out of the way. Everyone unpacks and then ambles down a busy pedestrianised street towards Galeries Lafayette in the dead centre of town. 'I've read there's a good food hall in here', Susan announces, and she jumps onto the escalator down to the basement. Paul agrees that so long as all the children stay together they can go for a bit of a wander, but they all have to meet back across the street in half an hour to help carry the shopping. As Susan puts the shopping in her trolley, she turns to Paul in the middle of the aisle. 'You know, in the supermarket at home I understand that all the stuff on the shelves comes from the delivery lorries, but you never really see them loading and unloading. Here it must be a nightmare – how do they get all this stuff through the narrow streets here?' Paul looks at her in some disbelief. 'I'm on holiday,' he replies. 'I couldn't care less.'

Accounting for around 20% of all mechanised journeys made in Britain, the freight sector plays a relatively small but by no means insignificant role in determining the characteristics of the UK's transport system. The term 'freight' is rather catch-all, referring not only to items on their way to and from factories, warehouses and retailers, but also to raw materials and fuels such as oil and gas. As is the case with passenger transport, private road vehicles are the most significant shippers of freight. Around 60% of goods are moved by lorries and vans, while rail carries approximately 9%, and pipeline and domestic shipping account for the rest. The number of moved 'freight tonne kilometres' (tkms) – this term takes into account both the net weight of the goods lifted and the distance they travel – has fluctuated in the past two decades. In 2010, just over 220 billion tkms were shifted, about the same as in 1990, although peaks of around 250 billion tkms were reached between 2000 and 2006 (DfT, 2012). The current economic downturn has certainly led to less freight being moved, and there is also some evidence of longer-term 'decoupling' (that is, weakening the relationship between economic growth and increasing tkms). For a period from the late 1990s, the number of tkms increased less quickly than the rate of growth of the economy, although McKinnon (2009) cautions against assuming that this trend will automatically continue once the economy recovers. As Britain's manufacturing base declined, much of the decoupling was due simply to the displacement of freight activity to other countries.

Concerted efforts by rail freight companies since privatisation in the mid-1990s have helped to achieve an impressive increase of more than 40% in the proportion of tkms moved by train, but notable in recent decades has been the unstoppable rise of the light goods vehicle (LGV). More commonly (but not necessarily accurately) known as 'white vans', LGVs are generally defined as vehicles under 3.5 tonnes. There are now more than three million LGVs registered in Britain, and each year they travel more than twice as far as the entire fleet of lorries (Browne et al, 2007). Several factors account for their popularity. Some of these, such as the imposition of weight restrictions on roads, are regulatory in nature, whereas others are down to operational convenience. It can be easier for freight businesses to recruit drivers without heavy goods vehicle licences, and the changing nature of distribution activities (see below) means that on some delivery rounds there is just not all that much stock to carry. At the same time, the time-critical parcels business has expanded significantly and the demand for home delivery has exploded since the advent of internet shopping. Broader changes in the economy and society have led to more outsourcing of service functions and 'rapid response servicing' has increased along with the range of services available. Compared to pre-privatisation days it is very quick to have your communications or energy infrastructure installed/serviced and it may or may not be your service provider who actually comes and does it. Compounding all of this is a sharp growth in the number of households, meaning that there are more places for delivery and service companies to go to (Browne et al, 2007). Nevertheless, because of their size and the kinds of jobs they do, LGVs still account only for under 10% of freight carriage, despite their high vehicle mileage.

The importance of the freight sector to the functioning of the country as a whole is clearly beyond doubt. Passenger transport supports the economy and society by enabling people to get where they need to go, but in the absence of a sophisticated freight sector there would be virtually nothing available for them to go and get. In this sense it is curious that across a range of constituencies freight transport tends to receive rather less attention than passenger modes. One such constituency is the government. Notwithstanding its advertised commitment to an integrated transport policy, when in power the Labour government rejected the House of Commons Transport Select Committee's (House of Commons, 2008) recommendation for a freight plan. The minister responsible did, though, admit that the government should have been able to 'explain much more clearly' how its policy approach met the needs of freight users, and a logistics section was included in the White Paper *Delivering a sustainable transport system* (DfT, 2008).

Freight transport is overlooked partly because it accounts for a relatively small proportion of British transport activity, and partly because, with the exception of a few key flows at certain times, Motorway Man and Woman are not especially aware of how it affects their daily transport lives. But another reason is that it requires only minimal government intervention. Since the privatisation of businesses such as the NFC, ABP and BR's railfreight companies in the 1980s and 1990s, the freight industry has operated almost entirely without government support. Some financial intervention in the form of capital grants is available to promote stated policy aims such as promoting modal shift from road to rail, but generally speaking, subject to applicable laws and safety regulations, freight shippers are left to their own devices on the basis that the sector is generally efficient and profitable.

It is also dynamic. Indeed, freight transport has been transformed in the last few decades and in global terms perhaps the largest single innovation has been the advent of containerisation. Introduced in the 1950s in Newark, New Jersey by Malcolm McLean, the container is a simple idea (it's easy to say this with hindsight, of course) that allows freight to be shipped in standard-sized 'boxes' that move unopened from producer to client (Fremont, 2013). Containers can be stacked seven deep in the holds of vast cargo ships capable of carrying up to 14,000 such boxes (Drewry, 2009) and then transferred by crane straight onto trains or lorries at purpose-built port facilities. The shift to containerisation replaced the laborious practice of taking freight to one port, packing it up and loading it onto a freighter that shipped it to another port where it would be unpacked and sorted before it could be loaded again onto surface modes. Capturing the significance of the freight revolution enabled by containerisation in the opening lines of *The box: How the shipping container made the world smaller and the world economy bigger*, Levinson (2006, pp 1–3) notes:

> Before the container, transporting goods was expensive – so expensive that it did not pay to ship many things half way across the country, much less half way across the world … The container made shipping cheap and by doing so changed the shape of the world economy. The armies of ill-paid, ill-treated workers who once made their livings unloading ships in every port are no more, their tight-knit waterfront communities now just memories. Cities that had been centers of maritime commerce for centuries [in Britain, London and Liverpool, for example] saw their waterfronts decline with startling speed, unsuited to the container trade … Even as it helped destroy the old economy, the container helped build a new one. Sleepy harbors such as Busan and Seattle moved into the front ranks of the world's ports, and massive new ports were built in places like Felixstowe in England and Tanjing Pelpas in Malaysia where none had been before.… Sprawling industrial complexes … gave way to smaller, more specialized plants that shipped components and half-finished goods to one another in ever-lengthening supply chains.… This new economic geography allowed firms whose ambitions had been purely domestic to become international companies, exporting their products almost as effortlessly as selling them nearby.

Even given the dangers inherent in attributing too much to any one innovation, Antoine Fremont (2013, p 47) has been moved to remark that 'it is safe to say … globalization could not have taken its present form without containerized international freight shipping'.

The 'new economic geography' of a global trading system centred increasingly on Asia is evident from Figure 6.1, but even in this context it will by now come as no surprise to learn that during the years leading up to the current economic slowdown Britain's ports ran into an 'era marked by the prospect of looming bottlenecks and consequent implications for economic stability' (Pinder, 2008, p 165). High-quality infrastructure is of course important in oiling the wheels of efficient world trade, but as supply chains have become more complex, so have the processes of logistics employed to manage them. Logistics is the integrated management of all the activities that are required to move goods through the supply chain. It is thus only *partly* about the movement of goods; also involved are storage, the handling of materials and the management of inventories and relevant information. Recycling and the disposal of waste generated throughout the supply chain (so-called reverse logistics) are also key. The main objective of logistics is to coordinate all of these processes in a way that both meets customer needs and minimises cost. Logistics managers have adapted to various cost-reduction innovations, including the shift to 'just-in-time' delivery requirements that enable firms to keep their stock levels to a minimum and thus keep expensive inventory and storage facilities as small as possible. Just-in-time obviously relies upon flexible and dependable freight transport links.

The spatially fragmented nature of many of today's supply chains has been criticised for being environmentally unfriendly because it involves moving freight over such large distances. The idea of food miles, for example, was developed as a means of calculating the full environmental cost of food production and distribution through identifying how far its constituent parts actually travel in any given supply chain. The implication is that more food miles results in less environmentally friendly logistics. Figure 6.2 shows Böge's (1995) mapping of a yoghurt supply chain in Germany, which reveals how some components of the final product, most notably the yoghurt cultures themselves, are sourced anything but locally. Interestingly, though, the assumption that the most environmentally friendly supply chains are locally or regionally focused is not necessarily sound because of the economies

Figure 6.1: Trade throughput of world container ports

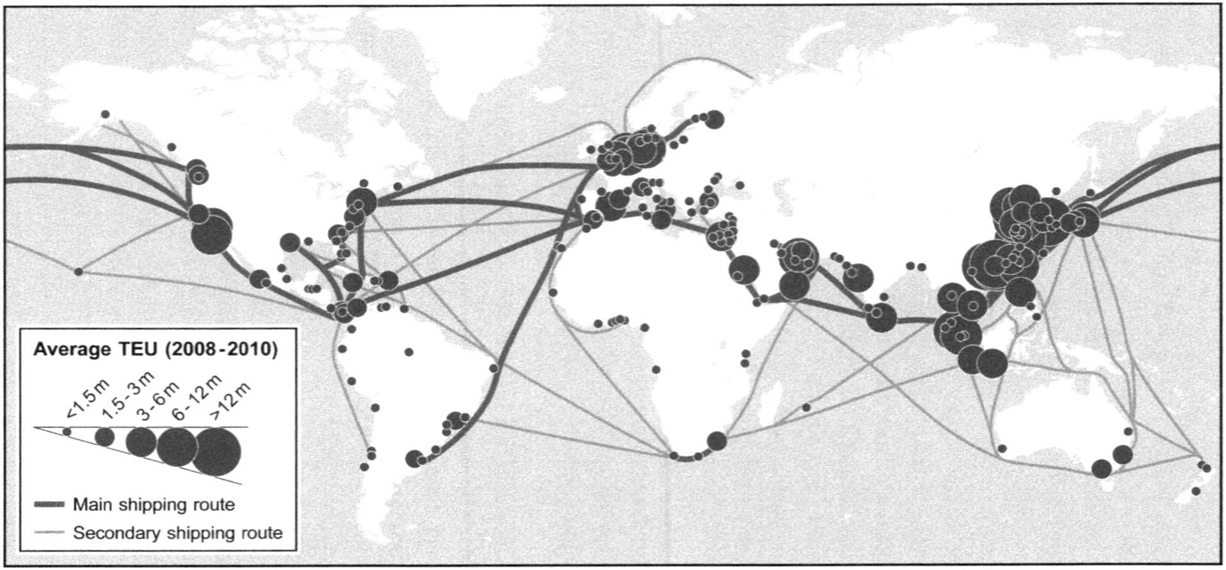

Source: After Rodrigue et al, (2013a).

Figure 6.2: Yoghurt supply chain in Germany

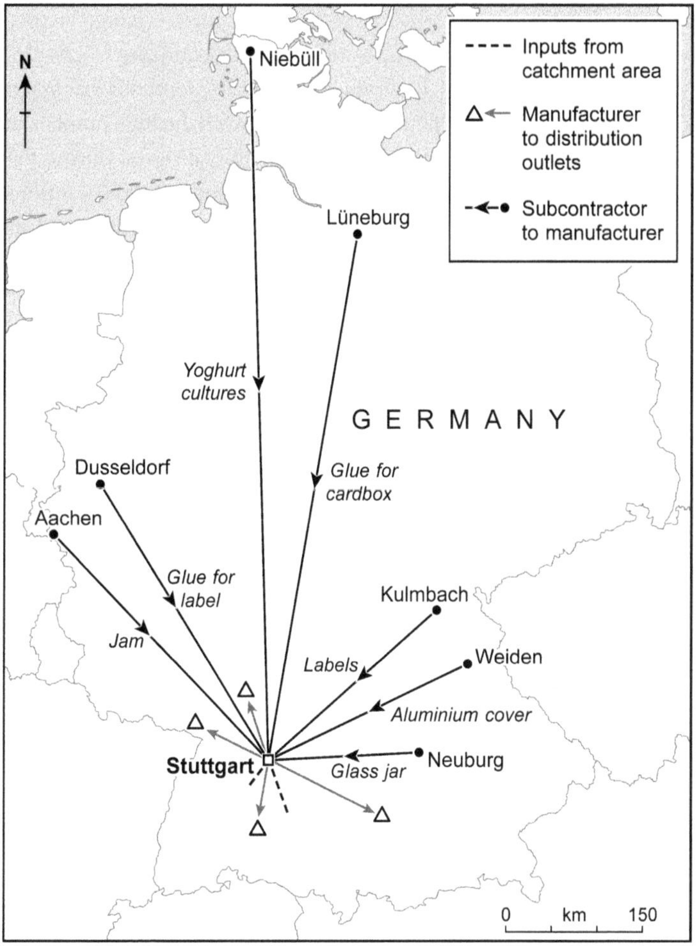

Source: After Böge (1995)

of scale that can be achieved by sourcing components of a product from a smaller number of larger suppliers.

In any event, recent years have witnessed logistics companies thinking much more about how to minimise their environmental impacts as well as their financial costs. In a move towards so-called green logistics, strategies have been developed to reduce the climate-change factors, pollution, safety risks and noise associated with companies' activities (Green Logistics, undated). Rodrigue et al (2013b) point out that green logistics can be extremely difficult to achieve, given the high number of participants in supply chains, but they do identify progress during the 2000s. Specifically in relation to Britain, McKinnon (2009) cautions against complacency, as, although the freight sector has reduced its emissions of oxides of nitrogen and particulates since the 1990s, new engines actually carry a CO_2 emissions penalty, and 'lading factors' – the proportion of carrying capacity that is used on paying trips – decreased from 66% to 58% between 1980 and 2008. Especially of late, though, rising fuel prices have resulted in the convergence of commercial and environmental interests, because the cost savings achieved by reducing packaging waste and diesel consumption have the happy side-effect of cutting emissions and pollution.

Such is the impact of economies of scale and (emerging) green logistics initiatives that the least carbon-efficient final link in the entire supply chain is actually the 'final mile' from the retailer to the consumer (Jespersen, 2004; Browne et al, 2008). Paul may not care all that much about how the goods he buys in the supermarket arrive on the shelves, especially when he's on holiday, but both hc and Susan would be intrigued to discover the significance of their shopping behaviour in terms of the carbon emissions associated with freight transport. Put simply, for any given consumer item personal shopping trips can use more energy than does the entire upstream supply chain, including production (Edwards et al, 2009). Studying the supply chain for bread in Denmark, for example, Jespersen (2004) found that the total distance travelled by ingredients on their way from suppliers to the manufacturer is around 11.5 miles per tonne. Less efficient transport, due to the use of different types of vehicles and less direct routing, doubles the figure for distribution from the manufacturer to retailers, to around 22.5 miles per tonne. Because much of the bread is then taken by consumers from the shops to their homes by car (Jespersen assumes that around half of these car journeys are dedicated 'freight' trips and the average shopping load is 20kg) the figure for this leg of the supply chain is an astonishing 44 miles per tonne. Browne et al (2008) examined the supply chains for fruit and furniture and confirmed the inefficiency of the final mile, although again assumptions were made with regard to consumer shopping behaviour. A trip made solely to pick up a small single item will be most inefficient, while a 'combined' trip could result in the energy used to fetch the shopping being close to zero if it is purchased on the way home from work or from a trip to the cinema with no route diversion.

In this context, Edwards et al (2009) investigated the environmental impacts of conventional and online shopping for non-food items. Online retailers have claimed that shopping on the internet is more environmentally friendly than going to the shops, although particular side-effects of internet shopping such as inefficient delivery practices associated with small, frequent orders and failed delivery attempts when no one is in do reduce the theoretical environmental advantages of buying things from home. The researchers found it difficult to profile a 'typical' high street shopper (Rotem-Mindali and Salomon, 2007), but were still able to estimate that on average a customer would have to buy up to 24 items before a dedicated conventional shopping trip became more carbon efficient than home delivery. By contrast, consumers who travel on the bus at busy times and make multiple purchases are responsible for lower emissions per item than when only one item is delivered. Research into the relative carbon intensity of different forms of retail distribution is on-going, but for our purposes the results of these initial studies reinforce the point that it is important to question the unthinking use of the private car, whatever the circumstance. Where people are genuinely dependent on their cars for certain journeys they may generate lower emissions (and contribute less to congestion) if they are able to chain certain trips outside of peak hours; in other cases, walking, cycling or taking public transport to the shops would be preferable when the prospect of real social interaction is more enticing than buying things online.

The boys (and girls) of summer

The sun shines on the Cote d'Azur for the whole of the Smiths' holiday and Paul and Susan's stresses have well and truly drifted away by the end of the first week. Paul's trip to Italy is, at least as he sees it, a tremendous success – he spends the return journey drunkenly trying to figure out what some of the graffiti daubed all over the train's interior means – and the girls find a spot on one of the beaches to claim as their own. Jack manages to rent a bike and find a great place to ride it, although Paul, who accompanies him into the mountains on the train, is struck by how infrequent the railway services are; on the way back they almost miss the train they are aiming for and a four-hour wait for the next one is not at all appealing. During the second week of the holiday even Susan gets a bit tired of the beach and joins Paul for a day wandering round the old town ('the square's been so beautifully done up, and you'd hardly even know the tram runs right through it!') and for a trip along the coast to Cannes ('look at that poor woman struggling up the stairs with her pram – is there no lift?').

It is with heavy hearts that everyone packs up their things and ambles to the station on the last day of their holiday. Tanned and reinvigorated after two weeks of sun and Mediterranean food and drink, the family boards the TGV service bound for Paris. Paul and Susan have arranged to meet up on their way back with Matthias, an old exchange student friend from Susan's university days, who's travelling with his family from Frankfurt for a short break in the French capital. Matthias is always travelling by train and suggested some time ago that the Smiths should go home by rail rather than fly. Of course they thought this was a ludicrous idea until they found out just how quick it was, and because they booked so early they got an absolute bargain in first class. They can't believe how smooth the ride is at nearly 200 mph, and as they head north at such speed Paul's mind drifts back to the bumpy and cramped hours in a Pendolino that he endures every month. Over dinner and a glass or two of Gewürztraminer in Terminus Nord, Paul laments to Matthias that he's a bit fed up with the thought of going back to life in 'Broken Britain'…

In Chapter One we referred to a statement made to one of us by a Treasury civil servant that the UK was correct *not* to invest as heavily in transport infrastructure as most other leading European countries. At the same time we have been clear that the evidence demonstrating direct causal links between transport investment and economic performance is not as persuasive as might at first be thought. But as Paul and Susan find out on their summer holiday, actually travelling around – the journey *experience*, in other words – in continental western Europe is often easier, cheaper and more comfortable than it is in the UK. This does not seem to us a trivial matter. The 40% more as a proportion of GDP spent on transport for 40 years by our closest neighbours has left them with vastly superior transport systems that make a real contribution to quality of life. This lesson has been learned loud and clear in London, where sustained investment in the transport network is transforming the quality of the system from visibly creaking to among the best of the major world cities (Chapter Four).

Elsewhere in Britain, comparisons with Continental equivalents are salutary, to say the least. Take Paul's home city of Birmingham, which is twinned with Milan, Lyon and Frankfurt on the European mainland. What passes for a modern transport system in England's second city and its surrounding settlements is a patched-together Victorian railway with a heavily overcrowded main station (albeit one that is finally being upgraded as we write), a single light rail line that will have taken 18 years from opening to reach the city centre (the other terminus in Wolverhampton has no interchange with any other public transport whatsoever) and a deregulated bus network with its ever-changing fares and routes. Meanwhile, Milan has an extensive regional rail network, with its own Crossrail-style tunnel and a three-line, 94-station metro system. Lyon has built four metro lines and four tram routes from scratch since the 1970s (with the TGV high speed line to Paris opening fully 45 years before HS2 is due to do so). And then there's Frankfurt, with its 11 tram lines, nine underground lines and nine S-Bahn lines (including a cross-city tunnel with services running every two minutes), all integrated with the bus network.

Once arguments about freedom, market choices and cultural preferences are exhausted, the more vociferous elements of the motoring lobby in the UK retreat to their last redoubt: that after 80 years or so of adjusting our society and economy to the car, it is just too late to turn the clock back, and that to effect major changes in the ways in which (and how much) we travel is impossible. The reality, though, is quite different. Certainly some countries made different choices a long time ago that maintained a better infrastructure inheritance, and the obvious example is Germany and the Low Countries' refusal to copy Britain and France's decisions to rip up their tramways in the 1950s and 1960s. But the much greater investment levels seen on the Continent in the second half of the 20th century have enabled substantial change to come about. Looking back on their first visits to France as students, Paul and Susan might remember a rather familiar transport scene: slow inter-city rail services, severe traffic congestion in the cities, a patchy public transport network dependent on the bus, and almost no provision for cyclists (and this in a country that regards cycling as its national sport). Fast-forward to their summer holiday in 2013, and the picture could not be more different. Two thousand kilometres of high speed railway line are in place (although plans to double this amount were rather abruptly put on hold in mid-2013 (*Independent*, 2013)), and more than 20 provincial cities have installed metro or tram systems that are closely integrated with the bus and new cycling facilities.

It is important to recognise that this divergence in the levels of public transport investment and the resulting quality of provision between the UK and France is the direct result of government policy decisions. Until the 1970s, both countries were extremely pro-car, with President Georges Pompidou predating even Margaret Thatcher's enthusiasm with his much-quoted statement that French 'cities must be adapted for cars' (see Guet, 2005). The reactions of the British and French governments during the subsequent recession were rather different, however. On this side of the Channel, ministers responded by cancelling most planned investment in major public transport projects in order to safeguard the motorway programme. In France, by contrast, the opportunity was taken to revisit the notion of a *politique tout-voiture* altogether. Partly this was driven by the logics of energy and industrial policy in a country without its own fossil fuel reserves, but none the less the phenomenon of the TGV that emerged as a result has transformed the way in which the French travel, and spawned a lucrative export industry to boot.

The same is true at the urban scale. Paul and Susan's enjoyment of the vibe in Nice owes much to the seminal intervention in 1975 by then transport minister Marcel Cavaillé, who wrote to the mayors of eight major cities inviting them to plan for the reintroduction of the tram. Ten years later the first implementation of the *Tramway Français Standard* was up and running in Nantes, with Grenoble following two years later. The positive influence of the tram (and in some cases metro) on French cities in the intervening years cannot be understated. Until recently, tourists pitching up in Nice would be in no doubt that they were in the Mediterranean, given the testosterone-fuelled mix of cars and mopeds that dominated the main city streets. The fact that the city centre of today is unrecognisable in comparison is just the latest success for the *tramway moderne*, the first line of the Niçois version having opened in 2007 as part of a larger project that completely renewed the public realm in the main square and shopping street (Ministère de l'Écologie, du Développement durable et de l'Énergie, 2012).

Two other policy elements are important in understanding the French public transport renaissance. The first is the existence of a dedicated payroll tax, the *Versement Transport*, directed to the funding of public transport infrastructure and services (see Docherty et al, 2009). First introduced in Paris in 1971 at a rate of 2.4% (now 2.6%), the tax has been progressively extended to all significant urban areas and provides an important incentive to the development and use of public transport (outside of Paris the maximum rate is 1.75%). Also of significance is the system of *Plans de Déplacements Urbains* (PDUs, urban travel plans), first introduced in 1982 and progressively strengthened through subsequent legislation. These delineate a quite different planning regime to that in place in the UK, with an explicit focus on road traffic reduction, a 'more rational' use of the car and integration between the needs of pedestrians, cyclists and public transport users. Subsequent legislative refinements mean that today's PDUs must also take account of the need to manage the demand for mobility so as to safeguard the environment and improve public health, and to favour the development of the least polluting and most energy-efficient transport modes. What is more, they incorporate freight management policies to ensure that the improved quality of place resulting from less traffic, better public transport and more high-quality pedestrian environments is not undermined by goods traffic.

Of course, not everything is *merveilleux*. As Paul was quick to notice, the levels of graffiti and general cleanliness of trains, trams and stops are noticeably worse than in the UK, and France has made comparatively little effort to make its existing infrastructure more accessible to mobility-impaired people, as compared to either Britain or Germany. Travel outside the main cities, and it will also be apparent that service frequencies are much lower than we are accustomed to in most of Britain, despite cutbacks in bus service provision since privatisation. It is not unusual in rural France for branch-line trains to run only a handful of times a day, or for some small villages to be served by the bus only once a week, on market day. Indeed, perhaps the most worrying aspect of French transport policy is the extent to which investment in the TGV has come at the expense of the existing railway network. This so-called 'dark side' of the French approach was all too sadly revealed in 2013 when a Limoges-bound inter-city service derailed at around 85 mph and crashed into Brétigny-sur-Orge station, south of Paris, killing six people and injuring a further 100. Transport minister Frédéric Cuvillier confirmed what earlier reports had already concluded, remarking that 'the situation is severe, with the deterioration in recent years of traditional lines because of a lack of resources' (*Guardian*, 2013b, unpaginated). As we make clear in the next chapter, the development of high speed rail in Britain cannot be to the detriment of the rest of the railway network, on which the majority of passengers will still rely.

But at least at the urban and trunk inter-urban levels the French have made a point of recognising and celebrating the role of good transport in improving quality of life. When speaking with planners in French cities contemplating the construction of a new tramway, it quickly becomes clear that they focus on the concept of its *insertion urbaine* – how the infrastructure will improve the urban fabric and quality of life – at least as much as on the technical details of how patterns of transport and mobility will change. The positive outcomes of this approach in terms of the quality of place are readily evident to anyone visiting these cities, as Susan appreciated. Such is the public enthusiasm for the benefits that well-designed public transport schemes can bring, that across the country cities now clamour and compete for increased investment in new tramways and other infrastructure designed to reduce the role of the car. The critical lesson from France is that *la politique tramway* has well and truly replaced *la politique tout-voiture* in a relatively short space of time.

Clearly, the cultural and political context across the Channel is rather more *dirigiste* than normally appeals to British tastes (Chapter Two), but French politicians are not unique in being able to achieve real change from inauspicious beginnings. A recent, obvious example in the UK is Margaret Thatcher, whose neoliberal revolution very definitely left its mark on transport policy in the form of spending cuts, successive waves of privatisation and deregulation and, of course, the great car economy. Among the reasons why Thatcher's approach appealed to British voters was its emphasis on freedom, choice and the symbolism of getting the state out of people's lives. Perhaps now in Britain we 'get the politicians we deserve' – and by extension, the decisions, priorities, projects and outcomes we deserve – in the sense of an electorate that likes to think of itself as individual and free to the point where it does not deal too well with learning that things might not be quite right in the green and pleasant land. By 'not quite right' we mean that some kind of shift in established norms and practices is required: at least in transport terms, the relatively low expectations of the British (Chapter One) seem to have combined with our sense of individuality to promote a doggedly competitive race to the bottom.

But change for a nation of individuals, especially when perceived as being enforced for the good of society as a whole, can at best be difficult and at worst an outrage (witness the front pages of the *Daily Mail* and *Daily Express* almost every day).

It is not difficult to see the links between individualism, a love affair with the car and a relative lack of enthusiasm for public transport. But if an over-reliance on private transport coupled with infrastructure and broader industry practices that are not fit for purpose have led to manifestly sub-optimal outcomes, perhaps it is time for us all to ask some searching questions about how we live our lives in relation to the transport choices we make and the level and type of mobility we consume.

In recent years very many of us, just like the Smiths, have been enormously privileged by the level of mobility we have been afforded, and by the myriad possibilities this mobility has opened up for more and more people. Yet in Britain more than other European countries we have chosen to consume our new levels of mobility by driving (and flying) in order to do more or less the same things, just in slightly different places that are further apart from each other. As our use of the car has increased, so we have considerably lengthened the distance we travel, even if the amount of time we spend travelling has remained more or less the same (Metz, 2008). We have exercised what we thought was our free choice, but as we saw in Chapter Five we have been labouring under something of a misapprehension. The pursuit for years of policies designed to favour the private car to the detriment of other modes has resulted in less rather than more transport choice, and at the same time the car has been used to underpin the provision of further choice in a range of related policy areas. This is a potent combination that has led to some pretty perverse policy outcomes. We send our children further to school, believing that exercising this choice will help them to succeed, yet our overall attainment continues to fall down international league tables. We drive longer distances to ever-expanding supermarkets that compete viciously with one another on the basis of bewildering choice and an extra penny off a 12-pack of fizzy drinks, yet we face the time-bomb of ill-health because we don't walk to the corner shop as much as we used to and our diet has become increasingly unhealthy. Such outcomes suggest to us that trying to address evident failures in education and health (and no doubt other) policies by deploying false choice in transport has not exactly been a success.

At the same time, Paul's admittedly rather tipsy insinuation to Matthias that Britain's transport is 'broken' is unduly pessimistic. Eddington (2006) rightly pointed out that the system runs well enough to accommodate more than 60 billion journeys a year and to support the functioning of our economy. Of course it needs to be much better, but there is already a reasonable amount of decent infrastructure and good practice upon which to build for the future. We hope we have highlighted some of the existing success stories in the pages of this book. And are there also signs of a desire for change among some of the travelling population, including Motorway Man himself? As you may by now have guessed, our central character, Paul Smith, is a case in point. Having constructed a happy and successful professional and family life for himself, he has begun to think about whether he and his family might be happier still if they adapted their transport habits even a little. In Paul's case, this process was prompted by the particular imperative of looking after his health, while at the same time he has become increasingly tired of long-haul flying for the sake of accessing something he could actually find much closer to home.

It is in reacting to such things that assumptions can be re-evaluated and behaviour can be changed. Crucially, too, Paul is not alone: early evidence on peak car is starting to hint at signs that the most mobile subgroups of the population, younger and more affluent men, have begun to lose their appetite for rushing around quite so much (LeVine and Jones, 2012; Goodwin 2012; Chapter Three). Women's mobility is still growing as the transport gender gap continues to close slowly, which is why in this book we have portrayed Susan as rather more of a 'die-hard motorist' than her husband. The trick will be to use the same suite of well-crafted policies designed to support Paul in his mobility transition – along with the Malcontented Motorists, Aspiring Environmentalists and Car Complacents (Anable, 2005) who also want to use their cars less than they currently do – to encourage Susan into one of her own in due course.

Making the move towards a more sustainable transport system, and with it a reduction or at least redistribution of overall mobility levels, requires reframing the transport debate away from that of an intractable 'wicked problem' (Rittel and Webber, 1973; Conklin, 2006) to the more positive question of how we get more out of the mobility and modes already available to us. We should not, after all, be afraid of celebrating mobility and all that it brings to individuals and the society of which we are part. It is simply fantastic to be able to travel in the ways offered by modern technology, and to do so is one of the hallmarks of a wealthy and civilised society; travel does indeed broaden the mind. The rather earnest nature of much of the discourse on sustainable transport means that the positives associated with modern transport are often not emphasised enough. While there is no doubt that we need to change the way we travel, we should do so in the context of crafting a transport and mobility culture that actively embraces the virtues of a technologically advanced transport system. It is time, in the next and concluding chapter, to advance our ideas of how this might be achieved.

Notes

[1] A legal agreement prevents the construction of a second runway at Gatwick before 2019.

[2] As the BBC's London Transport Correspondent, Tom Edwards, noted while reporting a BA flight's emergency landing at Heathrow in May 2013, 'When incidents like this have happened before, pro-expansion campaigners have claimed it proves why Heathrow should have a third runway … Campaigners against expansion use these incidents to say Heathrow is in the wrong place and shouldn't operate at 98% [capacity].' See http://www.bbc.co.uk/news/uk-england-22652718.

[3] Airlines at hub airports tend to have developed the concept of short-haul flights leaving in frequent 'waves' to connect with corresponding incoming 'waves' of long-haul flights (see Graham, 1995). This is passenger friendly but can be environmentally inefficient if planes fly relatively lightly loaded.

[4] Quieter aircraft technology will in any event help in this regard: the A380, for example, makes only half as much noise as the generation of aircraft it is replacing.

[5] This is something of a salutary tale, however. The bridges were required to protect the bats because the new road threatened to confuse them as they made their way along an established flight path. Unfortunately the bridges have had no effect at all, in part because, unlike the hedgerows they were supposed to mimic, they don't provide a home to insects. As such, the bats completely ignore them and in hindsight the bridges have proved a rather unwise investment (*Daily Telegraph*, 2012).

SEVEN

Conclusions: sorry for any inconvenience caused

The transport debate (reprise); what we can do about it; introducing 'progressive realism'

Heaven knows I'm (still) miserable now

We opened the book by suggesting that in the context of some recent, notable achievements in each of the major transport modes, some people might think that there is not much of a debate to be had about transport in Britain. We then spent the rest of the book suggesting reasons why, actually, there is. Politicians may at various times have talked a good game, but they have been hugely less successful at delivering schemes to improve the system on the ground, even when measured against their often rather modest policy objectives. The rhetoric of freedom and the 'great car economy' has bequeathed lots of privatisation and deregulation, but also the least well-developed and most congested road network of any major European economy.[1] After more than a decade and a half of 'integrated transport policy' we have the least integrated transport system of any of these same countries. Although few politicians or policy makers want to admit it, much of this is to do with privatisation and deregulation.

So which key transport debates have the Smiths uncovered during their journeys? Most often it has been our collective assumptions about how the economy works, and how transport can best contribute, that has shaped the choices facing Paul, Susan and their family. Our transport system provides the means of getting (most) people to work and goods to markets. It is preferable when these things can be done efficiently – that is, as quickly and reliably as reasonably possible and, even better, if the time spent travelling can be used productively – in order to minimise the external costs associated with poor transport and travel conditions. It is hard to imagine a major transport system without any congestion at all because there will always be occasions when the amount of traffic exceeds the amount of available road space. What is important is to find a reasonable balance between transport modes, or between transport and other means of communication, but apparently this balance remains elusive in the UK. We learnt in Chapter Two about the impacts of congestion in cities and on major routes, but Susan also experienced the difficulties that can be faced by those without access to a car in getting to work. Only when deprived of her own car through bad luck did she realise that many people without a car face significant impediments in getting around to work or wherever else all the time. Paul found his train journeys to and from London disrupted in Chapter Four, and all of the Smith family at one time or another during their journeys experienced the unreliability of transport facilities operating at or in excess of their capacity.

Transport also underpins a whole host of social activities. It allows people to reach basic and leisure services and, notwithstanding the advent of ICTs, to meet each other; transport is the glue that holds our social networks together. For many people, the car provides the means of accessing the things that they need and want, and this is especially the case following the increased dispersal of both services and social networks. But for those without access to their own car, such as Paul's mum's friend in Chapter Five, keeping up with others or getting to the shops can be somewhat more of an ordeal, often relying on lifts from friends and relatives or some kind of community transport service. We also saw that Paul's mum, along with all elderly and disabled people in each of the four constituent countries of the UK, receive their bus travel free of charge (some get free rail travel as well), while others such as jobseekers have no such luck. Yet free bus travel is useful only so long as there are actually buses to use, and in any event subsidising concessionary fares costs a fortune. It is legitimate to question whether this money might be better directed towards alternative investment capable of making bus travel better for everyone.

There are other social benefits to transport in addition to moving people around. For Sophie's classmate Neil, his modified Corsa plays a critical role in defining his identity. He is by no means alone, since many drivers, including regular car commuters, find the symbolic or affective value of their vehicles – how their cars make them *feel* – significant, as well as their instrumental value of providing a convenient means of travelling (Chapter Three). For Jack, a sporty teenager, it is not the internal combustion engine but the power provided by his own legs that is important. We discussed in Chapter Three how Jack is increasingly unusual in that rates of walking and cycling have been dropping for years, and that this is unfortunate because the active modes are excellent means of providing exercise and making people healthier, as well as enhancing city and townscapes as vibrant places of social interaction. Especially unfortunate is how much children use the non-active modes to get around, not least because of the potential for youngsters to become the next generation that sees itself as dependent on the car. Given the number of journeys made every year in Britain, our transport system is remarkably safe, but the cost to the health service of car dependence and the physical inactivity that results is in danger of running out of control.

There is then the extremely non-trivial matter of transport's environmental impact. Current transport trends are highly carbon intensive. We (think we) know that ICTs are never going to remove the need, or at least the strong desire, to travel, and levels of mobility are likely to remain high despite the possible trend towards peak car in some groups of the population (Le Vine and Jones, 2012). Part of the battle against carbon dioxide emissions will be won with technological development, but at the same time advances are unlikely to come quickly enough to make a significant dent in the global (or even the British) demand for non-renewable energy resources. Some form of behaviour change, where people alter their mobility patterns to use more energy-efficient transport modes and avail themselves of opportunities not to travel whenever this is appropriate, will also be necessary. In any case, it is worth remembering that a zero-emissions vehicle fleet does nothing to address the problems of congestion, social exclusion and obesity, and electric vehicles rely on scarce materials for their batteries and other technologies.

Thinking through the interaction of these economic, social and environmental benefits and costs in the round, we arrive at three rather fundamental questions that illuminate the transport debate: first, what is it, actually, that we want our transport systems to do? Second, what is the optimal balance between the different kinds of benefits and costs that arise from our transport systems? Third, how do we set about achieving this balance? In relation to the first question, much of the debate has tended to revolve around some rather sterile political contests: build more roads, build fewer roads; invest in public transport, don't invest in public transport. But what emerges from our discussion is that transport is about *so much more* than just transport. Even in the age of ICTs transport and the mobility it gives us still underpins much of what we do and (for many of us) who we are. It is fundamental to our very way – our very *quality* – of life in modern Western societies. Transport should, in our view, be better, but not just for the sake of having a better transport system: it should be capable of promoting economic development and social inclusion and cohesion while having as little detrimental impact as possible on the environment. This means that to the greatest extent reasonably practicable, where the development of a vibrant economy depends on mobility, it should be possible to undertake this more efficiently and more reliably, without the hindrance of too much congestion; where the ability of people to take a full part in society depends upon mobility, it should be possible for people to secure fair access to this, regardless of their income, gender, race and geographical location; and where effective means of reducing the pollution and carbon emissions associated with mobility exist, they should be actively promoted and embraced.

Within these rather broad (not to mention 'motherhood and apple pie') parameters there are clearly limits to the extent that a society can be mobile, and trade-offs that have to be made in relation to policy priorities. There will always be congestion at certain times in certain places, no matter how wide the road or appealing the alternatives to car use. Similarly there will always be communities whose transport services and infrastructure are minimal, owing to, for example, deep rurality. For the foreseeable future at least there will unavoidably be pollution and carbon dioxide emissions resulting from transport activity. But, as we have seen in the journeys we have described and the issues they have revealed, the costs of our current transport system are too high and the benefits are not as great as they could be. Moreover, these costs and the benefits are unevenly distributed among the population. Transport is fundamental to the quality of *all* of our lives, not just those of Mr and Mrs Smith and the rest of 'Middle England', and, in conceiving of transport policy as a means of playing to half a million voters in suburban middle-class constituencies, politicians – unwittingly or otherwise – run the risk of overlooking the needs, desires and preferences of everyone. Of course a poor-quality bus service is bad for existing bus users. But it also disadvantages those drivers who genuinely have no alternative and are forced to sit in traffic jams behind other drivers who might have been tempted to use the bus, had the service been better. Tacitly encouraging parents to give their children lifts to and from school may well promote safety for those in the car, but it prevents the development of an enhanced safety and fitness culture among all social groups that would improve public health and the well-being of millions of individuals. Better buses and more walking and cycling to school would cut carbon emissions, too.

Thus, our starting point is that our transport system should be viewed not in isolation but as being at the heart of public policy. It should be able to reliably accommodate large amounts of mechanised and non-mechanised mobility and be better than it currently is for the economy, society and the environment; these additional benefits should also be more evenly distributed. In a period of austerity, all of this will need to be brought about without a significant new burden on the public finances.

A thousand miles

Perhaps the first thing to say is that in defining a way forward we need to make the essential step of moving on from perennially diagnosing the transport problem. Despite repeated analysis *ad nauseam*, this has not fundamentally changed for years. For some, piecemeal developments might be enough, but for us (and we suspect many others) the need to do better than begin the same debate every time a new minister arrives (which is all too often) remains pressing. We would also argue that there is a strong case for retaining a normative position in terms of where we think transport policy should be going. Without such a strategic vision the temptation to cherry-pick politically attractive but probably unconnected and sub-optimal quick wins will be overwhelming. We have been clear that our thinking broadly aligns with the New Realist vision first properly articulated by Goodwin et al in 1991. Although there is excitement about the concept of 'peak car' having been reached, Le Vine and Jones's (2012) observation that the potential for car driving to further increase among key sections of the population means that in a 'do nothing' scenario motoring levels are likely to remain substantially above our ability to match road supply with demand. The New Realism – with its suite of approaches that includes improving public transport, promoting walking and cycling, investing in the public realm, making full use of available ICTs and embracing accessibility planning – is simply the best position yet set out to enable transport to realise much more of its economic, social and environmental potential.

At the same time, there is likely to be a case for considerably more new road building than might be envisioned by 'purist' advocates of New Realism. We do not see an inevitable contradiction between new road building in those circumstances where it is of real benefit, on the one hand, and the idea that demand management is an essential part of the overall picture, on the other. Britain's strategic road network remains under-developed in comparison with other major western European countries. As such, bypasses that reduce the impact of noise, vibration and local air pollution, safety enhancements or targeted action to address particular points of congestion, the 'completion' of the motorway and dual carriageway network to improve resilience and the construction of new routes to bring land (back) into productive use are still required to create the kind of roads provision that is regarded as standard in Germany and France. There is no need, in other words, *necessarily* to view roads as a 'means of the last resort' in addressing specific traffic problems, although clearly it is pointless to provide additional road space if the net result is little more than new congestion and pollution generated by induced traffic. New roads should be built only in the context of 'locking in' the benefits provided by the extra capacity, and this is where complementary demand management strategies can be at their most effective.

We resolve the potential tensions between New Realism and properly targeted road building with the twin aspirations of quality and choice. Our interest is first and foremost in good transport: good for the economy and society, and better for the environment. We do not think it outrageous to suggest that a good journey experience is the right of the traveller, and this will require investment across all the transport modes. For the reasons outlined in the preceding chapters, and notwithstanding the apparently limited expectations of the travelling British public, the 'good enough' is just not good enough. There are many benefits to be derived from enhanced infrastructure and the resulting improvements in the quality and reliability of journey opportunities. It is difficult to overestimate the importance of more widely available and comfortable alternatives to the car, although of course more and better ICT provision also has its role to play in improving access to goods and services.

Indeed, part of any quality journey experience is the ability of users to exercise choice in how their journey is made. The key point is that it needs to be *genuine* choice. We explained in Chapter Five how our understanding of choice differs very considerably from that based on the inherent flexibility of the car, which came to dominate transport thinking in much of the British government machine. Even after the Predict and Provide-style policies designed to build the 'great car economy' had become discredited in the 1990s, successive administrations backed away from doing anything that they thought would be construed as overtly 'anti-car'. For a while there was open talk of 'modal agnosticism' as the best approach for delivering choice in the transport realm: it was not for ministers to decide which mode of transport people should use for any given journey. This was convenient for the government. As most people chose the car, the status quo could remain and the votes of Motorway Man and his family would not be threatened, at least by transport policy. The DfT was reduced to producing an endless succession of unnecessary, underwhelming and rather unenlightening transport policy documents in want of finding something actually to do (Docherty and Shaw, 2011a).

In a free society, there is no reason why the state should be *telling* people how they should get around; it is good to have a choice. But the right conditions have to be in place in order to exercise genuine choice, and also to ensure that people are not overly disadvantaged by the choices of others.[2] The government's problem is that the present conditions are entirely, spectacularly wrong. Decades of transport policies favouring road transport and the associated, established car culture mean that for many journeys people have little practical choice, or at least perceive that they have little choice, other than to drive to where they want to go. Large sections of society have become car dependent to the point that it is a default reaction to reach for the car keys when any sort of journey needs to be made. Quite contrary to the expectations of numerous politicians and their adopted policy positions, this is a situation that can only constrain, rather than promote, transport choice. Instead, such freedom to choose exists when a range of means of accessing markets, goods, services and social interaction is widely available at most reasonable times. Alternatives to the car have to be credible, but they also have to be known about and to be appealing in more than an instrumental sense; it is worth remembering that people derive symbolic and affective value from their travel behaviour, and at present this is largely bound up with their automobiles.

This said, it is still the case that a significant factor in many people's decisions to drive is cost. Although motoring has become more expensive in recent years, its real cost remains rather higher than drivers currently pay once the full range of externalities is taken into account. Congestion in particular, but also negative social impacts, CO_2 emissions and various forms of pollution, impose a cost on the economy and society that is in excess of the total amount of tax taken through fuel duty, VED and VAT on new cars (Chapter Two). It is difficult to determine how much the externalities actually cost because some of the calculations used, despite their apparent elegance, rely on some pretty brave assumptions (such as in working out congestion's cost to the economy). This doesn't undermine the point that the fairest way of raising revenues from motorists is to charge, so far as it is possible, for those journeys that generate the most external costs, while discounting those that have little impact. This would require the introduction of some form of road-user charging scheme that was capable of capturing the costs of congestion and pollution. More broadly it would necessitate a wider exercise of charging for and subsidising all modes of transport that was roughly in line with the true costs and benefits of using them. The net effect would be to help create equality between modes and free up each to play to its strengths in meeting the mobility needs of the economy and society.

Throughout the book we have made reference to research by Jillian Anable and others that points to the rather significant numbers of people who would like to use their cars less than they currently do. Those categorised as Malcontented Motorists find current road conditions stressful and would like to reduce their car use but can't see how they might do this, given the lack of practical alternatives. Aspiring Environmentalists already do use other modes of transport and are looking for ways to still further reduce the amount they use their cars. We know from Smarter Choices that some people will switch to the active modes and/or public transport solely as a result of being told what alternatives exist. Crafting and delivering upon a transport strategy that actually enhances the quality and availability of these alternatives should thus have a far greater impact on existing transport problems, and would more than likely persuade some Car Complacents – that is, those who generally don't consider other transport modes but have no fundamental objection against so doing – to drive less than they do now. In this context, Die-Hard Drivers would be welcome to carry on using their cars as much as they wanted, provided that they paid the full external costs of their journeys.

These are the fundamental principles of our 'Progressive Realism' for transport. It represents a definite move away from Predict and Provide and relates the New Realism to a national as well as an urban context. It also challenges the opposition to large-scale road building that is fundamental to Goodwin et al's (1991) thinking. We advance Progressive Realism as inherently positive in outlook, and fully cognisant of the economic, social and environmental imperatives associated with transport activity. How might it look in practice, and what would it cost to deliver?

Land of hope and dreams

Introducing the then Labour government's new transport policy in 1997, John Prescott, the newly installed and grandiosely titled Secretary of State for Transport, Environment and the Regions, offered his most famous hostage to fortune: 'I will have failed if in five years' time there are not many more people using public transport and far fewer journeys by car. It is a tall order but I urge you to hold me to it' (quoted in Friends of the Earth, 2000, p 1). What 'far fewer journeys by car' actually meant in numbers was never made clear, but targets to increase bus and train patronage did emerge (passenger rail kilometres in Great Britain should increase by 50% and bus journeys in England by 10%), along with the aspiration to treble the number of cycling trips. Prescott was no doubt buoyed by the *Consensus for change* (Labour Party, 1996) that seemed to be sweeping through the British political establishment as the Conservatives were dislodged for the first time in 18 years, but he was swiftly forced to realise just how tall an order bringing about change in people's transport behaviour was going to be. Towards the end of Labour's term of office, the number of car, van and taxi trips had fluctuated but remained more or less constant (and the distance travelled had increased), passenger rail kilometres were up by nearly 35% but bus patronage had fallen by nearly 3%. The number of cycling trips had also fluctuated but ended up being 4% fewer than in 1997. We do not doubt that Prescott's intentions were genuine, but his deeds and those of his successors were not capable of matching his words (Docherty and Shaw, 2011a).

In seeking to rebalance Britain's transport system to encourage fewer journeys by car and more by other modes, we need to be realistic about what can be achieved in the short to medium term. Given that overall traffic levels have roughly stabilised (and might indeed have peaked), and that the accomplishments of transport policy in London since 2000 have shown what might be done, a 10% overall reduction in private car kilometres by 2027 – the year after the first stretch of HS2 is supposed to open – is not beyond the realm of possibility. Greater reductions would of course be desirable in places and at times that are particularly congested. Some of this reduction might come from greater car sharing, bringing the average car occupancy rate closer to two people per vehicle per journey. A further 50% increase in passenger rail kilometres would also be realistic, but on its own this would be nowhere near enough to accommodate the kind of modal shift from the car that a 10% decrease in private car kilometres would imply, even in the event of more car sharing. The biggest reductions in urban congestion and pollution will be derived from modal shift from cars to buses and the active modes; *at least* a doubling of bus and walking kilometres would be necessary, and the *New deal for transport* (DETR, 1998) target of trebling the number of cycling trips seems conservative. With regard to freight transport, a reduction in road-based freight is a desirable policy goal and support for, say, rail freight and green distribution initiatives should be provided where quick environmental wins and safety wins can feasibly be delivered (see McKinnon et al, 2010). Our preference, though, is to concentrate on passenger transport in the first instance because this accounts for the large majority of journeys and their related impacts. As road congestion eases, so freight transport will become more efficient, and in the longer term significant increases in rail capacity will provide further opportunities for modal shift.

In the current financial climate, a strong element of realism is also needed in relation to the amount of money any government is going to make available for capital and revenue spending on transport. This strongly implies that it is necessary to generate funding for expenditure over and above that which is currently provided by Westminster and the devolved administrations. One means of doing this would be to introduce a national road-user charging scheme. Road-user charging has been described as 'being 10 years away' for decades. But its time must surely come before too long, especially since the trend for more fuel-efficient (including electric) vehicles means that the Treasury will soon have to find an alternative to VED and fuel duty if it is to safeguard the overall revenue from transport taxes. At the same time it would not be politically acceptable to introduce such a scheme (particularly if the objective is to charge motorists *more* to use their cars) until some quite significant improvements to the existing road network and to public transport capacity had been made. Borrowing against future revenues – even £1 billion a year would be extraordinarily conservative if the charging scheme ultimately deployed was designed to capture the full costs of congestion (see Glaister and Graham, 2005) – would help to pay for up-front investment in both road schemes and better public transport.

Another means would be to pay for the targeted expansion of the strategic road network through tolls associated with particular pieces of infrastructure. The most recent large-scale example of this is the M6 Toll. Traffic levels on this stretch of road are only just over half of those initially forecast, which indicates a reluctance on the part of motorists to pay to use road infrastructure. If such behaviour were replicated across the network, this could tip the balance in favour of national road-user charging because of its potential to reduce congestion overall, rather than along a collection of under-used strips of infrastructure that did little to combat traffic jams elsewhere. What is clear, though, is that a national road-user charging scheme and selective tolling cannot easily be pursued concurrently. It would be contradictory to set up one scheme that penalises people for using existing congested stretches of road while at the same time establishing another that seeks to charge them the same or more for using uncongested new ones. It is even more clear that recently vaunted (and then hidden again) plans to privatise the English trunk road network and fund it through a regime of 'shadow tolls' are completely absurd, since this would only incentivise commercial road infrastructure operators to *increase* traffic levels across the network in order to maximise their revenue (see also Shaoul et al, 2006).

At the sub-national level, local authorities across Great Britain are heavily dependent on funding from Westminster, Holyrood and Cardiff Bay for major capital schemes in their respective areas. Certainly this can hamper councils in their pursuit of better transport, but while the prospect of financial devolution is ostensibly appealing, the 'single capital pot' system in operation means that local authorities are actually free to spend monies they receive from central government however they wish. Perhaps it is better to retain some form of central government funding arrangement, but in conjunction with enhanced powers for local authorities to raise their own revenue for transport projects; much more opportunity for the joint funding of projects, as is common elsewhere in Europe, would arise in this scenario. In the absence of national road-user charging, or if a national scheme were adopted only on the inter-city trunk road network, conurbations could be encouraged to introduce their own London-style congestion charging schemes (legislation is already in place to allow this) and borrow against future revenue. Things are possibly more difficult for smaller towns and cities, although a re-evaluation of parking policy might be an ideal substitute for congestion charging in some, especially given that it is much easier to administer. Ending the vast, hidden subsidy of supermarkets and out-of-town retail parks by heavily taxing their car parks (which often have the same number of spaces as are available in a decent-sized town) is more clear cut. This would help to reduce traffic immediately, support struggling neighbourhood centres (to which people are more likely to walk and cycle) and send out an unambiguous signal that change is to be made (especially because it was the first progressive measure to be abandoned by Labour under heavy lobbying from the supermarkets).

On top of these targeted measures, American-style public bond issues could be used to develop strategic investment plans. A bond issue was the Mayor of London's preferred alternative instrument to the disastrous and ultimately untenable Public Private Partnership that Gordon Brown insisted should finance the revitalisation of the Tube network. Transport for London has now terminated the PPP and taken the entire upgrade project back in-house after Brown's favoured scheme collapsed (Shaoul, 2002; Wolmar, 2002; House of Commons, 2010b). There is also the potential to devolve and increase business rates (these are currently levied by central government at a uniform rate and then passed back to local authorities according to population), as well as to ring-fence other locally raised monies. A very good example is the French *Versement Transport* (Chapter Six), but further mechanisms include land value taxation, which captures a percentage of wide land value rises resulting from infrastructure such as a new light rail or underground line; a hypothecated (proportion of) sales tax, such as that in the Denver metropolitan area which is being used to fund a multi-billion-dollar rapid transit expansion; and local increases in fuel duty, an example being Washington DC's two cents per gallon petrol tax. In Britain, it would be important to differentiate sales and fuel taxes at the regional level, so as to avoid significant distortion of consumption patterns, and hence wildly fluctuating tax revenues, across boundaries between closely neighbouring towns or cities.

We can show the size of each of these new revenue streams by applying each of them in turn to an 'average' British conurbation (Table 7.1). We assume a population of two million people, 700,000 full-time equivalent (FTE) jobs, a median annual salary of £23,000 per FTE employee, total annual retail sales of £10 billion and total fuel sales of 1.65 billion litres.[3] It would seem that business rates uplift and congestion charging produce modest returns, while sales and payroll taxes provide significantly greater revenue. Neither has been used in Britain before, but both are well-established means of funding local and regional transport schemes in Europe and North America. Levying either of these taxes at a starting rate of 1% would deliver enough revenue to finance the major capital projects identified by transport plans in all of the UK's city regions as essential prerequisites for enhanced competitiveness (Docherty et al, 2009).

Table 7.1: Potential annual revenue from transport and related taxes

Mechanism	Rate	Annual revenue (£m)
Business Rates Uplift	4p local supplement	45
Congestion Charge	£5 per day	50
Fuel duty top-up	1p per litre	16.5
	5p per litre	82.5
Payroll Tax	1%	161
	1.75%	281.75
Sales Tax (all transactions)	1%	100

Source: Docherty et al (2009)

Even if the opportunities to raise such additional funding were taken, it would remain incumbent upon ministers to ensure that the existing transport budget was spent more efficiently. We saw in earlier chapters that compared with other European countries the cost of building new infrastructure in Britain is truly scandalous, and that revenue expenditure can also represent poor value for money. Reform will be needed to address this 'efficiency gap', but the problems that exist would not be insurmountable, given the necessary political will. Indeed, some attempts have already been made, such as Labour's move to address the cumbersome nature of the planning process in England. A non-departmental Infrastructure Planning Commission (IPC) was established in 2008 to deal in a more streamlined fashion with large-scale infrastructure projects deemed to be in the national interest. The feeling was that such schemes were being held up by the tendency of the planning process to over-privilege the NIMBY interests of the well-educated middle class in particular locations with easy access to money to pay for professional representation. This delayed the development of projects and usually came at vast expense to the public purse. For reasons apparently to do with its 'localism agenda', the Coalition government abolished the IPC and repoliticised the large-scale infrastructure planning process by transferring decision-making powers to the relevant Secretary of State.

The problem of incompetent procurement has received rather less attention, at least in Whitehall and among local authorities. Examples of overspend associated with a lack of expertise in this area abound: large-scale undertakings such as the Jubilee Line Extension and the Edinburgh trams project have in one way or another suffered from the public sector's inability to understand and/or specify deliverable project outcomes. At the same time, the private sector's ability to outwit its public sector counterpart during project negotiations can result purely and simply in the government being ripped off. This is one of the principal reasons why three-mile dual carriageways such as the Dobwalls bypass in Cornwall (see also Chapter Six) cost an eye-watering £45 million, and why new Intercity Express Programme (IEP) trains procured to replace aged InterCity 125s on the Great Western and East Coast main lines will cost twice as much to run as the Pendolinos currently operated by Virgin Trains (*Rail Business Intelligence*, 2012).[4] A railway industry insider memorably commented to one of us that the IEP trains are so expensive because the deal was brokered by 'a world class negotiating team … and the DfT'.

Creating executive delivery agencies or departments staffed with carefully chosen procurement experts is one way around this mess, and perhaps the best example in Britain exists in Transport for London. Mackinnon et al (2008) found that when putting its teams together TfL sought to avoid appointing applicants from local authority backgrounds because they did not possess the skills necessary to deliver schemes to the standards demanded by the Mayor (see also Docherty and Shaw, 2011a on DfT 'displacement activity'). Instead TfL paid highly competitive salaries to skilled recruits from all over the world (Ken Livingstone once pointed out that there were more than 100 people employed by TfL who earned more than he did); its track record of on-time, on-budget project delivery speaks for itself, although we are sure TfL feels it could secure still better value for money. The DfT does not yet seem to have realised that paying each member of a highly expert, in-house procurement team a handsome premium over the civil service norm is excellent value for money if together their work saves taxpayers tens or hundreds of millions of pounds in project delivery costs. Indeed, on the subject of value for money, it may well be that the current process of CBA and its battery of supporting assumptions are just not fit for the purpose of distinguishing between investments in the context of promoting significantly better transport. Metz's (2008) suggestion that projects should be appraised on the basis of their capacity to meet stated transport policy aims rather than spurious value-for-money tests is probably worth investigating (Chapter Four).

Equally, neither Labour nor the Coalition has seen fit to address the fragmentation and unnecessary complexity that dogs the transport industry and its governance. The privatised railway is the best case in point. Having been split up into over 100 companies and several regulators at the time of privatisation and subject to endless tinkering by ministers, it is now all but impossible to deal with relatively straightforward tasks like procuring new rolling stock without astonishingly lengthy delays and cost over-runs. A major problem is that there is no efficient means of making decisions because so many different actors are involved at almost every level of operation. The privatised railways have cost vastly more to run than BR ever did, and neither the extent of the maintenance backlog nor the fact that BR ran far fewer trains than the TOCs can account for this discrepancy. What is required is more fundamental reform to simplify the structure of the industry. It *may* be sensible to retain an element of vertical separation, perhaps even splitting up Network Rail into three entities and combining these with the Highways Agency and its equivalents in Scotland and Wales to create genuinely strategic infrastructure authorities (as was done in Sweden in 2010). But fewer train operators, subject to a different and much more straightforward type of franchising under the control of a strategic rail authority staffed by expert railway industry managers, are definitely needed. One attractive approach would be to move to a 'concessionaire' system, whereby operators are effectively given rolling stock, a timetable and a fares structure, and contracted to run the railway punctually, reliably and to a high-quality standard. And regardless of the structure, consistent above-inflation fares increases need to stop (a message that politicians seem finally to have begun to understand).

One point we should make here is that in some quarters the debate over the future of the railways seems to have deteriorated into a bun-fight between those who support privatisation and those who oppose it. To us the issue is more nuanced and ownership seems rather less important per se than how the industry is organised and controlled; even under the current system the actual commercial profit made by the operators is a very small proportion of industry turnover. There are plenty of examples where private sector operation of transport services works well. In Britain, London's buses, Overground and DLR – all of which are let on a concessionaire basis – spring to mind, and similar contracts have been let in mainland Europe. The German *Länder*, for example, have adopted a system of contracting out rural railway services that has resulted in large annual savings and forced national operator Deutsche Bahn to become more lean and competitive. Comparable examples can be found in Denmark and Sweden. The problem with the British franchising system, as with the PPP on London Underground, is that it tries to involve the private sector too much; it remains highly ideological in purpose, trying to ape market conditions where they do not and cannot naturally exist, and as a result trips itself up on a morass of unnecessary and expensive complexities (Parker, 2013). Private sector operation of public transport services can certainly save money and introduce exciting innovations, but there is nothing to be gained from an evangelical fixation with privatisation purely and simply for privatisation's sake.[5]

Finally in terms of the transport budget, it is also possible to redirect current spending towards different ends capable of achieving a higher impact than those that are currently supported. A good example here is the £1 billion or so spent on concessionary bus travel for the elderly. We suggested in Chapter Five that, particularly in times of economic difficulty, this expenditure should at least be re-examined because the introduction of a flat fare of 50p per single journey would free up more than £500m a year for investment in improving the quality of bus services for everyone. Holders of concessionary passes would still retain a significant discount on the standard single fare across all UK jurisdictions, but they, along with all other bus users, would enjoy a step-change in the quality of service unprecedented in the UK bus sector outside of London. As with the railway industry, a concessionaire system of contracting out seems most sensible as a means of combining public sector control over a strategic public service with private sector expertise in actually running it. This is already provided for, but not acted upon, by legislation that allows the establishment of Quality Contracts. An added benefit of Quality Contracts is that they place a legal duty on local authorities to provide substantial infrastructure improvements in exchange for imposing strict regulation and operating conditions upon the bus companies. By our calculations, for £500m annually it would be possible to roll out state-of-the-art, European-style bus service quality across the equivalent of up to 20 cities the size of Plymouth (250,000 inhabitants) within 10 years; borrowing against guaranteed future expenditure could re-equip the whole country within this period (Table 7.2). Further savings might then be realised from school travel budgets if far better bus networks reduced the need for dedicated school buses or taxi runs for pupils travelling longer distances.

In our discussion so far we have identified some ways of increasing the available spend on transport and securing better value for money from that which we do spend. At a conservative estimate our suggestions would realise £2–£2.5 billion per year in new money (up to £1 billion from national road-user charging or tolled road improvements, £1 billion from local revenue-raising schemes depending on uptake and £500 million from redirected Concessionary Fares spending). Regarding the 'value for money' savings, lobbying by vested interests and basic politics will render it beyond expectation for any government to fight waste on all fronts simultaneously, and in any case we cannot rule out poor and/or delayed decision making in the future that might undo early gains; as such, perhaps the best that can be hoped for in the medium term is £1 billion per year. Still, this is an *additional* £3–£3.5 billion per year, or up to £35 billion over the decade, to be spent on new and/or improved transport infrastructure and services outside of London. This represents at least a 15% uplift on current transport expenditure, which itself needs to be maintained

Table 7.2: Potential investment in a new bus Quality Contract regime for a city of 250,000 people

Capital items	Description	Estimated costs
300 buses	Mix of single- and double-deckers, each with separate boarding and alighting doors, comfortable seats with 34" pitch, real-time information system on board; only 300 needed for considerable capacity uplift as higher proportion of double-deckers and new buses deployed more efficiently because wasteful competition removed.	300 x £200k = £60m
Real-time information	Provided at all 'timed' stops (where buses wait until scheduled departure time if they are running early) and at least half of all bus stops with shelters. Some additional info screens at 'flag and pole' stops where deemed appropriate.	600 x £15k = £9m
High-quality shelters at most bus stops	These can be provided free of charge with an advertising deal, although it might be easier to specify high standards of design and upkeep – cleaning, maintenance etc – by buying them up-front and recouping some of this investment through advertising revenue.	1,000 x £30k = £30m
Ticketless travel	Full smart card system with complete inter-operability, that is, cards can be used on all buses (and trains, boats and so on) within the local area and are compatible with every other smart card system throughout the country.	Reasonable share of the £17m it will cost to equip the whole of the south-west of England = £4m
New park and ride sites	The number and cost will depend on particular local conditions and site availability. It is assumed that two already exist and a further two are needed.	2 x £7.5m = £15m

Capital items	Description	Estimated costs
New bus lanes	These need to be provided at all points of congestion along all routes in order to guarantee competitive and reliable journey times at all times of day. The amount of mileage is less significant than the location, but is (probably rather generously) estimated at 10 miles and some engineering works are assumed to be necessary	£15m
Total capital cost = £133m		
Revenue costs	**Description**	**Estimated costs**
New fares structure	£1 flat fare per single journey;* £3 daily maximum; £10 weekly maximum. A starting point of 20m journeys per year, 6m of which are on the Concessionary Fares scheme, is assumed. This suggests annual revenue of ~£25m (around 80p per single concession journey and £1.50 for the rest). Thus revenue would initially fall by £6m–£7m per year and operating costs would increase by around £3m because of the extra buses, but the shortfall should be made up in future years by substantially increasing patronage.	£10m per year, declining to £5m and ultimately to zero; current subsidy including Concessionary Fares runs at around £6m.
Staff to run tendering process and manage contracts	This could probably be done without additional staff but would require retraining and at least initially would involve consultants as in-house expertise is built back up	£?
Extras	Running costs for real-time info and back-office support for smart card system; maintenance of shelters and so on.	£0.5m

Note: * By 'single journey' is meant the mainland European standard of a one-way trip from a point of origin to a destination, not the typical British one-way trip that requires the purchase of another single ticket with each change of bus.

Source: Information is derived from conversations with staff from different local authorities and the (former) Government Office for the Regions network, and should be regarded as indicative.

in real terms, at no cost to central government over and above what is already disbursed through the DfT, TfL and the Scottish, Welsh and Northern Irish governments. We assume that this extra amount is not enough to trigger significant project-cost inflation, especially in the context of much better project procurement.

What, then, would we prioritise for investment? Any attempt at managing transport demand needs to be multi-modal in character and to utilise a complementary suite of 'hard' and 'soft' approaches (see Ison and Rye, 2008). It should also be about paying more attention to those who have missed out as a result of the slavish political pursuit of Motorway Man. Starting with public transport, we have already mentioned the complete overhaul of the bus system. For the railways we have suggested a different model of franchising and a new Strategic Rail Authority to oversee it. We also support the delivery of an HS2 that is *properly planned and integrated* into national and urban economic development strategies. This would provide a massive shot in the arm for the urban cores of our major provincial cities. At the same time, HS2 cannot be allowed to compromise other transport investment. It is important to deliver all of the major schemes in Network Rail's (2013) *Strategic business plan*, plus the further electrification required to fully wire the inter-city and urban 'metro' networks across the country. This would permit much improved operations and release massive economies of scale in train procurement.

Perhaps rather predictably, the DfT has been slow to follow up its stated willingness to promote devolution in the administration of the railways with action to make it happen, and this should be rectified. A good model to follow in this regard is that of the London Overground (and the long-standing local aspirations for Merseyrail); in our view, all of London's suburban railways (and the necessary funding to improve them) should be turned over to TfL to be run as Overground lines, and this approach exported to all other cities in England so that the Overground brand can be developed along the lines of the German S-Bahn system to provide easily identifiable, high-quality metro services across the country (the devolved administrations, Scotland in particular, have moved in the opposite direction, towards more integrated 'national' systems reminiscent of the Netherlands'). All of this should be perfectly possible so long as the proposed HS2 budget is kept under control, the current annual spend of £4 billion on the railways is at least maintained rather than progressively reduced and McNulty's efficiency savings are actually achieved and then recycled into investment.

On the subject of urban transport, all of Britain's major cities should have tram *networks*, rather than just single lines, that are fully integrated with other modes of transport (including high speed rail stations where appropriate) and built to link places that people actually want to go to; it is important also to link the development of these networks with public realm improvement projects that enhance the pedestrian environment in key locations. Fifteen new lines (we realise this still fails to reach the number originally envisaged in *A new deal for transport* in 1998) at an average of £500 million each would cost £7.5 billion. At the same time other less costly but, in the fragmented world of UK public transport, difficult-to-deliver schemes should not be lost sight of, especially where they make the system much easier to use. We are thinking here of reliable real-time information; standardised, integrated smart-ticketing infrastructure; and, relatedly, simple ticketing schemes such as flat-fare bus journeys in urban areas and an easy-to-understand fares regime like that used by Deutsche Bahn for longer journeys. In a world of Quality Bus Contracts (see Chapter Four) and concessionaire rail franchises, all of this would be much more readily achievable.

On the road network, the introduction of charging will be essential, although, as we have said, it could only take place after significant improvements to the transport system on the ground. At the strategic level, road improvements already identified by the Highways Agency and its equivalents as the most likely to reduce congestion and improve safety are the obvious place to start. The removal of at-grade junctions on trunk routes would do a great deal to assist the reliability of traffic, at least on these routes themselves. At the local level, the maintenance of roads to a much higher standard (fix the potholes, make sure the white lines are properly painted and visible and so on), and the pursuit of *proper* pedestrian and cycling enhancement schemes, as outlined in

Chapter Three, is more important than major road building. In relation to air transport, it is time to reform Air Passenger Duty to reflect the availability of alternatives to particular air routes and to incentivise airlines to fly their planes as full as possible, albeit that the economic importance of some routes could justify a lower rate. There might be a case for privately funded second runways at Stansted and, particularly, Gatwick on operational and environmental grounds, while at Heathrow existing capacity could be better used (especially in the longer term, once HS2 is fully up and running), and a third runway might again be justified for operational and environmental reasons.

These 'hard' measures, which we estimate will cost the government around £33 billion (Table 7.3), will be in need of support from 'softer' policies such as educational campaigns and PTP initiatives like Smarter Choices. The potential for using social media to develop nuanced and sophisticated PTP interventions is tremendously exciting, but at the same time the hardware has to be there in order to prevent such things backfiring. There is nothing particularly smart about leaving your car on the drive if the alternative bus journey is expensive, slow and unreliable. Finally, more effective joint working between transport planners and those in other areas of public policy is needed to promote a better understanding of the relationship between transport and land use, employment, health, education, social inclusion and so on. It would be wrong to say that efforts are not already under way in this regard (see Davis and Annett, 2013), but much more can still be done to promote flexible home working and the active modes, and the days of siting major new pieces of public infrastructure in places that are difficult to get to without a car will simply have to come to an end: indeed, the public sector needs to demonstrate leadership here and stop locating critical facilities such as new hospitals, schools and colleges at the edge of town. The difference that this would make in terms of its likely impact on modal shift, would be very noticeable indeed.

We accept that achieving change on such a scale would not be easy and would represent a considerable shift in mindset for many in the UK government machine. But large-scale change is perfectly possible, even in the British political system. We noted in the last chapter that

Table 7.3: Approximate cost breakdowns for transport schemes over a 10-year period, funded through additional revenue raised by various mechanisms explained in the chapter text

Intervention	**Approximate additional cost over 10 years (£bn)**
Rail improvements: Electrification, rolling stock, capacity enhancements (including new tracks and resignalling), station improvements	7.5
Light rail: 15 new tram lines	7.5
Buses: Up to 20 new city networks	5
Roads: various schemes	10
Walking/cycling schemes	3
Total	33

the entire basis of thinking about the role and scope of government was radically altered in the 20 years following the election of Margaret Thatcher's Conservatives, to the point where large sections of society now struggle to view the world without the aid of neoliberal-tinted glasses. Of more immediate relevance to our discussion is that large-scale change in the transport sector has also taken place, and has involved both major political parties and mayors of wildly diverging political starting points. Since London's devolution in 2000, Ken Livingstone and Boris Johnson have instigated (Livingstone) and perpetuated (Johnson) a remarkable turnaround in the fortunes of the city's transport system. The introduction of congestion charging, unprecedented investment across the public transport system and massive support for a cycling revolution are all transforming Londoners' travel experiences. By 2019, after the completion of Crossrail, Thameslink and most of the Tube's modernisation programme, London's transport system will be genuinely world class.

Why has this occurred in London to an extent as yet unimaginable in the rest of the UK? One story has it that Gordon Brown was terrified to hear that important bankers found travelling in 'third world' London a chore to the point that they were thinking of relocating to Frankfurt, where, as we noted in Chapter Six, it is very easy indeed to get around. On this basis he authorised a generous funding arrangement for TfL and sanctioned the rebuilding of the Tube (albeit with his signature and completely unworkable PPP). This would certainly help to explain why Ken Livingstone, reviled by the Labour Party hierarchy of the day, was able to extract so much money from the Treasury to invest in London's transport services and infrastructure. Funding is undoubtedly one of the principal reasons why so much transport investment has taken place in London in recent years, but it is by no means the only one. As Mackinnon et al (2008) found out, also important have been: the devolution settlement itself, which allowed a different policy trajectory from central government to be developed; the setting up of a highly competent technocracy in TfL, under the leadership of respected practitioner Bob Kiley (and subsequently Sir Peter Hendy), that was capable of both determining and realising a strategic vision; and the personal capacity of both Livingstone and Johnson to lead from the front. That Livingstone would prioritise transport as a focus for significant investment was largely unsurprising, since he had championed it when he was leader of the Greater London Council and it was one of the few policy areas in which the Mayor of London has sufficient leeway to bring about real change. Nevertheless, as one TfL Board member speaking to Mackinnon et al (2008, p 115) observed, while devolution may 'open the door' for change, people have actually got to walk through the door to effect that change. He speculated on what might have happened if the preferred candidate of the Labour 'machine', Frank Dobson, had been elected as Mayor of London:

> I am trying to work out … what's the lesson here? The lesson is, it's the people that drive it, isn't it? You needed the legislation of the devolved structure to create the platform but then [also] the key people. I mean, if Frank Dobson had been Mayor of London, let's work this one through, right? Frank [imposing] a £5 tax to drive into London …? I mean, would Frank Dobson have [set up] Transport for London? No. Firstly, he wouldn't have got Kiley in, despite all the [potential] on the salary. He would have got some jobsworth

> who was competent. He wouldn't have got all that political and [would have] been officer-driven.

It is worth pointing out here something we might well have revealed at the start of this chapter, or even the book. While we have made a big play of being able to increase the overall UK transport budget by a maximum of 15%, in fact transport expenditure went up by considerably more than this across the UK in the 2000s. In England the increase was 83%, Wales and Northern Ireland witnessed increases of around 50% and in Scotland the spend rose by fully 145%. This was of course very welcome. But much of this increased expenditure was accounted for by massive investment in London, the need to address chronic, historic underinvestment in the railways and the expansion of Concessionary Fares schemes. We also know that at least 30% of this increase was wasted by inefficient spending. Imagine what could happen across the whole country and all transport modes if the rest of the UK government machine developed the same 'strategic capacity' – the identification of transport as fundamental to the economy and society, the political will to make things happen, the mechanisms to raise the finance to pay for investment and the technocracy to deliver schemes on time and on budget – as now exists in London.

Throughout the book we have seen how our Motorway Man, Paul Smith, has begun to change his travel behaviour for various reasons. We know that there are many more drivers who to varying degrees want to have a go at changing theirs. What we are proposing in this chapter is the pursuit of means designed to encourage rather than enforce change among those people who want to change their existing travel habits. High-quality alternatives to driving, with genuine economic, social and environmental benefits, should help to achieve more sustainable travel behaviour as people see the benefits of change for themselves. Once the projects we outline have been completed – and we would of course see these as a foundation for further improvements in the longer term, not least to capitalise on economies of scale that stable and continuous investment programmes bring about – the introduction of road-user charging across the country would provide both a 'stick' to promote additional modal shift and a means of capturing the true cost of motoring for those who want or need to continue driving their cars. The aim is for Sophie and Lucy to grow up not thinking that the car is their default mode of transport; for Jack to continue using the active modes for commuting and business journeys as well as for leisure trips; for Susan to be able to take the bus more easily to work and to realise that it's actually rather a good way to travel; and for Paul to want to leave the car (and the plane) behind more and more often. None of this means that they shouldn't use the car or the aeroplane when these are obviously the best, or the only, means of getting from A to B. Both are, after all, wonderful inventions that bring enormous benefits.

Bemoaning his political bosses' apparent unwillingness to commit to the visions they had set out in an ever-expanding number of transport policy documents, a government official confided in us one day there are two types of public policy: that which you put in your policy documents and that which you spend your money on. British government ministers and officials have produced all too many policy documents but have delivered too little on the ground. It is time to pursue a progressive realism that makes transport better and fairer for all of us. We think Motorway Man and his family might actually approve of that.

Notes

[1] As defined by the proportion of the total network that is of motorway standard. See Chapter One.

[2] Which, of course, is one of the main reasons why we have a taxation mechanism in the first place.

[3] These estimates are derived from National Statistics survey data for the indicators concerned, using 2006 data/prices; fuel sales data are derived from http://www.publications.parliament.uk/pa/cm200506/cmhansrd/cm051219/text/51219w08.htm.

[4] This is to say nothing of the fact that they have taken years to order and have been imposed on TOCs that do not want to run them.

[5] It is for this same reason that we did not include Public Private Partnerships (PPPs) in our discussion of how to raise additional funds for transport investment. See also Shaoul and Edwards (2004).

References

Aaranovitch, D. (2012) 'Welcome to Britain, the ludicrous Land of No', http://www.thetimes.co.uk/tto/opinion/columnists/davidaaronovitch/article3472804.ece. Accessed 20 May 2013.

Adams, J. (1993) 'No need for discussion – the policy is now in place!', in P. Stonham (ed) *Local transport today and tomorrow*, London: Local Transport Today Ltd, pp 73–7.

AEA (2012) *2012 Guidelines to Defra/DECC's GHG conversion factors for company reporting*, London: Department of Energy and Climate Change and Department for Environment, Food and Rural Affairs', http://www.defra.gov.uk/publications/files/pb13773-ghg-conversion-factors-2012.pdf. Accessed 10 January 2013.

Airports Council International (2013) *Annual traffic data*, http://www.aci.aero/Data-Centre/Annual-Traffic-Data. Accessed 22 May 2013.

Aldred, R. (2010) '"On the outside": constructing cycling citizenship', *Social & Cultural Geography*, vol 11, no 1, pp 35–52.

Amin, A., Massey, D. and Thrift, N. (2003) *De-centering the nation: A radical approach to regional inequality*, London: Catalyst.

Anable, J. (2005) 'Complacent car addicts or aspiring environmentalists? Identifying travel behavior segments using attitude theory', *Transport Policy*, vol 12, pp 65–78.

Anable, J. and Gatersleben, B. (2005) 'All work and no play? The role of instrumental and affective factors in work and leisure journeys by different travel modes', *Transportation Research Part A*, vol 39, pp 163–81.

Anable, J. and Shaw, J. (2007) 'Priorities, policies and (time)scales: the delivery of emissions reductions in the UK transport sector', *Area*, vol 39, no 4, pp 443–57.

Andrews, G., Parkhurst, G., Susilo, Y. and Shaw, J. (2012) 'The grey escape: investigating older people's use of the free bus pass', *Transportation Planning and Technology*, vol 35, no 1, pp 3–15.

Appleyard, D. and Lintell, M. (1969) 'The environmental quality of city streets: the residents' viewpoint', *Journal of American Planning Association*, vol 35, pp 84–101.

Association of Train Operating Companies (2013) *Airline-style discounting by rail cuts aviation's market share*, http://www.atoc.org/media-centre/latest-press-releases/airline-style-discounting-by-rail-cuts-aviations-market-share-100822. Accessed 21 May 2013.

Atkins (2010) *An evaluation of the 'Travelling to School Initiative' programme*, London: Atkins.

Banister, C. and Gallent, N. (1998) 'Trends in commuting in England and Wales – becoming less sustainable?', *Area*, vol 30, no 4, pp 331–42.

Banister, D. (1985) 'Deregulating the bus industry in Britain – (A) the proposals', *Transport Reviews*, vol 5, no 2, pp 99–103.

Banister, D. and Berechman, Y. (2001) 'Transport investment and the promotion of economic growth', *Journal of Transport Geography*, vol 9, no 3, pp 209–18.

Banks, N., Bayliss, D. and Glaister, S. (2007) *Motoring towards 2050: Roads and reality*, London: RAC Foundation, http://www.racfoundation.org/assets/rac_foundation/content/downloadables/roads_and_reality-glaister_et_al-041207.pdf. Accessed 23 May 2013.

Baslington, H. (2008) 'School travel plans: overcoming barriers to implementation', *Transport Reviews*, vol 28, no 2, pp 239–58.

Baslington, H. (2009) 'Children's perceptions of and attitudes towards transport modes: why a vehicle for change is long overdue', *Children's Geographies*, vol 7, no 3, pp 305–22.

BBC (2004) *'We want to keep our rail line'*, http://news.bbc.co.uk/1/hi/uk/4033269.stm. Accessed 19 January 2013.

BBC (2012a) *Inactivity 'killing as many as smoking'*, http://www.bbc.co.uk/news/uk-wales-politics-18876880?print=true. Accessed 18 July 2012.

BBC (2012b) *George Osborne in 'first class ticket row'*, http://www.bbc.co.uk/news/uk-politics-20008342. Accessed 9 January 2012.

BBC (2013a) *Type 2 diabetes rise in under-40s, says Cardiff research*, http://www.bbc.co.uk/news/uk-wales-22543559. Accessed 20 May 2013.

BBC (2013b) *The great London airport debate*, http://www.bbc.co.uk/news/business-20679148?print=true. Accessed 12 March 2013.

BBC (2013c) *Boris Johnson announces plans for ultra low emissions zone*, http://www.bbc.co.uk/news/uk-england-london-21443439. Accessed 22 May 2013.

Beesley, M. and Glaister, S. (1985) 'Deregulating the bus industry in Britain – (C) a response', *Transport Reviews*, vol 5, no 2, pp 133–42.

Bissell, D. (2010) 'Passenger mobilities: affective atmospheres and the sociality of public transport', *Environment and Planning D: Society and Space*, vol 28, no 2, pp 270–89.

Böge, S. (1995) 'The well-travelled yogurt pot: lessons for new freight transport policies and regional production', *World Transport Policy & Practice,* vol 1, pp 7–11.

Bos, I., Van der Heijden, R., Molin, E. and Timmermans, H. (2004) 'The choice of park and ride facilities: an analysis using a context-dependent hierarchical choice experiment', *Environment and Planning A*, vol 36, pp 1673–86.

Brake, J., Nelson, J. and Wright, S. (2004) 'Demand responsive transport: towards the emergence of a new market segment', *Journal of Transport Geography*, vol 12, no 4, pp 323–38.

Breheny, M. (1995) 'The compact city and transport energy consumption', *Transactions of the Institute of British Geographers*, vol 20, pp 81–101.

Breheny, M. (1997) 'Urban compaction: feasible and acceptable?', *Cities*, vol 14, pp 209–18.

British Medical Association (1992) *Cycling: Towards health and safety*, Oxford: Oxford University Press.

British Railways Board (1963) *The reshaping of British Railways. Part 1: Report*, London: HMSO.

Brown, R. (2013) *The Brown review of the rail franchising programme*, Cmnd 8526, London: The Stationery Office, https://www.gov.uk/government/uploads/system/uploads/attachment_data/file/49453/cm-8526.pdf. Accessed 19 January 2012.

Browne, M., Rizet, C., Leonardi, J. and Allen, J. (2008) *Analysing energy use in supply chains: The case of fruits and vegetables and furniture*, http://www.greenlogistics.org/SiteResources/bcf4484f-4fd2-45b2-954a-d77de10951d9_LRN%202008%20-%20Supply%20chain.pdf. Accessed 20 May 2013.

Browne, M., Allen, J., Woodburn, A. and Piotrowska, M. (2007) *Literature review WM9: Part II – light good vehicles in urban areas*, London: University of Westminster.

Buck, N., Gordon, I., Hall, P., Harloe, M. and Kleinman, M. (2002) *Working capital: Life and labour in contemporary London*, London: Routledge.

Burgess, K. (2012) 'Cameron backs "excellent" #cyclesafe campaign', *Times*, 23 February, http://www.thetimes.co.uk/tto/public/cyclesafety/article3328193.ece. Accessed 10 January 2013.

Burgess, S., Briggs, A., McConnell, B. and Slater, H. (2006) *School choice in England: Background facts*, CMPO working paper series number 06/159, Bristol: CMPO.

Butcher, L. (2009) *Buses: Concessionary fares*, Standard Note SN/BT/1499, House of Commons Library.

CAA (Civil Aviation Authority) (2006) *No-frills carriers: Revolution or evolution?*, CAP770, London: CAA.

Cabinet Office (2009) *An analysis of urban transport*, http://webarchive.nationalarchives.gov.uk/+/http://www.cabinetoffice.gov.uk/media/308292/urbantransportanalysis.pdf. Accessed 7 February 2013.

Cahill, M. (2010) *Transport, environment and society*, Maidenhead: McGraw-Hill.

Cairncross, F. (1997) *The death of distance: How the communications revolution will change our lives*, Boston, MA: Harvard Business School Press.

Camagni, R., Gibelli, M. and Rigamonti, P. (2002) 'Urban mobility and urban form: the social and environmental costs of different patterns of urban expansion', *Ecological Economics*, vol 40, no 2, pp 199–216.

Carrabine, E. and Longhurst, B. (2002) 'Consuming the car: anticipation, use and meaning in contemporary youth culture', *The Sociological Review*, vol XX, pp 181–96.

Carver, A., Timperio, A. and Crawford, D. (2008) 'Playing it safe: the influence of neighbourhood safety on children's physical activity – a review', *Health and Place*, vol 14, pp 217–27.

CfIT (Commission for Integrated Transport) (2001a) *A study of European best practice in the delivery of integrated transport*, London: CfIT.

CfIT (2001b) *Key issues in rural transport*, London: CfIT.

CfIT (2002) *Paying for road use*, London: CfIT, http://webarchive.nationalarchives.gov.uk/20060130194436/http://cfit.gov.uk/docs/2002/pfru/pfru/index.htm. Accessed 26 January 2013.

CfIT (2007) 'Transport and climate change', http://webarchive.nationalarchives.gov.uk/20110304132839/http://cfit.independent.gov.uk/pubs/2007/climatechange/index.htm. Accessed 7 February 2013.

Charlesworth, G. (1984) *A history of British motorways*, London: Thomas Telford.

Clark, C. and Stansfeld, S. (2007) 'The effect of transportation noise on health and cognitive development: a review of recent evidence', *International Journal of Comparative Psychology*, vol 20, pp 145–58.

Clark, J. (2010) *Social inclusion and the urban renaissance – without the car*, unpublished PhD thesis, University of Glasgow.

Clifton, P. (2012) 'Coping with climate change', *Rail*, vol 716, pp 62–7.

Conklin, J. (2006) *Dialogue mapping: Building shared understanding of wicked problems*, Chichester: Wiley.

Crafts, N. (2009) 'Transport infrastructure investment: implications for growth and productivity', *Oxford Review of Economic Policy*, vol 25, pp 327–43.

Cresswell, T. (2006) *On the move*, Oxford: Blackwell.

Crime Concern (2004) *The school run: A training programme for bus drivers focusing on conflict resolution with school pupils*, London: DfT.

Daily Mail (2009) 'Every driver milked for £300-a-year as fuel tax is not NOT spent on our roads', http://www.dailymail.co.uk/news/article-2060140/Every-driver-milked-300-year-fuel-tax-NOT-spent-roads.html. Accessed 7 February 2013.

Daily Telegraph (2009) 'Road pricing killed off by transport secretary, Lord Adonis', http://www.telegraph.co.uk/motoring/news/5625034/Road-pricing-killed-off-by-Transport-Secretary-Lord-Adonis.html. Accessed 7 February 2013.

Daily Telegraph (2012) 'Utterly bats', http://www.telegraph.co.uk/comment/telegraph-view/9329259/Utterlybats.html. Accessed 22 May 2013.

Daley, M. and Rissel, C. (2010) 'Perspectives and images of cycling as a barrier or facilitator of cycling', *Transport Policy*, vol 18, pp 211–16.

Davis, A. and Annett, H. (2013) 'Transport, travel and health in public policy: a journey begun', in J.-P. Rodrigue, T. Notteboom and J. Shaw (eds) *The Sage handbook of transport studies*, London: Sage, in press.

Davis, A., Valsecchi, C. and Fergusson, M. (1997) *Unfit for Purpose: How Car Use Fuels Climate Change and Obesity*. London: Institute for European Environmental Policy.

de Hartog, J., Boogaard, H., Nijland, H. and Hoek, G. (2010) 'Do the health benefits of cycling outweigh the risks?' *Environmental Health Perspectives*, vol 118, no 8, pp 1109–16.

Delbosc, A. and Currie, G. (2012) 'Using online discussion forums to study attitudes toward cars and transit among young people in Victoria', *Australasian Transport Research Forum 2012 Proceedings*, 26–28 September, Perth.

Department for Education (2006) *Education and Inspections Act 2006*, https://www.education.gov.uk/publications/standard/publicationDetail/Page1/DCSF-10544006X. Accessed 7 February 2013.

Department of Enterprise, Trade and Investment (2006) *Air route development fund ends on a successful note*, news release, 20 December 2006, Archive.nics.gov.uk/eti/061220g-eti.htm. Accessed 3 July 2007.

Department of Health (2013) *Reducing obesity and improving diet*, https://www.gov.uk/government/policies/reducing-obesity-and-improving-diet. Accessed 20 May 2013.

DETR (Department of the Environment, Transport and the Regions) (1998) *A new deal for transport: Better for everyone*, Cmnd 3950, London: DETR.

DfES (Department for Education and Skills) (2003) *Travelling to school: An action plan*, London: DfES.

DfT (Department for Transport) (2004) *Feasibility study of road pricing in the UK – Full report*, http://webarchive.nationalarchives.gov.uk/20090505152230/http:/www.dft.gov.uk/pdf/pgr/roads/introtoroads/roadcongestion/feasibilitystudy/studyreport/feasibilityfullreport. Accessed 14 February 2013.

DfT (2006) *Concessionary bus travel*, http://webarchive.nationalarchives.gov.uk/20060829143900/http://dft.gov.uk/stellent/groups/dft_localtrans/documents/divisionhomepage/032412.hcsp. Accessed 20 January 2013.

DfT (2007) *Understanding the travel aspirations, needs and behaviour of young adults*, London: DfT.

DfT (2008) *Delivering a sustainable transport system*, http://webarchive.nationalarchives.gov.uk/+/http:/www.dft.gov.uk/about/strategy/transportstrategy/dasts/. Accessed 12 March 2013.

DfT (2009) *Transport trends: 2009 edition*, London: DfT and Office for National Statistics, http://webarchive.nationalarchives.gov.uk/20100406130654/http:/www.dft.gov.uk/adobepdf/162469/221412/190425/220778/trends2009.pdf. Accessed 27 January 2013.

DfT (2010) *National travel survey: 2010*, London: DfT.

DfT (2011) *Public attitudes to transport and the impact of climate change in 2011*, https://www.gov.uk/government/uploads/system/uploads/attachment_data/file/11508/climate-change-2011-report.pdf. Accessed 12 March 2013.

DfT (2012) *Transport Statistics Great Britain*, London: DfT, https://www.gov.uk/government/organisations/department-for-transport/series/transport-statistics-great-britain. Accessed 10 January 2013.

DfT (undated) *Attitudes to, and potential take-up of, additional home to school transport*, http://webarchive.nationalarchives.gov.uk/20090511232132/http://www.dft.gov.uk/pgr/sustainable/schooltravel/research/attitudestoandpotentialtakeu5747?page=1. Accessed 7 February 2013.

DfT and Office of Rail Regulation (2011) *Realising the potential of GB rail: Report of the rail value for money study. Summary report*, http://assets.dft.gov.uk/publications/report-of-the-rail-vfm-study/realising-the-potential-of-gb-rail-summary.pdf. Accessed 26 June 2013.

Dini, P., Milne, C. and Milne, R. (2012) *Costs and benefits of superfast broadband in the UK*, London: LSE, www2.lse.ac.uk/businessandconsultancy/lseconsulting/pdf/costs-and-benefits-of-superfast-broadband.pdf. Accessed 21 May 2012.

Disdier, A. and Head, K. (2006) 'The puzzling persistence of the distance effect on bilateral trade', *Review of Economics and Statistics*, vol 90, no 1, pp 37–48.

Dobbs, L. (2005) 'Wedded to the car: women, employment and the importance of private transport', *Transport Policy*, vol 12, no 3, pp 266–78.

Dobruszkes, F. (2013) 'The geography of European low-cost airline networks: a contemporary analysis', *Journal of Transport Geography*, vol 28, pp 75–88.

Docherty, I. and Mackie, P. (2010) 'Planning for transport in the wake of Stern and Eddington', *Regional Studies*, vol 44, pp 546–67.

Docherty, I. and Shaw, J. (2011a) 'The transformation of transport policy in Great Britain? "New Realism" and New Labour's decade of displacement activity', *Environment and Planning A*, vol 43, no 1, pp 224–51.

Docherty, I. and Shaw, J. (2011b) 'Transport in a sustainable urban future', in J. Flint and M. Raco (eds) *The future of sustainable cities: Critical reflections*, Bristol: The Policy Press, pp 131–52.

Docherty, I., Giulano, G. and Houston, D. (2008) 'Connected cities', in R. Knowles, J. Shaw and I. Docherty (eds) *Transport geographies: Mobilities, flows and spaces*, Oxford: Blackwell, pp 83–101.

Docherty, I., Shaw, J. and Gray, D. (2007) 'Transport strategy in Scotland since devolution', *Public Money and Management*, vol 27, no 2, pp 141–8.

Docherty, I., Shaw, J., Knowles, R., and Mackinnon, D. (2009) 'Connecting for competitiveness: future transport in UK city regions', *Public Money and Management*, September.

Doganis, R. (2001) *The airline business in the 21st century*, London: Routledge.

Downs, A. (2004) *Still stuck in traffic: Coping with peak-hour traffic congestion*, Washington, DC: Brookings Institution.

Drewry Shipping Consultants (2009) *Container market 2009/10, annual review and forecast*, London: Drewry.

Economist (2009) 'We did it!', http://www.economist.com/node/15174489. Accessed 14 February 2013.

Eddington, R. (2006) *The Eddington transport study: The case for change: Sir Rod Eddington's advice to the government*, London: HM Treasury.

Edwards, E., McKinnon, A. and Cullinane, S. (2009) *Carbon auditing the "last mile": Modelling the environmental impacts of conventional and online non-food shopping*, paper presented at the 14th Annual Logistics Research Network Conference, 9–11 September, Cardiff.

Ellaway, A., McKay, L., Macintyre, S., Kearns, A. and Hiscock, R. (2004) 'Are social comparisons of homes and cars related to psychosocial health?' *International Journal of Epidemiology*, vol 33, no 5, pp 1065–71, http://eprints.gla.ac.uk/2610/. Accessed 26 June 2013.

European Commission (2011a) *Survey on passengers' satisfaction with rail services*, http://ec.europa.eu/public_opinion/flash/fl_326_en.pdf. Accessed 8 January 2012.

European Commission (2011b) *EU transport in figures: statistical pocketbook 2011*, http://ec.europa.eu/transport/facts-fundings/statistics/doc/2011/pocketbook2011.pdf. Accessed 19 July 2013.

European Rail Research and Advisory Council (2004) *Light rail and metro systems in Europe: current market, perspectives and research implication*, http://www.errac.org/IMG/pdf/LRailandMetroinEU-042004.pdf. Accessed 19 July 2013.

Evening Standard (2008) 'Comment (David Cameron): I won't back Gordon's great Heathrow con', http://www.standard.co.uk/news/comment-i-wont-back-gordons-great-heathrow-con-6928482.html. Accessed 22 May 2013.

Falconer, R. and Kingham, S. (2007) '"Driving people crazy": a geography of boy racers in Christchurch, New Zealand', *New Zealand Geographer*, vol 63, no 3, pp 181–91.

Farrington, J. (2007) 'The new narrative of accessibility: its potential contribution to discourses in (transport) geography', *Journal of Transport Geography*, vol 15, pp 319–30.
Farrington, J. and Farrington, C. (2005) 'Rural accessibility, social inclusion and social justice: towards conceptualisation', *Journal of Transport Geography*, vol 13, no 1, pp 1–12.
Felstead, A. (2011) 'Rapid change or slow evolution? Changing places of work and their consequences in the UK', *Journal of Transport Geography*, vol 21, pp 31–8.
Flyvberg, B., Bruzelius, N. and Rothengather, W. (2003) *Megaprojects and risk: An anatomy of ambition*, Cambridge: Cambridge University Press.
Foresight (2007) *Tackling obesity: Future choices*, London: Department of Business, Innovation and Skills, http://www.bis.gov.uk/foresight/our-work/projects/published-projects/tackling-obesities. Accessed 10 January 2013.
Forsyth, A. and Southworth, M. (2008) 'Cities afoot – pedestrians, walkability and urban design', *Journal of Urban Design*, vol 13, pp 1–3.
Fremont, A. (2013) 'Containerization and intermodal transportation', in J.-P. Rodrigue, T. Notteboom and J. Shaw (eds) *The Sage handbook of transport studies*, London: Sage, pp 47–62.
Friedman, M. (1980) *Free to choose*, New York: Avon.
Friends of the Earth (2000) *Paved with good intentions? Government transport plans*, press release, 20 July, London: Friends of the Earth.
Friends of the Earth Scotland, Transform Scotland and WWF Scotland (2006) *Parliamentary briefing on the air route development fund*, Edinburgh: FoE Scotland, Transform Scotland and WWF Scotland.
Fu, M., Kelly, A., Clinch, P. and King, F. (2012) 'Environmental policy implications of working from home: modelling the impacts of land-use, infrastructure and socio-demographics', *Energy Policy*, vol 47, pp 416–23.
Gatersleben, B. and Appleton, K. (2007) 'Contemplating cycling to work: attitudes and perceptions in different stages of change', *Transportation Research Part A*, vol 41, pp 302–12.
Gatersleben, B. and Uzzell, D. (2007) 'Affective appraisals of the daily commute', *Environment and Behaviour*, vol 39, pp 416–31.

Gaunt, M., Rye, T. and Allen, S. (2007) 'Public acceptability of road user charging: the case of Edinburgh and the 2005 referendum', *Transport Reviews*, vol 27, pp 85–102.

Glaister, S. and Graham, D. (2005) *Pricing our roads: Vision and reality*, London: Institute of Economic Affairs, http://papers.ssrn.com/sol3/papers.cfm?abstract_id=664421##. Accessed 26 January 2013.

Glaister, S., Nurnham, J., Stevens, H. and Travers, T. (2006) *Transport policy in Britain*, Basingstoke: Palgrave.

Goodwin, P. (1992) *A quality margin in transport*, Oxford: Transport Studies Unit, University of Oxford.

Goodwin, P. (1995) *Car dependence: A report for the RAC Foundation for motoring and the environment*, London: RAC Foundation.

Goodwin, P. (2004) *The economic costs of road traffic congestion*, London: The Rail Freight Group, http://eprints.ucl.ac.uk/1259/. Accessed 10 January 2013.

Goodwin, P. (2010) *Opportunities for improving transport and getting better value for money, by changing the allocation of public expenditures to transport*, Bristol: Centre for Transport & Society, University of the West of England.

Goodwin, P. (2012) *Peak travel, peak car and the future of mobility: Evidence, unresolved issues, and policy implications, and a research agenda*, Paris: International Transport Forum, http://www.internationaltransportforum.org/jtrc/DiscussionPapers/DP201213.pdf. Accessed 26 June 2013.

Goodwin, P. (2013) 'Peak car – themes and issues', *Transport Reviews*, vol 33, pp 243—254.

Goodwin, P. and Lyons, G. (2010) 'Public attitudes to transport: interpreting the evidence', *Transportation Planning and Technology*, vol 33, no 1, pp 3–18.

Goodwin, P., Hallett, S., Kenney, F. and Stokes, G. (1991) *Transport: The new realism*, Transport Studies Unit, University of Oxford.

Graham, B. (1995) *Geography and air transport*, Chichester: John Wiley.

Graham, B. and Shaw, J. (2008) 'Low cost airlines in Europe: reconciling liberalisation and sustainabilily', *Geoforum*, vol 39, pp 1439–51.

Graham, D. (2009) 'Identifying urbanisation and localisation externalities in manufacturing and service industries', *Papers in Regional Science*, vol 88, no 1, pp 63–84.

Graham, S. (1998) 'The end of geography or the explosion of place? Conceptualising space, place and information technology', *Progress in Human Geography*, vol 22, pp 165–85.

Gray, D., Docherty, I. and Laing, R. (2013) *Delivering lower carbon transport choices: Lessons for the UK from northern Europe*, working paper available from the authors.

Gray, D., Shaw, J. and Farrington, J. (2006) 'Community transport, social capital and social exclusion in rural areas', *Area*, vol 38, no 1, pp 89–98.

Gray, D., Farrington, J., Shaw, J., Martin, S. and Roberts, D. (2001) 'Car dependence in rural Scotland: transport policy, devolution and the impact of the fuel duty escalator', *Journal of Rural Studies,* vol 17, pp 113–25.

Green, A. (1997) 'A question of compromise? Case study evidence on the location and mobility strategies of dual career households', *Regional Studies*, vol 31, pp 641–57.

Green Logistics (undated) *Green logistics: Research into the sustainability of logistics systems and supply chains*, www.greenlogistics.org. Accessed 12 March 2013.

Griefahn, B., Marks, A. and Robens, S. (2006) 'Noise emitted from road, rail and air traffic and their effects on sleep', *Journal of Sound and Vibration*, vol 295, pp 129–40.

Guardian (2008) 'Manchester says no to congestion charging', http://www.guardian.co.uk/politics/2008/dec/12/congestioncharging-transport. Accessed 20 May 2013.

Guardian (2009) 'Lib Dems back road-pricing despite fears of "poll tax on wheels" accusations', http://www.guardian.co.uk/politics/2008/sep/16/libdemconference.transport. Accessed 14 February 2013.

Guardian (2010) 'Air pollution leads to premature deaths of more than 4,000 Londoners a year', http://www.guardian.co.uk/environment/2010/jun/30/london-air-quality-premature-deaths. Accessed 22 May 2013.

Guardian (2013a) 'HS2 project has £3.3bn funding shortfall, warns spending watchdog', http://www.guardian.co.uk/uk/2013/may/16/hs2-rail-report-watchdog. Accessed 21 May 2013.

Guardian (2013b) 'Paris train disaster highlights dark side of French railway dream', http://www.guardian.co.uk/world/2013/jul/17/paris-train-disaster-dark-side-railway-tgv?CMP=twt_gu. Accessed 19 July 2013.

Guet, J.-F. (2005) *French urban planning tools and methods renewal*, IsoCaRP Congress, http://www.certu.fr/fr/_Activites_Internationales-n33/approches_thematiques-n170/IMG/pdf/isocarp05paper.pdf. Accessed 23 May 2013.

Guo, Z. and Wilson, N. (2011) 'Assessing the cost of transfer inconvenience in public transport systems: a case study of the London Underground', *Transportation Research Part A: Policy and Practice*, vol 45, no 2, pp 91–104.

Gwilliam, K., Nash, C. and Mackie, P. (1985) 'Deregulating the bus industry in Britain – (B) the case against', *Transport Reviews*, vol 5, no 2, pp 105–32.

Hall, D. (2008) 'Transport, tourism and leisure', in R. Knowles, J. Shaw and I. Docherty (eds) *Transport geographies: Mobilities, flows and spaces*, Oxford: Blackwell, pp 196–211.

Hart, J. and Parkhurst, G. (2011) 'Driven to excess: impacts of motor vehicles on the quality of life of residents of three streets in Bristol UK', *World Transport Policy & Practice*, vol 17, pp 12–30.

Hass-Klau, C. (1993) 'Impact of pedestrianisation and traffic calming on retailing', *Transport Policy*, vol 1, no 1, pp 21–31.

Hayek, F. (1960) *The constitution of liberty*, London: Routledge Kegan Paul.

Headicar, P. (2011) *Transport planning and policy in Great Britain*, Abingdon: Routledge.

Heathrow Airport (undated) *About Heathrow Airport: Facts and figures*, http://www.heathrowairport.com/about-us/company-news-and-information/company-information/facts-and-figures. Accessed 22 May 2013.

Heinen, E., Van Wee, B. and Maat, K. (2010) 'Commuting by bicycle: an overview of the literature', *Transport Reviews*, vol 30, no 1, pp 59–96.
Hillman, M., Adams, J. and Whitelegg, J. (1990) *One false move … A study of children's independent mobility*, London: Policy Studies Institute.
Hine, J. (2008) 'Transport and social justice', in R. Knowles, J. Shaw and I. Docherty (eds) *Transport geographies: Mobilities, flows and spaces*, Oxford: Blackwell, pp 49–61.
HM Treasury (2010) *National infrastructure plan 2010*, http://webarchive.nationalarchives.gov.uk/20130129110402/http://www.hm-treasury.gov.uk/d/nationalinfrastructureplan251010.pdf. Accessed 20 May 2013.
HM Treasury (2012) *Public expenditure statistical analyses*, London: HM Treasury.
House of Commons (2008) *Freight transport*, Eighth report of Session 2007–08, HC 249, http://www.publications.parliament.uk/pa/cm200708/cmselect/cmtran/249/24903.htm. Accessed 12 March 2013.
House of Commons (2009a) *School travel*, Second report of Session 2008–09, London: The Stationery Office, http://www.publications.parliament.uk/pa/cm200809/cmselect/cmtran/351/35102.htm. Accessed 15 February 2013.
House of Commons (2009b) *Improving road safety for pedestrians and cyclists in Great Britain*, Forty-ninth report of Session 2008–09, London: The Stationery Office, http://www.publications.parliament.uk/pa/cm200809/cmselect/cmpubacc/665/665.pdf. Accessed 10 January 2013.
House of Commons (2009c) *The future of aviation*, First report of Session 2009–10, http://www.publications.parliament.uk/pa/cm200910/cmselect/cmtran/125/125i.pdf.
House of Commons (2010a) *Environmental Audit Committee Fifth Report: Air quality*, http://www.publications.parliament.uk/pa/cm200910/cmselect/cmenvaud/229/22902.htm. Accessed 22 May 2013.

House of Commons (2010b) *Update on the London Underground and the public–private partnership (PPP) agreements*, Seventh report of Session 2009–10, London: The Stationery Office, http://www.publications.parliament.uk/pa/cm200910/cmselect/cmtran/100/100.pdf. Accessed 10 January 2013.

House of Commons (2011) *Transport and the economy*, Third report of Session 2010–11, London: The Stationery Office, http://www.publications.parliament.uk/pa/cm201011/cmselect/cmtran/473/47302.htm. Accessed 15 February 2013.

House of Commons (2012a) *Road safety*, Second report of Session 2012–13, London: The Stationery Office, http://www.publications.parliament.uk/pa/cm201213/cmselect/cmtran/506/506.pdf. Accessed 22 May 2013.

House of Commons (2012b) *Plug-in vehicles, plugged in policy?* Fourth report of Session 2012–13, http://www.publications.parliament.uk/pa/cm201213/cmselect/cmtran/239/239.pdf. Accessed 3 June 2013.

House of Commons (2013) *Aviation strategy*, First report of Session 2013–14, http://www.publications.parliament.uk/pa/cm201314/cmselect/cmtran/78/78i.pdf. Accessed 22 May 2013.

Houston, D. (2001) 'Testing the spatial mismatch hypothesis in the United Kingdom using evidence from firm relocations', *European Research in Regional Science*, vol 11, pp 134–51.

Hull, A. (2005) 'Integrated transport planning in the UK: from concept to reality', *Journal of Transport Geography*, vol 13, no 4, pp 318–28.

Independent (2013) 'France shunts new TGV projects into a siding', http://www.independent.co.uk/news/world/europe/france-shunts-new-tgv-projects-into-a-siding-8676909.html. Accessed 19 July 2013.

Inside Government (2013) *20 years since rail privatisation*, https://www.gov.uk/government/speeches/20-years-since-rail-privatisation. Accessed 18 July 2013.

Institution of Civil Engineers (2009) *The state of the nation: Defending critical infrastructure*, London: ICE.

International Transport Forum (2012) *12 ways to make roads safer for pedestrians*, Paris: OECD.

ipayroadtax.com (undated) *The oddly fascinating history of 'road tax' and the Road Fund*, http://ipayroadtax.com/no-such-thing-as-road-tax/bring-back-the-road-fund/. Accessed 20 May 2013.

Ison, S. and Rye, T. (eds) (2008) *The implementation and effectiveness of transport demand management measures: An international perspective*, Aldershot: Ashgate.

Jacobs, J. (1968) *The death and life of great American cities*, London: Penguin.

Jain, J. (2011) 'The classy coach commute', *Journal of Transport Geography*, vol 19, no 5, pp 1017–22.

Jain, J. and Lyons, G. (2008) 'The gift of travel time', *Journal of Transport Geography*, vol 16, no 2, pp 81–9.

Jaroszweski, D., Chapman, L. and Petts, J. (2010) 'Assessing the potential impact of climate change on transportation: the need for an interdisciplinary approach', *Journal of Transport Geography*, vol 18, pp 331–5.

Jespersen, P. (2004) 'The transport content of products', *World Transport Policy & Practice*, vol 10, no 3, pp 28–35.

Jones, K. and Rhodes, D. (2009) *Aircraft noise, sleep disturbance and health effects: A review*, London: CAA, http://www.caa.co.uk/docs/33/ERCD1208.pdf. Accessed 22 May 2013.

Jones, P. (2005) 'Performing the city: a body and bicycle take on Birmingham, UK', *Social & Cultural Geography*, vol 6, no 6, pp 813–30.

Jones, P. (2012) 'Performing sustainable transport: an artistic RIDE across the city', *Cultural Geographies*, OnlineFirst, DOI 10.1177/1474474012466016.

Jupe, R. (2010) 'A model or a policy muddle? An evaluation of rail franchising in the UK', *Public Money & Management*, November, pp 347–54.

Kenyon, S., Lyons, G. and Rafferty, J. (2002) 'Transport and social exclusion: investigating the possibility of promoting inclusion through virtual mobility', *Journal of Transport Geography*, vol 10, pp 207–19.

King, J. (2008) *The King review of low carbon cars. Part II: Recommendations for action*, London: HM Treasury, http://webarchive.nationalarchives.gov.uk/+/http:/www.hm-treasury.gov.uk/d/bud08_king_1080.pdf. Accessed 23 May 2013.

Kingham, S. and Donohoe, S. (2002) 'Children's perceptions of transport', *World Transport Policy & Practice*, vol 8, no 1, pp 6–10.

Knowles, R. and Abrantes, P. (2008) 'Buses and light rail: stalled en route?', in I. Docherty and J. Shaw (eds) *Traffic jam: Ten years of 'sustainable' transport in the UK*, Bristol: The Policy Press, pp 97–116.

Kuhnimhof, Y., Buehler, R., Wirtz, M. and Kalinowska, D. (2012) 'Travel trends among young adults in Germany: increasing multimodality and declining car use for men', *Journal of Transport Geography*, vol 24, pp 443–50.

Kwan, M.-P. (2007) 'Mobile communication, social networks and urban travel: hypertext as a new metaphor for conceptualising spatial interaction', *The Professional Geographer*, vol 59, pp 434–46.

Labour Party (1996) *Consensus for change*, London: Labour Party.

Laidlaw, S. (2012) *Report of the Laidlaw Inquiry into the lessons learned for the Department for Transport from the InterCity West Coast Competition*, HC 809 Session 2012–13, London: The Stationery Office, https://www.gov.uk/government/uploads/system/uploads/attachment_data/file/29866/report-of-the-laidlaw-inquiry.pdf. Accessed 19 January 2013.

Laurier, E. (2004) 'Doing office work on the motorway', *Theory, Culture & Society*, vol 21, pp 261–77.

LeVine, S. and Jones, P. (2012) *On the move: Making sense of car and train travel trends in Britain*, London: RAC Foundation.

Levinson, M. (2006) *The box: How the shipping container made the world smaller and the world economy bigger*, New Jersey: Princeton University Press.

Line, T., Jain, J. and Lyons, G. (2011) 'The role of ICTs in everyday mobile lives', *Journal of Transport Geography*, vol 19, pp 1490–9.

Local Transport Today (2012a) 'In passing: just how much does congestion cost the economy?', http://www.transportxtra.com/magazines/local_transport_today/news/?id=30150. Accessed 9 January 2013.

Local Transport Today (2012b) 'London Mayor plans £1bn investment in cycling', 4 December, http://www.transportxtra.com/magazines/local_transport_today/news/?id=32900. Accessed 10 January 2013.

Lonely Planet (2009) *Great Britain*, London: BBC Worldwide.

Lucas, K. (2013) 'Transport and social exclusion', in J.-P. Rodrigue, T. Notteboom and J. Shaw (eds) *The Sage handbook of transport studies*, London: Sage, in press.

Lucas, K. and Jones, P. (2009) *The car in British society*, London: RAC Foundation, http://www.racfoundation.org/assets/rac_foundation/content/downloadables/car_in_british_society-lucas_et_al-170409.pdf. Accessed 7 February 2013.

Lucas, K. and Jones, P. (2012) 'Social impacts and equity issues in transport', *Journal of Transport Geography*, vol 21, pp 1–3.

Lucas, K., Blumenberg, E. and Weinberger, R. (eds) (2011) *Auto motives: Understanding car use behaviours*, Bingley: Emerald.

Lyons, G. (2004) 'Transport and society', *Transport Reviews*, vol 24, no 4, pp 485–509.

Lyons, G. and Urry, J. (2005) 'Travel time use in the information age', *Transportation Research Part A*, vol 39, no 2–3, pp 257–76.

Lyons, G., Holley, G. and Jain, J. (2008) 'The business of train travel', in D. Hislop (ed) *Mobility and technology in the workplace*, London: Routledge.

McDowell, L. (2004) 'Work, workfare, work/life balance and an ethic of care', *Progress in Human Geography*, vol 28, no 2, pp 145–63.

McDowell, L., Ward, K., Fagan, C., Perrons, D. and Ray, K. (2006) 'Connecting space and time: the significance of transformations in women's working lives and the structure of cities', *International Journal of Urban and Regional Research*, vol 30, pp 141–58.

Mackett, R. (2001) 'Are we making our children car dependent?', lecture presented at Trinity College Dublin, 17 May.

Mackett, R. (2002) 'Increasing car dependency of children: should we be worried?', *Proceedings of the Civil Institution of Engineers: Municipal Engineer*, vol 151, no 1, pp 29–38.

McKinnon, A. (2009) *Transport challenges and opportunities: Briefing paper on the freight transport sector*, London: Commission for Integrated Transport.

McKinnon, A., Cullinane, S., Browne, M. and Whiting, A. (eds) (2010) *Green logistics: Improving the environmental sustainability of logistics*, London: Kogan Page.

McKinnon, A., Edwards, J., Piecyk, M. and Palmer, A. (2009) 'Traffic congestion, reliability and logistical performance: a multi-sectoral assessment', *International Journal of Logistics Research and Applications*, vol 12, pp 331–45.

Mackinnon, D. and Cumbers, A. (2011) *An introduction to economic geography: Globalisation, uneven development and place*, Harlow: Pearson.

Mackinnon, D., Shaw, J. and Docherty, I. (2008) *Diverging mobilities? Devolution, transport and policy innovation*, Oxford: Elsevier.

McLennan, P. and Bennetts, M. (2003) 'The journey to work: a descriptive UK case study', *Facilities*, vol 21, pp 180–7.

Massey, D. (1988) 'What's happening to UK manufacturing?', in J. Allen and D. Massey (eds) *The economy in question*, London: Sage, pp 45–90.

Meaton, J. and Kingham, S. (1997) 'Children's perceptions of transport modes: car culture in the classroom?', *World Transport Policy & Practice*, vol 4, no 2, pp 12–16.

Meek, S. (2008) 'Park and ride', in S. Ison and T. Rye (eds) (2008) *The implementation and effectiveness of transport demand management measures: An international perspective*, Aldershot: Ashgate, pp 165–88.

Met Office (2013) *Statistics for December and 2012 – is the UK getting wetter?*, http://www.metoffice.gov.uk/news/releases/archive/2013/2012-weather-statistics. Accessed 21 May 2013.

Metz, D. (2008) *The limits to travel: How far will you go?*, London: Earthscan.

Middleton, J. (2010) 'Sense and the city: exploring the embodied geographies of urban walking', *Social & Cultural Geography*, vol 6, pp 575–96.

Ministère de l'Écologie, du Développement durable et de l'Énergie (2012) *Le renouveau du tramway en France*, http://www.developpement-durable.gouv.fr/IMG/pdf/tramway_FR_08-06-2012.pdf. Accessed 23 May 2013.

Ministry of Transport (1963) *Traffic in towns*, London: HMSO.

Mitchell, G., Hargreaves, A., Namdeo, A. and Echenique, M. (2011) 'Land use, transport, and carbon futures: the impact of spatial form strategies in three UK urban regions', *Environment and Planning A*, vol 43, no 9, p 2143.

Mokhtarian, P. and Handy, S. (2009) 'No particular place to go: an empirical analysis of travel for the sake of travel', *Environment and Behavior*, vol 41, pp 233–57.

Mokhtarian, P. and Tal, G. (2013) 'Impacts of ICT on travel behaviour: a tapestry of relationships', in J.-P. Rodrigue, T. Notteboom and J. Shaw (eds) *The Sage handbook of transport studies*, London: Sage, in press.

Moore, S. (2011) 'Understanding and managing anti social behaviour on public transport through value change: the considerate travel campaign', *Transport Policy*, vol 18, no 1, pp 53–9.

Morgan, K. (2004) 'The exaggerated death of geography: learning, proximity and territorial innovation systems', *Journal of Economic Geography*, vol 4, no 1, pp 3–21.

Mumsnet (undated) 'Surviving the school run', http://www.mumsnet.com/education/surviving-the-school-run. Accessed 8 October 2012.

NAEI (National Atmospheric Emissions Inventory) (2013) 'Emissions of air quality pollutants, 1970–2011', http://uk-air.defra.gov.uk/reports/cat07/1305031312_EoAQP1970-2011_pq.pdf. Accessed 20 May 2013.

National Audit Office (2012) *Lessons from cancelling the InterCity West Coast franchise competition*, HC 796 Session 2012–13, http://www.nao.org.uk/publications/1213/intercity_west_coast_franchise.aspx. Accessed 19 January 2013.

Network Rail (2011) *Britain relies on rail*, www.networkrail.co.uk/contents/aboutus/documents/11865_britainreliesonrail.pdf. Accessed 21 May 2103.

Network Rail (2013) 'Strategic business plans: a better railway for a better Britain', London: Network Rail, http://www.networkrail.co.uk/publications/strategic-business-plan-for-cp5/. Accessed 26 January 2013.

Neuman, M. (2005) 'The compact city fallacy', *Journal of Planning Education and Research*, vol 25, pp 11–26.

Oberholzer-Gee, F. and Weck-Hannemann, H. (2002) 'Pricing road use: politico-economic and fairness considerations', *Transportation Research Part D: Transport and Environment*, vol 7, no 5, pp 357–71.

OEF (Oxford Economic Forecasting) (2006) *The economic contribution of the aviation industry in the UK*, Oxford: OEF, http://www.gacag.org/images/gacag/pdf/The%20Economic%20Contribution%20of%20the%20Aviation%20Industry%20in%20the%20UK.pdf. Accessed 19 January 2013.

ONS (Office for National Statistics) (2012) '2011 census, population and household estimates for the United Kingdom', http://www.ons.gov.uk/ons/rel/census/2011-census/population-and-household-estimates-for-the-united-kingdom/index.html. Accessed 16 January 2013.

Ogilvie, D., Egan, M., Hamilton, V. and Petticrew, M. (2004) 'Promoting walking and cycling as an alternative to using cars: systematic review', *British Medical Journal*, vol 329, 763–6.

O'Rourke, P.J. (1987) 'A cool and logical analysis of the bicycle menace', in *Republican Party reptile: The confessions, adventures, essays and (other) outrages of PJ O'Rourke*, London: Picador.

Oullette, J. and Wood, W. (1998) 'Habit and intention in everyday life: the multiple processes by which past behaviour predicts future behaviour', *Psychological Bulletin*, vol 124, no 1, pp 54–74.

Paez, A. and Whalen, K. (2010) 'Enjoyment of commute: a comparison of different transportation modes', *Transportation Research Part A*, vol 44, pp 537–49.

Pain, R. (1997) 'Social geography of women's fear and crime', *Transactions of the Institute of British Geographers*, vol 22, pp 231–44.

Parker, D. (2013) 'The privatized railways: problems foreseen', *Public Money & Management*, vol 33, pp 313-319.

Parkin, J. (ed) (2012) *Cycling and sustainability*, Bingley: Emerald.

Passenger Focus (2009) *England-wide concessionary bus travel: The passenger perspective*, http://www.passengerfocus.org.uk/research/englandwide-concessionary-bus-travel-the-passenger-perspective. Accessed 10 January 2013.

Passenger Focus (2012) *Bus passenger survey*, http://www.passengerfocus.org.uk/research/publications/bus-passenger-survey-summary-march-2012. Accessed 7 February 2013.

Pickard, J. (2010) 'British Parties in election drive to track down motorway man', *Financial Times*, 22 January, http://www.ft.com/cms/s/0283fcbe-06f5-11df-b058-00144feabdc0,Authorised=false.html?_i_location=http%3A%2F%2Fwww.ft.com%2Fcms%2Fs%2F0%2F0283fcbe-06f5-11df-b058-00144feabdc0.html&_i_referer=http%3A%2F%2Fen.wikipedia.org%2Fwiki%2FMotorway_man. Accessed 10 January 2013.

Pinder, D. (2008) 'Economic versus environmental sustainability for ports and shipping: charting a new course?', in I. Docherty and J. Shaw (eds) *Traffic jam: Ten years of 'sustainable' transport in the UK*, Bristol: The Policy Press, pp 161–82.

Pooley, C. and Turnbull, J. (2000) 'Commuting, transport and urban form: Manchester and Glasgow in the mid-twentieth century', *Urban History*, vol 27, no 3, pp 360–83.

Potter, S. and Bailey, I. (2008) 'Transport and the environment', in R. Knowles, J. Shaw and I. Docherty (eds) *Transport geographies: Mobilities, flows and spaces*, Oxford: Blackwell, pp 29–48.

Potter, S., Berridge, C., Cook, M. and Langendahl, P. (2013) 'Transport and energy use', in J.-P. Rodrigue, T. Notteboom and J. Shaw (eds) *The Sage handbook of transport studies*, London: Sage, pp 397–411.

Preston, J. (2012) 'High speed rail in Britain: about time or a waste of time?', *Journal of Transport Geography*, vol 22, pp 308–11.

Preston, J. (2008) 'Is Labour delivering a sustainable railway?', in I. Docherty and J. Shaw (eds) *Traffic jam: Ten years of 'sustainable' transport in the UK*, Bristol: The Policy Press, pp 75-96.

Pucher, J. and Buehler, R. (2008) 'Making cycling irresistible: lessons from the Netherlands, Denmark and Germany', *Transport Reviews*, vol 28, no 4, pp 495–528.

RAC Foundation (2013) *800,000 homes spend more than a quarter of their income on running a car*, London: RAC Foundation, http://www.racfoundation.org/media-centre/800000-households-spend-quarter-of-income-on-cars. Accessed 17 July 2013.

Rail (2013) 'High court rejects anti-HS2 campaigners' objections', vol 719, pp 8–9.

Rail Business Intelligence (2012) 'IEP will cost twice as much as a Pendolino', vol 425, 1 November.

Read, R. (2012) 'New study offers more proof that Gen Y just isn't that into cars', *The Car Connection*, 23 November, http://www.thecarconnection.com/news/1069808_new-study-offers-more-proof-that-gen-y-just-isnt-that-into-cars. Accessed 10 January 2013.

Retail Gazette (2011) 'Amazon takeover of book depository tightens its grip on the market', 28 October, http://www.retailgazette.co.uk/articles/14412-amazon-takeover-of-book-depository-tightens-its-grip-on-market.

Rietveld, P. and Vickerman, R. (2003) 'Transport in regional science: The "death of distance" is premature', *Papers in Regional Science*, vol 83, no 1, pp 229–48.

Rittel, H. and Webber, M. (1973) 'Dilemmas in a general theory of planning', *Policy Sciences*, vol 4, pp 155–69.

Roberts, J., Hodgson, R. and Dolan, P. (2011) 'It's driving her mad – gender differences in the effects of commuting on psychological health', *Journal of Health Economics*, vol 30, pp 1064–76.

Rodrigue, J.-P., Notteboom, T. and Shaw, J. (eds) (2013a) *The Sage handbook of transport studies*, London: Sage.

Rodrigue, J.-P., Slack, B. and Comtois, C. (2013) 'Green supply chain management', in J.-P. Rodrigue, T. Notteboom and J. Shaw (eds) *The Sage handbook of transport studies*, London: Sage, pp 427–38.

Rosenbloom, S. (2011) 'Driving off into the sunset: the implications of the growing automobility of older travellers', in K. Lucas, E. Blumenberg and R. Weinberger (eds) *Auto motives: Understanding car use behaviours*, Bingley: Emerald, pp 173–92.

Rotem-Mindali, O. and Salomon, I. (2007) 'The impacts of e-tail on the choice of shopping trips and deliver: some preliminary findings', *Transportation Research Part A*, vol 41, pp 176–89.

Rye, T. and Mykura, W. (2006) 'Concessionary bus fares for older people in Scotland: are they achieving their objectives?', *Journal of Transport Geography*, vol 17, no 6, pp 441–6.

Ryley, T. and Chapman, L. (eds) (2012) *Transport and climate change*, Bingley: Emerald.

SACTRA (Standing Advisory Committee on Trunk Road Assessment) (1994) *Trunk roads and the generation of traffic*, London: Department of Transport, http://webarchive.nationalarchives.gov.uk/+/http:/www.dft.gov.uk/pgr/economics/rdg/nataarchivedocs/trunkroadstraffic.pdf. Accessed 10 January 2013.

SACTRA (1999) *Transport and the economy: Full report*, http://webarchive.nationalarchives.gov.uk/20050301192906/http:/dft.gov.uk/stellent/groups/dft_econappr/documents/pdf/dft_econappr_pdf_022512.pdf. Accessed 10 January 2013.

Santos, G. (2008) 'London congestion charging', *Brookings Wharton Papers on Urban Affairs*, pp 177–234, http://muse.jhu.edu/journals/brookings-wharton_papers_on_urban_affairs/v2008/2008.santos.html.

Schaeffer, K. and Sclar, E. (1975) *Access for all: Transportation and urban growth*, London: Penguin.

Schwanen, T. (2008) 'Managing uncertain arrival times through sociomaterial associations', *Environment and Planning B: Planning and Design*, vol 35, pp 997–1011.

Schwanen, T. (2011) 'Car use and gender: the case of dual-earner families in Utrecht, The Netherlands', in K. Lucas, E. Blumenberg and R. Weinberger (eds) (2011) *Auto motives: Understanding car use behaviours*, Bingley: Emerald, pp 151–72.

Schwanen, T. and Kwan, M.-P. (2008) 'The internet, mobile phone and space-time constraints', *Geoforum*, vol 39, pp 1362–1377.

Scottish Enterprise (2004) *FAQs and useful links*, www.scottish-enterprise.com/sedotcom_home/services-to-the-community/stc-keyprojects/transportprojects/routedevelopmentfund/routedevelopmentfund-faq.htm. Accessed 3 July 2007.

Scottish Executive (2004) *Scotland: National Rural Network*, www.ruralgateway.org.uk. Accessed 14 December 2004.

Scottish Executive (2005) *Transport research series: Cycling in Scotland*, Edinburgh: Scottish Executive.

Shaoul, J. (2002) 'A financial appraisal of the London Underground Public-Private Partnership', *Public Money and Management*, vol 22, no 2, pp 53–60.

Shaoul, J. (2004) 'Railpolitik: the financial realities of operating Britain's national railways', *Public Money and Management*, vol 24, no 1, pp 27–36.

Shaoul, J. (2006) 'The cost of operating Britain's privatised railways', *Public Money and Management*, vol 26, no 3, pp 151–8.

Shaoul, J. and Edwards, E. (2004) 'Public Private Partnerships: troublesome relationships', *Spectra, The Journal of the Management Consultancies Association*, pp 56–7.

Shaoul, J., Stafford, A. and Stapleton, P. (2006) 'Highway robbery? A financial analysis of Design, Build, Finance and Operate (DBFO) in UK roads', *Transport Reviews*, vol 26, no 3, pp 257–74.

Shaw, J. (2000a) 'Designing a method of rail privatisation', in R. Freeman and J. Shaw (eds) *All change: British railway privatisation*, Maidenhead: McGraw-Hill, pp 1–29.

Shaw, J. (2000b) *Competition, regulation and the privatisation of British Rail*, Aldershot: Ashgate.

Shaw, J. and Walton, W. (2001) 'Labour's new trunk-roads policy for England: an emerging pragmatic multimodalism?', *Environment and Planning A*, vol 33, pp 1031–56.

Shaw, J., Mackinnon, D. and Docherty, I. (2009) 'Divergence or convergence? Devolution and transport policy in the United Kingdom', *Environment and Planning C: Government and Policy*, vol 27, no 3, pp 546–67.

Sloman, L., Cairns, S., Newson, C., Anable, J., Pridmore, A. and Goodwin, P. (2010) *The effects of smarter choice programmes in the sustainable travel towns: Summary report*, London: DfT.

Smeed, R. (1964) *Road pricing: The economic and technical possibilities*, London: HMSO.

Social Exclusion Unit (2003) 'Making the connections: final report on transport and social exclusion, London: Office of the Deputy Prime Minister, http://webarchive.nationalarchives.gov.uk/+/http://www.cabinetoffice.gov.uk/media/cabinetoffice/social_exclusion_task_force/assets/publications_1997_to_2006/making_transport_2003.pdf. Accessed 21 January 2013.

Starkie, D. (1972) *The motorway age*, Oxford: Pergamon.

Steer Davies Gleave (2006) *Air and rail competition and complementarity*, London: SDG, http://ec.europa.eu/transport/rail/studies/doc/2006_08_study_air_rail_competition_en.pdf. Accessed 23 May 2013.

Steg, L. (2005) 'Car use: lust and must. Instrumental, symbolic and affective motives for car use', *Transportation Research Part A*, vol 39, no 2–3, pp 147–62.

Stern, N. (2006) *Stern review on the economics of climate change*, London: HM Treasury, http://webarchive.nationalarchives.gov.uk/+/http:/www.hm-treasury.gov.uk/sternreview_index.htm. Accessed 21 January 2013.

Stradling, S. and Anable, J. (2008) 'Individual transport patterns', in R. Knowles, J. Shaw and I. Docherty (eds) *Transport geographies: Mobilities, flows and spaces*, Oxford: Blackwell, pp 179–95.

STV (2012) 'Aberdeen bypass to cost £300m more than previously estimated', http://news.stv.tv/north/197258-aberdeen-bypass-to-cost-more-than-300m-more-then-previously-estimated/. Accessed 14 February 2013.

Supreme Court (2012) *Walton (Appellant) v The Scottish Ministers (Respondent) (Scotland)* [2012] UKSC 44. Press summary, http://www.supremecourt.gov.uk/decided-cases/docs/UKSC_2012_0098_PressSummary.pdf. Accessed 20 May.

Sutton Trust (2005) *No more school run: Proposal for a national yellow bus scheme in the UK*, London: The Sutton Trust.

TfL (Transport for London) (2008) *Central London congestion charging impacts monitoring. 6th annual report*, www.tfl.gov.uk/assets/downloads/sixth-annual-impacts-monitoring-report-2008-07.pdf. Accessed 21 May 2013.

TfL (2012) 'Annual report and statement of accounts, 2011/2012', http://www.tfl.gov.uk/assets/downloads/corporate/tfl-annualreport-2012.pdf. Accessed 12 February 2013.

Thérival, R. and Partidário, M. (1996) *The practice of strategic environmental assessment*, London: Earthscan.

Thomson, A. (2012) 'The Rolls-Royce has become an Italian tank', *The Times*, 31 October, http://www.thetimes.co.uk/tto/opinion/columnists/alicethomson/article3584787.ece. Accessed 10 January 2013.

Tight, M., Timms, P., Banister, D., Bowmaker, J., Copas, J., Day, A., Drinkwater, D., Givoni, M., Gühnemann, A., Lawler, A., Macmillen, J., Miles, A., Moore, N., Newton, R., Ngoduy, D., Ormerod, M., O'Sullivan, M. and Watling, D. (2011) 'Visions for a walking and cycling focussed urban transport system', *Journal of Transport Geography*, vol 19, pp 1580–9.

Tolley, R. (2008) 'Walking and cycling: easy wins for sustainable transport policy?', in I. Docherty and J. Shaw (eds) *Traffic jam: Ten years of 'sustainable' transport in the UK*, Bristol: The Policy Press, pp 117–38.

TRACY (Transport Needs in an Ageing Society) (2012) *Work package 2: Determining the state of the art*, Transport Needs for an Ageing Society, http://www.tracy-project.eu/fileadmin/tracy/deliverables/wp2_report.pdf. Accessed 20 May 2013.

Urry, J. (2000) *Sociology beyond societies: Mobilities for the twenty-first century*, London: Routledge.

Urry, J. (2007) *Mobilities*, Cambridge: Polity Press.

Vande Walle, S. and Steenbergen, T. (2006) 'Space and time related determinants of public transport use in trip chains', *Transportation Research Part A: Policy and Practice*, vol 40, no 2, pp 151–62.

Vanderbilt, T (2008) *Traffic: Why we drive the way we do (and what it says about us)*, Penguin, London.

Velaga, R., Beecroft, R., Nelson, D., Corsar, D. and Edwards, P. (2012) 'Transport poverty meets the digital divide: accessibility and connectivity in rural communities', *Journal of Transport Geography*, vol 21, pp 102–112.

Watts, L. (2008) 'The art and craft of train travel', *Social and Cultural Geography*, vol 9, no 6, pp 711–26.

Wener, R. and Evans, G. (2011) 'Comparing stress of car and train commuters', *Transportation Research Part F*, vol 14, pp 111–16.

White, P. (2008) 'Transport for London: success despite Westminster', in I. Docherty and J. Shaw (eds) *Traffic jam: Ten years of 'sustainable' transport in the UK*, Bristol: The Policy Press, pp 183–204.

White, P. (2009) *Public transport: Its planning, management and operation*, 5th edition, Abingdon: Routledge.

Wolmar, C. (2002) *Down the tube: The battle for London's Underground*, London: Aurum Press.

Wolmar, C. (2005) *On the wrong line: How ideology and incompetence wrecked Britain's railways*, London: Aurum Press.

World Bank (2013) *GDP per capita, PPP (current international $)*, http://data.worldbank.org/indicator/NY.GDP.PCAP.PP.CD. Accessed 19 July 2013.

World Health Organisation (2013) *Global status report on road safety 2013*, http://www.who.int/violence_injury_prevention/road_safety_status/2013/en/. Accessed 19 July 2013.

Young, R. (1999) 'Prioritising family health needs: a time–space analysis of women's health-related behaviours', *Social Science & Medicine*, vol 48, no 6, pp 797–813.

Index

Page references for notes are followed by n

L

M

Q

R

S

T

Lightning Source UK Ltd.
Milton Keynes UK
UKHW02f0113110718
325533UK00006B/357/P

9 781847 428561